I0902282

Willem de Kooning Nonstop

Willem de Kooning Nonstop

Cherchez la femme

Rosalind E. Krauss

The University of Chicago Press
Chicago and London

Rosalind E. Krauss is University Professor at Columbia University, where she was previously the Meyer Schapiro Professor of Modern Art and Theory in the Department of Art History and Archaeology. She is the cofounder of *October* and has written many essays and books. She has also curated many exhibitions at leading museums.

The University of Chicago Press, Chicago 60637
The University of Chicago Press, Ltd., London
© 2015 by Rosalind Krauss
All rights reserved. Published 2015.
Printed in China

24 23 22 21 20 19 18 17 16 15 1 2 3 4 5

All text by Willem de Kooning © Estate of Lisa de Kooning.

ISBN-13: 978-0-226-26744-9 (cloth)
ISBN-13: 978-0-226-26758-6 (e-book)
DOI: 10.7208/chicago/9780226267586.001.0001

Library of Congress Cataloging-in-Publication Data
Krauss, Rosalind E., author.
Willem de Kooning nonstop : cherchez la femme / Rosalind E. Krauss.
pages : illustrations ; cm
Includes bibliographical references and index.
ISBN 978-0-226-26744-9 (cloth : alk. paper) — ISBN 978-0-226-26758-6 (e-book) 1. De Kooning, Willem, 1904–1997—Criticism and interpretation. 2. De Kooning, Willem, 1904–1997—Themes, motives. 3. Women in art. 4. Abstract expressionism—United States.
I. Title.
N6537.D43K73 2015
759.13—dc23

2015028491

♾ This paper meets the requirements of ANSI/NISO Z39.48-1992 (Permanence of Paper).

In memory of Anne Hollander

Contents

Illustrations

Willem de Kooning Nonstop

1

In Lieu of a Preface

In 1960, his preeminence secured by his series of *Woman* paintings, de Kooning told an interviewer about finishing a work: "I always have a miserable time over it. But it is getting better now. . . . I just stop."[1]

Commentators pounce on this "I just stop" as a way of demonstrating de Kooning's freedom from the strictures of European modernism. We cannot imagine Mondrian, in the midst of titrating the size of his planes and the placement and scale of his colors, "just" stopping. Walking away from that preciosity, de Kooning is seen as freeing American art from the scale and enclosure of easel painting[2] with everything primly secured in place behind the frame. Bigger scale, more aggressive attack, a turbulent embrace of the viewer—all became available with this truculent "stop."[3]

But de Kooning was famous for being *unable* to "stop," neither while working on the individual canvases in his major *Woman* series—*Woman I* to *Woman VI* and *Woman with Bicycle*—nor to put the entire theme of the Woman to rest (figs. 1–10). *Woman I*, begun in 1950, was only "completed" when Sidney Janis whisked it away in 1953 for an exhibition at his gallery in March; and for a moment before that when the art historian Meyer Schapiro visited his studio in late January to insist that the artist return the discarded *Woman, I* to the chassis so as to hold a long, analytical colloquy with him on the formal virtues of the work.[4]

In that stage, with only a few changes, *Woman I* made its way outside de Kooning's studio and into the art world.

De Kooning's inability to "stop" was not limited, however, to the nearly interminable work on *Woman I*. Six large Women followed and, in the summer of 1952, as he was unable to break his momentum, the rich series of pastels he drew of women in an improvised studio on the porch of Leo Castelli and Ileana Sonnabend's East Hampton house (fig. 11).

Twelve years later, in 1964, as he was completing his own studio in the Springs, a group of hollow-core doors were delivered to the construction site and instantly became the supports and format for yet more Women, including *Woman, Sag Harbor* (fig. 12).[5] De Kooning could not desert his Women even though they interrupted the important breakthrough to abstraction represented by his black-and-white paintings (1946–49) and by *Excavation* (1950), the latter widely considered a masterpiece (figs. 14–15). It was this interruption that led Jackson Pollock to attack de Kooning at the Janis Gallery opening of the 1953 *Women* show (which included *Woman, I* through *Woman V*, and *Woman with Bicycle*): "Bill, you betrayed it," Pollock jeered. "You're doing the figure, you're still doing the same goddamn thing. You know you never got out of being a figure painter."[6]

If de Kooning couldn't "just stop" but had to repaint his Women obsessively, in Pollock's eyes the opposite was the case. He saw de Kooning as indeed "stopped," or stalled: unable to reconnect with the famed successes of abstractions like *Excavation*.

De Kooning's reputation as a major artist was sealed by *Excavation*. Challenged already at its moment of completion by the struggle opened by *Woman, I* in June 1950,[7] the enormous abstract canvas (80 by 100 inches, the largest he would ever make) was sent by Alfred Barr to the Venice Biennale and placed by Barr among the work of a "predominant vanguard."[8] The following year *Excavation* won the Logan Medal and Purchase Prize at the Art Institute of Chicago, where it hangs today.

Speculation over the title's meaning has led some writers to examine the excavation needed for the dismantling of the Third Avenue El then under way in New York, with hoardings erected to protect the open pit. These wooden palisades had small "windows" cut into their surfaces, making it possible for passersby to study the spectacle of the rubble.[9] De Kooning, whose studio at the time was at 85 Fourth Avenue on the east side of Greenwich Village between Tenth and Eleventh Streets, was an inveterate late-night walker and would have, it is reasoned, passed these windows onto the site many times a night. The square cutouts would have provided the painter with a series of ready-made pictures, a sequence of "views" giving onto the landscape of debris. In this sense they combine two painterly problems that had begun to haunt de Kooning. Frame and depth are superimposed on the implicit surface of the "cut," as though the actual vista were no more than a representation of itself, a perspectival prolongation of vision already vortexed onto the implicit surface laterally stretched within the opening's frame. This is to say that the representation of depth is always-already a picture, flattened onto the surface as duplication, and nothing more. Paintings traditionally challenge the opacity of the picture plane with foreshortened drawing: lines oblique to the surface penetrate through it into depth.

The view through the hoardings presented the problem of depth in its purest, most "abstract" form. It was not the depth of *something*: receding body part; half-open door; reclining violin. The *painter's* problem of "depth" is, however, the depth of *nothing*. It is an abstract problem—the invention of a formal connection between a figure and its ground. Edwin Denby, de Kooning's neighbor at his Chelsea studio, was witness to de Kooning's struggles. The essential paradox of de Kooning's work in the late 1930s, said Denby, was how sophisticated his understanding was of every style and artistic idea—"I often heard him say that he was beating his brains out about connecting a figure and a background."[10] The readymade "picture-surfaces" cut into the hoardings around the excavations, with the representational depth spread laterally across the opening, would be acknowledged in de Kooning's later comment about *Woman V*: "I get the paint right on the surface. Nobody else can do that."[11]

Hans Hofmann, in his role as eminent teacher, had defined negative space for many young artists as that part of the painting often considered merely the background that exists behind and around the central or positive image.[12] The critic Dore Ashton said Hofmann brought two important ideas to America. The first was respect for the "grammar of painting,"[13] a "rigorous technical and formal understanding of visual meaning—apart from the overt subject-matter of a picture."[14] The second important idea was Hofmann's "imperturbably art-for-art's sake urbanity,"[15] which, Ashton said, "made the rhetoric of social realism sound shrill and tinny, and gave hope to the city's modernists."[16]

De Kooning's friends Arshile Gorky and John Graham described his focus on the formal problems of 'negative space,' how it had "its own power and how he sought a seamless image in which each received its due."[17] It was in de Kooning's black-and-white abstractions that he breached these possibly flaccid gaps to produce just such a "seamless" image between positive and negative. *Painting* (1948; fig. 14), the black-and-white work Alfred Barr acquired for the Museum of Modern Art, achieved the seamlessness of analytic cubist paintings, as its suggestive bodily fragments, with their lush contours, seem to advance and recede in relation to the lateral spread of the picture plane. Denby said that de Kooning's working idea at the time was to master "the plainest problems of painting."[18]

Accordingly, de Kooning's friend Joop Sanders explained *Excavation*'s surface in terms of his ambition to succeed in animating the entire canvas by creating a detailed but *seamless* work "without the 'hot spots' that he complained sometimes stopped the eye in a painting—the figure's ill-fitting pieces that troubled him."[19]

De Kooning could have been describing the goal he set himself with *Excavation* when he told Denby that a masterpiece succeeded in keeping the figures and the voids equally active, which "squeezed everything dramatically but somehow the picture opened itself way out, changing the center and the frame."[20] *Excavation* tendered a resistance similar to what the Women would do. Joan Mitchell reported, "He worked on a single painting all that winter long. I'd go up there and say to myself, Why doesn't he stop? It's finished! But it wasn't and he didn't."[21]

But in June 1950, amidst the accolades pouring in for *Excavation*, de Kooning pinned two long sheets of paper to the wall of his studio and began the drawings of standing women that heralded *Woman I*, his notoriously endless painting (fig. 16).[22] The reasons for this problem—his incapacity to "stop"—are at the center of much of the discussion of the artist. Perhaps de Kooning can enlighten us on this subject with his own statement of the problem foreshortening placed in his path: The *Woman* "became compulsive in the sense of not being able to get hold of it and the idea that it really is very funny . . . to get stuck with a woman's knees, for instance. You say, 'What the hell am I going to do with that now?' . . . it's really ridiculous."[23]

Woman I is a seated figure, her posture developed over the many stages through which the painting evolved—her knees projecting more and more toward the viewer and, a fortiori, the painter (figs. 17–22). Denby recalls de Kooning explaining his difficulty in capturing the proportions of the live model before him: "He spoke to me about the trouble he had with the projecting thighs of a full-face seated figure. I pointed out that he avoided foreshortening. He said vehemently that it made him sick to his stomach, not in other people's pictures but when he did it himself."[24] This implicit stance of the painter in front of the model, so as to look at her while he works, sets up two of the terms of representation necessary to any depiction of the artist at work in a studio. The third term of that depiction is, of course, the canvas on which the artist labors, a canvas that may already figure forth the model's developing replication. Picasso, de Kooning's idol, stated this tripartite arrangement—in all its purity—in *The Studio* and *Painter and Model*, both of 1928 and in the collection of the Museum of Modern Art (figs. 23–24). In *Painter and Model*, Picasso shows the artist holding his palette with one hand while his reified "line of vision" points, arrowlike, to the canvas on which the silhouette of his model already takes shape. The model herself is on the left, her embodiment falling like a shadow onto the canvas and thus becoming representation before our very eyes. Picasso hadn't come to this tripartite composition entirely on his own. Ingres's *Raphael and the Fornarina* (1814) combines artist and model in an embrace while the artist turns away from her to observe the sliver of the Fornarina's representation sketchily developing on the easel-born canvas behind him (fig. 25).

With Gorky, de Kooning traveled uptown in the late 1930s to see the exhibitions in the Fifty-Seventh Street galleries and to visit the Museum of Modern Art and the Met. Their analyses of the pictures they looked at were indefatigable. At the Museum of Modern Art, Picasso's *Studio* served de Kooning as template, even though other synthetic cubist Picassos suggest the three figures as compressed into overlapping layers in depth rather than laterally splayed. This is particularly true of Picasso's 1915 *Harlequin*: the painter in the quilted diamond patterned dress of the comedia dell'arte character; the plane behind him a rectangle of the easel bearing its canvas, itself with curvilinear shapes cut from it to suggest the artist's palette (fig. 26). One hand holds a white plane onto which the faint profile of the model is cast.

Two of de Kooning's studies for WPA murals transcribe Picasso's tripartite arrangement of *The Studio* in starkly programmatic form. In *Untitled* (circa 1939), the model, on the left, is caricatured as head and buttocks; the representational field of the introjected canvas registers as a red lozenge perched atop the legs of an easel at the center; then the painter himself, on the right, is reduced to a pair of staring eyes (fig. 27). The other, *Study for the Williamsburg Project* of 1935 (fig. 28), had already organized this triplex arrangement, the only variation being the painter's line of sight penetrating the canvas, as in Picasso's *Painter and Model*. With these schematic lines of vision—implying the point of view of perspective—both de Kooning and Picasso rotated the horizontal panorama of artist/canvas/model ninety degrees to layer them one behind the other, the painter at the forefront as implicit point of view.

This very same transformation—from lateral panorama to perspective into depth—was given aesthetic prestige in the classical theme of the Three Graces, in which three Greek goddesses submit themselves to the judgment of the shepherd Paris. The traditional representation of the Three Graces concentrates on the nude as artist's model, a single figure triplicated by rotating her 360 degrees before the artist-observer (fig. 29). The Three Graces traditionally represent the Judgment of Paris, demanding that the viewer imagine the painter in front of the triplicate nudes as both observer and judge. Picasso's 1925 synthetic cubist painting *The Three Dancers* (*Les Trois Danseues*) repeats this composition of the Graces, frontal nude in the center flanked by profiled figures on either side (fig. 30). Behind the dancers large windows open onto a blue exterior, the shadows of the dancers spilling over onto the window panes as though onto a receptive surface of representation.

De Kooning's awareness of the necessity of the artist's vantage point as ballasting the figurative array in pictorial space was stated in his brilliant 1950 lecture "The Renaissance and Order," a treatment of the visual vectors internal to Western painting that surpasses anything written to that point on the implications of perspective:

> As a matter-of-fact, it was depth which made it possible for the world to be there altogether. . . . It was more intriguing [for the Renaissance artist] to imagine himself busy on that floor of his—to *be*, so to speak, on the inside of his picture. He took it for granted that he could only measure things *subjectively*, and it was logical therefore that the best way was from the inside. It was the only way he could eventually project all the happenings on the front-most plane. He became, in a way, the idea, the center, and the vanishing point himself—and all at the same time. He shifted, pushed, and arranged things in accordance with the way he felt about them.[25]

In his 1972 interview with de Kooning, Harold Rosenberg spoke of this principle of the artist as vantage point: "Suppose you have the idea that you'd like to paint a tableau of a tree with people or cats sitting under it. Isn't it true that while you are painting you must see yourself come into it? The action of painting has to catch the totality of object and subject." De Kooning replied, "That's right!"[26]

In "The Renaissance and Order," the lucidity and precision of de Kooning's treatment of perspectival construction, in which viewing and vanishing point oppose artist and depth, all the while each *presupposing* the other, bears out Denby's assessment of the sophistication of de Kooning's "understanding of every style and artistic idea." As I examine de Kooning's development of the triplex template of the *Woman* series here, the formulations of his "Renaissance and Order" will be referred to repeatedly.

Besides his WPA studies, de Kooning pursued the triplex composition in *Pink Landscape* (1942), *Father, Mother, Sister, Brother* (1937), and *Secretary* (1948). As *Willem de Kooning Nonstop* will argue throughout, the triplex structure dominated *all* de Kooning's Women.

De Kooning certainly saw Gorky's *Organization* (1933–36), which hung in Gorky's Union Square studio in 1935 (fig. 31). *Organization* is itself a variant on *The Studio*'s triplex arrangement with painter on the left, his palette in hand, and model in the center captured on the white canvas that fills the upper right quadrant of the surface.[27]

In their exploration of art uptown, de Kooning and Gorky visited the Frick Collection. There they examined the works by Ingres especially.[28] In the context of a model paired with her representation, Ingres's *Comtesse d'Haussonville* (1845) is particularly arresting (fig. 32). Her arms folded across her chest, the countess leans on a credenza, the back of her head and shoulders reflected in a rectangular mirror in perfect detail, where, in contrast to the body's presence, they become pure *representation*. The superimposed mirror and canvas would be what de Kooning's student Pat Passlof reported:

> Speaking of Ingres or Cézanne, he initiated me into the world of artists' concerns: finding and consolidating the picture plane; the role of movement, speed, and stillness in creating space; what paint does. Bill preferred to leave a door, a place in the plane to let you in—akin perhaps to the American Indian taboo against closing circumferences, although one is three-dimensional, the other two—a sort of asymptotic space.[29]

In a photograph of his studio from 1950, the still unfinished *Excavation* leans against the wall, with de Kooning standing in front of it as he shows Rosenberg what appears to be a compositional sketch for the work, arranged as an abstract series of flattened color planes, two of them rectangular (fig. 33). The sketch is as far as one could imagine from the roiling, interlocked pieces of the finished painting—their thickly smeared surfaces dispersed as so many body parts, profile, full face, nose and smiling jaw, which Tom Hess termed "a savage rending"[30] and Paul Brach declared "the fleshy crush of *Excavation*."[31] The compacted surface recalls that of *Attic* (1949), which de Kooning had interrupted to begin *Excavation* (fig. 34).

Across the bottom third of *Excavation* appears a sequence of rectangular openings, with the small "door," as he called it, added as he was finishing the work.[32] The break in the flat plane functions like the doors Passlof remembers him analyzing as the artist's goal of "finding . . . a place in the plane to let you in."[33] If these planes are the openings in the hoardings to protect passersby from the yawning pits of the excavation, they are also the mirrors reflecting tiny representations of the "savage rendings" of body parts, a memory of the *Comtesse d'Haussonville* perhaps, or of the profile captured on Picasso's canvas inserted into *Painter and Model*. The door in the plane "to let you in" completes the triplet of painter, canvas, and model, swiveled 90 degrees. Like the artist's sight-line in Picasso's *Painter and Model*, the perspectival window situates a tacit viewer before the depicted opening—whether picture frame or canvas: a viewer who was originally the artist himself now reduced to nothing more than an implicit point of view, the outset of Western perspective in what is termed the "viewing point" standing in opposition to its "vanishing point."

In every state of *Woman I*, as well as in the Women to follow, a window fills the upper right corner of the painting, inserted above the model's left shoulder. Through most of these States the "window" frame holds constant: a square with struts dividing it into four quadrants, mimicking the stretcher bars of a canvas seen back to front. In the reading of this constant square, the struts enforce an ambiguity between window and canvas. From the first, then, the window in the interior wall of the studio is envisioned as a support for the representation of the model, placed to the side of the central Woman but clearly doubling her.[34] By the third state, this canvas begins to support a rapidly brushed representation that could be of the model herself.

The slashing brushstrokes that sit atop the model's left shoulder in the final painting like an explosive epaulette, and then catapult down her side in a thick green smear that extends from her arm to the edge of the easel (fig. 3), confirms de Kooning's predilection for "a nice, juicy, greasy surface."[35] That surface demanded an invented medium combining turpentine, stand oil, and damar varnish, which, according to de Kooning's working procedure was constantly scraped down and sanded so that a new version could be layered over it. Ashton acknowledges this process: "De Kooning's reputation for working slowly, scraping out, starting all over again, and never really finishing a painting was legendary already in 1943."[36] Denby describes the typical jumps in de Kooning's process in essentially the same terms:

A new picture of his, a day or two after he had started it, had a striking, lovely beauty. . . . But at that point Bill would look at his picture sharply like a choreographer at a talented dancer, and say bitterly, "Too easy." A few days later the picture looked puzzled; where before there had been a quiet place for it to get its balance, now a lot was happening that belonged to some other image from the first. Soon the unfinished second picture began to be pushed into by a third. After a while a series of rejected pictures lay one over the other. One day the accumulated paint was sandpapered down, leaving hints of contradictory outline in a jewel-like haze of iridescence. . . . And then on the sandpapered surface Bill started to build up the picture again.[37]

By the fifth state both the model and her surroundings had been submerged in a bath of white paint that isolated and frontalized the figure. At this stage de Kooning felt himself to be at an impasse, unable to separate the flattened figure from its ground, unable to activate what he would eventually call "negative space." He had hit exactly that stone wall where, he confessed to Denby, "he was beating his brains out about connecting a figure and a background."[38] Connection here couldn't mean just continuity across a planar surface; it had to resonate with the underneath of a represented depth.[39]

This is one of the "painter's problems," he explained to Denby: de Kooning "talked about how a masterpiece made the figures active and the voids around them active as well, as active as possible."[40] It was in this context that de Kooning stated his great enthusiasm for the work of Miró: "He cut the Gordian knot. . . . The idea of in and out, forward and backward.He didn't talk about it, he just did it."[41] As he explained to his brother-in-law Conrad Fried, "'Edges are what we see. It's between the edges that it's difficult. That's what Vermeer is good at.' He'd say, 'What we're going to do is go look at a Vermeer. See how he painted between the lines.' So we'd go up to the Met."[42]

From de Kooning's Rotterdam days at the Academy, with its exercises of drawing from the figure,[43] he had modeled and shaded the spaces between the difficult "edges" of objects with the hatch marks of the draftsman's hardest of lead pencils—the 6H graphite tools he forced Passlof to use. "The thing is, when you're working like that it's hard to change," she said. "It's practically like working with an etching needle.He wanted that control."[44] The *Woman* series would put an end to that careful, academic shading. In 1950 the Museum of Modern Art mounted an exhibition of Chaim Soutine, whose expressive and explosive brushwork de Kooning admired. "Maybe it's the lushness of the paint," de Kooning said.[45] "He builds up a surface that looks like a material, like a substance. There's a kind of transfiguration, a certain fleshiness, in his work"[46] (fig. 35).

In the new vocabulary he was developing, his earlier parallel penciled hatch marks were exchanged for the explosive smear of housepainter's brushes. By the 1950s this brushstroke had become so seductive—de Kooning once said of it that he was "selling his own image now"[47]—that Jasper Johns, when he saw *Bolton Landing* (1957; fig. 36), called it a "wonderful painting. . . . [It] made me want to go out and buy a big brush."[48] In the 1960s de Kooning began to buy more varied brushes; Lou Rosenthal of NY Central Art Supply later reported to de Kooning's biographers that the artist had asked him to construct a brush "so he could do the swirling strokes."[49]

> The result was the aptly named "de Kooning brush," a round brush with stiff three-inch-long bristles and a long handle that enabled de Kooning to stand back from the canvas to see the effect he produced. "But he also liked some of the ordinary brushes that you buy in hardware stores,'" said [Michael] Wright. "He liked brushes with long bristles that had a lot of snap. He liked to soak them in water until they were really soft and pliable. They gave him a line that he liked. . . . He wanted them kind of floppy—a little resistance, but not too much. He'd buy three or four dozen of those. He'd order stuff for about a year, and it would sit around in these benches waiting to be used."[50]

The wide housepainter's brushes created the background transition between the "edges" with one juicy swipe. Since de Kooning painted wet-into-wet, the strokes smeared into a suave transition from light to dark, suggesting the tonal modeling of classical volumes. If this satisfied de Kooning, it was because of what he had wanted Conrad Fried to observe in Vermeer, to "see how he painted between the lines." This was the "negative space" that one smear of the brush could bridge, suggesting—at the same time as it evacuated—atmospheric shading.

Denby explained the effect of negative space as he had learned this lesson from de Kooning: according to Denby, de Kooning had told him that "keeping the figures and the voids equally active 'squeezed everything dramatically but somehow the picture opened itself way out, changing the center and the frame.'"[51] "The space between the figures becomes a firm body of air, a lucid statement of relationship, in the way intervening space does in the modern academy of Cézanne, Seurat, and Picasso."[52] De Kooning was proud of the way his explosive brushstrokes patterned the space between the lines, speaking of this manipulation as "fitting in."[53]

De Kooning's brushstrokes had become famous by the time *Excavation* ceded place to his Women. For many of his fellow painters, the strokes symbolized the individuality they wished to honor by imitation, leading to what Rosenberg disparaged as "the herd of independent minds."[54] If de Kooning's brushstroke "celebrated a kind of personal handwriting, a living record of one's feelings and sensations . . . , at a certain moment, to move a brush like de Kooning seemed to represent the epitome of grace under pressure. His brushstroke was manly, beautiful, despairing, and he attracted followers much as Hemingway did."[55]

Clement Greenberg lamented the host of de Kooning's imitators, comparing his brushwork to the lure of the Pied Piper. "De Kooning really took a whole generation with him," said Greenberg, "like the flute player of the fairy tale."[56] Hilton Kramer worried that the "cult of personality seemed to increase in exact ratio to the decline of the artist's work," adding, "The fabrication of synthetic de Koonings has become a 10th Street industry."[57] The snap and smear of de Kooning's brushes gave the impression of the paint being applied with lightning speed, or, as de Kooning expressed it, "so fast you couldn't think."[58] Like Greenberg, many critics did not admire this turbulent way of marking. When Manny Farber reviewed *Young Painters in the U.S. and France*, a Sidney Janis exhibition in autumn 1950, he restricted his account to the American participants, to whom he attributed a collective "speed fetish." They would, he wrote, "use every line and color as a speed-up connection in an endlessly linked journey over anonymous terrain."[59]

De Kooning admitted to Fried that he did indeed have a "speed fetish." Fried reported him saying: "I might work on a painting for a month, but it has to look like I painted it in a minute."[60] Farber criticized De Kooning's *Woman I* as a "maelstrom of black lines which lends a false excitement to a static, familiar composition," adding,

"These lines caught between illustration and ferocity, hide their glibness with an excess of shock and movement."[61] Many of de Kooning's critics comment on the artist's discomfort with his own facility and the pitfalls it might open not only to self-imitation but to banality. Elaine de Kooning underscores this point: "Bill was very irritated with his facility and he was constantly struggling against it."[62] Since de Kooning himself stressed the need for lightning speed in his delivery—"so fast you couldn't think"—many of his commentators interpret this as a way to outsmart the failure of self-repetition.

In reality, however, as many witnesses at his studio reported, de Kooning worked with the painstaking deliberateness that was manifested in the starts and stops of the puzzlelike discontinuity of the paintings' surfaces. In 1955 he gave voice to this: "I spend most of the time sitting there, studying the picture, and trying to figure out what to do next."[63] "What to do next" seems to have meant returning to an almost-blank canvas on which there were only faint traces of the earlier version of the work. De Kooning famously scraped down each day's activity, leaving the surface Denby had termed an "iridescence."[64] The surface formed by combining traces of earlier shapes with details of the eradicated work pocketed the painting with collagelike discontinuities and shifts of focus (fig. 37).

It was Tom Hess who had described de Kooning's process of cutting and pasting as a form of collage:

> Shapes do not meet or overlap or rest apart as planes; rather there is a leap from shape to shape; the "passages" look technically "impossible." This is a concept which comes from collages, where the eye moves from one material to another in similar impossible bounds. De Kooning often paints "jumps" by putting a drawing into a work-in-progress. Sometimes painting over part of it and then removing it, using it as a mask or template, sometimes leaving it in the picture.[65]

Contemplating each stage of his work, de Kooning would find areas he both liked and wanted to save but found to be the "hot spots" he was determined to avoid. At that point, according to Joop Sanders, who often observed de Kooning painting in the 1940s, "he would trace [the form] in charcoal on tracing paper" (fig. 38).[66] After each day's work, he would scrape down the canvas of all the built-up paint, leaving only a ghostly trace of the undercoat. Deliberately he would then lay the traced detail over different sections of the work until he found its satisfying location. Then, when he went over the edges on the front again with the charcoal, the charcoal lines on the back were transferred directly onto the paint. As Sanders explained, "When you take off the paper, you get an outline of the form. . . . Then he would paint the form another color or even use parts of the lines underneath to flatten out the shape so you get the structural lines of what was underneath. Which brings in a great deal of abstraction."[67] Of the pieces of paper, Sanders reported that "[de Kooning] would say, 'That looks interesting,' and cut it out and put it into something else and have that be a starting point."[68]

In his reading of the states of *Woman I*'s development, E. A. Carmean traces the changes wrought to the lower half of the model as her legs progress from silhouetted appendages—emphasized in State 2 by a drawing's flattened plane, lifted from State 1 and now collaged onto nearly a third of the surface—from which newly conceived legs, protruding from the collage plane, turn into projections outward toward the viewer, as seen in the final state.[69] The apex of these projections are, of course, the troublesome knees that led to de Kooning's problem of "not being able to get hold of" the *Woman*.[70]

The knees of *Woman I* repeat those of *Seated Woman* (circa 1940) and of *Woman* (1949), in which one knee is parallel to the picture plane while the other is the apex of the leg projecting outward, toward the viewer (figs. 17–22). In "De Kooning Paints a Picture," Hess lays out the progress de Kooning made from June 1950 to his discouragement a year and a half later that led him to discard the nearly finished *Woman I*. Hess's story continues, "A few weeks later, the art historian Meyer Schapiro visited de Kooning and asked to see the abandoned painting. It was brought out and re-examined. Later it was put back on the frame, and after some additional changes was declared finished."[71]

Perhaps it was Schapiro who analyzed the perspectival extension from de Kooning's position in front of the painting to the seated model, herself backed by her double on the truncated "canvas." This perspective onto the model from the painter's vantage point accords with the statement de Kooning made at this very time: "I am always in the picture somewhere. The amount of space I use I am always in, I seem to move around in it, and there seems to be a time when I lose sight of what I wanted to do, and then I am out of it. If the picture has a countenance, I keep it. If it hasn't, I throw it away."[72]

Although it has been speculated that Schapiro's intervention took place as he and the artist faced State 6,[73] Hess's more proximate account of the visit clearly states that Schapiro and de Kooning talked as they faced the almost completed picture in which the layered positions of knees protruding from torso had been developed, achieving the visual necessity of the implicit presence of the artist (as vantage point) in front of her.

Years later, in 1967, among the works that de Kooning delivered to M. Knoedler and Company for an upcoming exhibition were several *Woman on a Sign* paintings, painted on hollow-core doors.[74] The implication of the title (a billboard or advertising image) underscored the erotic impact of the spread-eagled pose of the woman, which de Kooning himself called "sexy," but added, "That's not the main issue for me. I'm working on a pose with which I can explore foreshortening and perspective."[75] Painting himself into the picture, even if only as implied point of view, is what de Kooning had explained in his lecture "The Renaissance and Order": "It was more intriguing to imagine himself busy on that floor of his—to *be*, so to speak, on the inside of his picture. He took it for granted that he could only measure things subjectively, and it was logical therefore that the best way was from the inside."[76] De Kooning described his admiration for Cézanne to Rosenberg, quoting Cézanne as saying "that every brushstroke has its own perspective. He didn't mean it in the sense of Renaissance perspective, but that every brushstroke has its own point of view."[77]

De Kooning's astonishingly precise analysis of the relation between viewing and vanishing point in Renaissance perspective, added to his comments about Vermeer to Conrad Fried, give us a measure of the heated intelligence of the formal discussions the 10th Street artists had among themselves either at the club or around their tables at the artists' hangout Romany Marie's. De Kooning's biographers report that "in the early 1930s, Cézanne remained an inspiration. How had he flattened the picture plane? How had the cubists taken his depiction of space still further? Matisse, Uccello, and especially Ingres, whom [John] Graham and Gorky revered, were held up for admiration. Hours were spent over cigarettes and three percent beer discussing the mysteries of space, perspective, and illusion."[78]

Just before shipping off *Woman I* for exhibition in 1953, de Kooning restored eight inches of canvas to its right edge (cropped off from the original decision about the picture's size). This last-minute enlargement reinforces the artist-model-canvas template that had held steady through all the stages of *Woman I*.

The extension makes room for a smeared gray parallelogram that overlaps the extension's plane, thereby suggesting a canvas and easel to the model's left, with dark, loosely brushed passages conveying the gestating representation of the woman. If the projecting knee does indeed imply the presence of the painter himself in front of both model and canvas, this composition reminds us of Vermeer's 1965/66 *The Art of Painting*, in which Vermeer's back is toward us as he faces both his canvas and his model (fig. 41). Dressed as Klio, the model wears a laurel wreath on her head, the wreath taking shape on the canvas beneath the artist's hand and brush, and visible as well in the swag of tapestry hung along the left side of the painting. Undoubtedly de Kooning would have described such a painting as enlivening the passages between the three elements—painter/model/representation—in terms of the space linking and separating their edges, as in the jigsawlike "negative" shape unfolding between the model's back and hip and the left-hand silhouette of the painter, its pale tint burgeoning forth as a "positive" surface. As we remember him explaining to Fried, "It's between the edges that it's difficult. That's what Vermeer is good at."

The use of aggressively smeared strokes of heavy paint to depict the representation of the model's body on the canvas in the final version of *Woman I* reminds us of the artist's statement from his 1950 lecture "The Renaissance and Order," in which he declares that for sixteenth-century Venetian painting, "the interest in the difference of textures—between silk, wood, velvet, glass, marble—was there *only in relation to flesh*. Flesh was the reason why oil painting was invented."[79] Perhaps the artist's inability to desert the subject of Woman stemmed from his commitment to his painterly craft and its medium—oil—since "flesh was the reason why oil painting was invented." For de Kooning, Rubens represented the ultimate capture in oil of women's flesh. As he said, "I'm crazy about Rubens, all those voluptuous women. He was the ultimate of the Baroque period—all hallelujah."[80]

Even in some drawings from the mid-1940s onward, the figures are twinned, with the model doubled by her representation. Once again the artist is given an implicit place by the model's silhouetted leg and projecting knee: see, for example, *Two Women in the Country* (1954; fig. 42). In *Untitled (Three Women)* (ca. 1948; fig. 43), the arrangement of the central figure's legs and knees presages the final state of *Woman, I*. In both, the posture can be seen to be explicitly based on the nude—second from the left—of Picasso's 1907 *Les Demoiselles d'Avignon* (fig. 44). This is the nude Leo Steinberg names the "rampant gisant"—a figure that is seen as alternately lying down (the gisant) and rearing up (rampant, in the language of heraldry). This rocking back and forth—itself the focus of the sharply triangular table that is thrust spearlike into the painting's space as a prolongation of the artist's stance before it—becoming, as de Kooning had said, "the idea, the center and the vanishing point himself."[81] This spearlike projection of the *Demoiselles'* table appears in the summer pastel *Two Women with Still Life* (1952) and in *Two Women in the Country*, as a triangular incursion into the space between the two nudes. Such a projection creates what Steinberg sees as the sexual impact of the work: "male *complicity* in an orgy of female exposure, the *direct axial address*, the spasmodic action, the explosive release in a constricted space, and the reciprocity of engulfment and penetration."[82]

Untitled (Three Women) enunciates the triplicate of artist/canvas/model differently from that of the larger *Woman* series. Here the painter is actually depicted before his canvas, on which the fragmented representation of the model's face can be seen.

The important State 5 of *Woman I*, where the model's frontal position is reinforced by the white ground that flattens and submerges her body—itself sketchily outlined in black—bears a curious resemblance to Matisse's *Mademoiselle Yvonne Landsberg* (1914), with the sitter hovering between her physical presence and the linear aureoles that encircle her as in a cocoon of pure gestation (fig. 45). The centrality of Matisse for de Kooning's art makes its presence felt in the contours of suggested bodies within *Attic* (fig. 34) and *Excavation* with their curvaceous limbs and supple torsos. But, even more, the Matisse example appears—as in *Excavation*—in the importance for de Kooning of the windows opened into the paintings' surfaces, as introjected repetitions of the canvas as a whole. The green window cut into the left side of *Asheville* (1948; fig. 46), flanked by half-opened violet shutters, both echoes the submerged rectangle with its bisected struts-as-suggested-canvas in *Special Delivery* (1946) and recalls its central position in the 1946 *Backdrop for "Labyrinth."*

Matisse's *Interior with Egyptian Curtain* (1948) juxtaposes a large window opening onto a profusion of palm fronds to a curtain within which the fronds are repeated as a curvilinear pattern, thereby producing ambiguity as to which is model and which is copy (fig. 47). This ambiguity repeats in *View of Notre-Dame* (1914), where the window of the painter's studio facing the cathedral is itself shaped like the famous twin bell towers, making the window/canvas into an always-already representation of the exterior object (fig. 48). The stained-glass windows of Matisse's Chapel of the Rosary in Vence, France (1948–51), with their depiction of the fronds in the garden just beyond the chapel's walls, thus repeat the ambiguity between inside and outside, as the light flooding the interior both includes and surrounds the body of the viewer/painter (fig. 49). The suggestion of the painter as subsumed within the field of representation is caused by the luminous aureole of the windows seeming to circulate around the artist as a plane both before and behind him.[83] The Vence Chapel takes the idea of the artist submerged in the midst of his represented space—"it was more intriguing to imagine himself busy on that floor of his—*to be*, so to speak, on the inside of his picture"—to a breathtaking pitch of specificity. In the Museum of Modern Art's *Piano Lesson* (1916), Matisse famously repeats the scrollwork of the instrument's music stand by the wrought-iron decoration of the window's balcony; the same wrought-iron décor opens out from *The Painter in His Studio* (1916–17; fig. 50), where the tripartite overlay recalls the all-important Picasso *Studio* composition pivoted 90 degrees to project the artist at his easel with the model in her chair already echoed in the representation on the canvas. Matisse was the painter of windows-rhymed-with-canvases, as in the Museum of Modern Art's *The Blue Window* (1913).

Doubts about de Kooning's specific interest in Matisse can be put to rest by awareness of de Kooning's avid inspection of old master art, reflected in his comments about Vermeer to Fried and his visits to the Met and the Frick, where he and Gorky would have been able to study Ingres.[84]

De Kooning's notorious painterly bravura was often viewed as a way of warding off the repetitive solutions that might be induced by his spectacular mastery of drawing. Some of his struggles led him to draw and paint with his left hand while watching television. De Kooning commentators often interpret this resistance as a rejection not only of theorizations about art but of his own compositional solutions as well—solutions, they claim, that de Kooning thought of as falling into the grip of *habit*.

Continually looking for ways to escape the deadening reflex of habit, de Kooning is seen as searching for techniques to produce the shock of an immediate onrush of sensation. "Action Painting" was

Rosenberg's term to evoke this immediacy, famously expressed thus: "At a certain moment the canvas began to appear to one American painter after another as an arena in which to act—rather than as a space in which to reproduce, re-design, analyze or 'express' an object, actual or imagined. What was to go on the canvas was not a picture but an event."[85]

To capture the immediacy of sensation, de Kooning's compositional practice depended on masking, which induced visual jumps from one part of the planar surface to another. In addition, he would rotate his canvas while working on it, the shifting orientations dispersing the structure of the figure. As he drew he often saw a shape that he wanted to save for later or move somewhere else in the picture.

The question why de Kooning could not lay the image of *Woman* to rest has elicited various answers—such as the relation exemplified by Rubens between woman's flesh and oil paint, the medium to which de Kooning was immovably committed. Denby reports that de Kooning's friends took up this struggle with him: "His friends would say, 'Listen Bill, you have a psychological block about finishing; you're being very self-destructive, you ought to see an analyst.' He burst out laughing, 'Sure, the analyst needs me for his material the way I need my pictures for mine.'"[86]

None of these explanations, however, is powerful or satisfying enough to account for the repetitions displayed here, and thus this study will offer other suggestions. But first we need to take up the repetition of de Kooning's compositional template as testimony to his formal control of his art.

2

Triplex-Nonstop

Willem de Kooning Nonstop has been arguing, contrary to the claim about *habit*, that de Kooning's commitment to the woman-as-model template held steady over four decades of his career, having produced, indeed, a compositional solution, begun while working in the WPA, that had become, if not habit, the nexus of what he, canny reader of pictures, wanted to say about the status of painting as representation. Its very repetition is another instance of the artist's inability to "stop."[1]

From the very beginnings of his work as a painter, the theme of the female model dominating his rectangular field held steady for three decades. This is true of *Seated Woman* (ca. 1940; fig. 39), *Woman Sitting* (1943–44), *Queen of Hearts* (1943–46), *Pink Lady* (1944), *Woman* (1949; fig. 40), and *Pink Angels* (ca. 1945; fig. 51). In every one of these, the head and torso are backed by a plane in the shape of a canvas. Thus the double of artist's model and field of representation was already operative. This needs only the insertion of the artist himself to fill in the triplicate elements of the composition de Kooning had put in place in the WPA and could not "stop."

3

The Shadow Knows

De Kooning had consistently said that the artist enters the picture as point of view, the linchpin of perspectival depth, and thus as the artist's desire to *be* on the inside of his picture.[1]

Picasso's *Painter and Model* (fig. 24) had served as the basis for de Kooning's faith in his tripart template; but Picasso's *The Shadow* (*L'Ombre*) of twenty-five years later (1953; fig. 52) creates an even more arresting model for de Kooning's conviction that the point of view need not be materialized through an actual representation of the artist. In *The Shadow* the artist casts himself as a mere shadow poised on the threshold of his bedroom, facing inward toward Françoise Gilot asleep on their bed. Picasso is reduced to pure vantage point, but the nude Gilot, asleep, is unconscious of his presence, her ignorance of his stance reducing him to an unstable "absence."[2] The simultaneous presence/absence of this disunity breaks what de Kooning had called the perspectival "subjectivity" that the Renaissance artist sought, as he understood that "the best way was from the inside." Picasso's shadow is cast onto Gilot's body in a layering that repeats the simultaneous overlap of model, artist, palette of his 1916 *Harlequin* (fig. 26). His commitment here to the tripartite organization of the studio is echoed by the three-part stratification of artist, model, and the canvas on which she will be represented, a canvas established by the luminous tabletop's rectangle, itself echoed by the frame (of mirror or stretcher bars) at the table's upper left corner.

The series of artist's models that derive from de Kooning's early years of life drawing at the Academy[3] includes *Pink Angels* (ca. 1945), two weightless nudes elevated as if in sleep (fig. 51). As Picasso had uncannily demonstrated in *The Shadow*, the sleeping model deprives the artist of his possibility of *being* "so to speak on the inside of his picture." Her refusal of recognition enforces his exile from the template. But elsewhere de Kooning *forces* his women's acknowledgment. The index of this pressure is registered by the hideous toothy grimace of

Woman I, as her transfixing stare acknowledges the painter's place before her (fig. 2). De Kooning's Women trouble their viewers by what is seen as his insistence on their ugliness, their brutality. The violent grimace as de Kooning's Women, including *Woman with Bicycle* (fig. 10), recognize their viewers with a distorted oral rictus was acknowledged by him in interviews: "I cut out a lot of mouths. . . . Maybe it was like a pun . . . maybe it's even sexual. . . . Maybe the grin. It's rather like the Mesopotamian idols. . . . They always stand up straight looking to the sky with this smile, like they were just astonished about the forces of nature, you feel—not about problems they had with one another. That I was very conscious of; [the smile] was something to hang on to."[4] The acknowledgment of the viewer as surrogate for the artist's vantage point was a crucial element of the tripartite template.

For, as we have seen, de Kooning's drive toward perspective, as when he said, "I'm working on a pose with which I can explore foreshortening and perspective,"[5] meant that he had to be present as point of view, a presence that had necessarily to be acknowledged by his model. Tom Hess reports, "The artist suggests a further complication of meaning, and points out that his 'idolized' Woman reminds him strongly of a landscape—with arms like lanes and a body of hills and fields, all brought up close to the surface, like a panorama squeezed together."[6]

Another artist who insisted on his presence before the canvas, his vantage point, his address, even taking up the very image of Picasso's *The Shadow*, was Jasper Johns, who in *Summer* (1985) adopted this not so much as the emblem of the artist's effacement as of the engagement with the surface emblematized by his cast shadow falling onto the field of vision (fig. 53). To the right of the artist's shadow, Johns painted the circular swipe of his own hand smearing the paint into a tonal gamut that mimes de Kooning's famous brushstroke. Johns's hand and its imprint had figured importantly as an index of his own presence to his canvas, as in his masterfully smeared *Diver* (1962–63), the smudged index of the artist sliding down the height of his charcoal-covered sheet, to end in the imprint of his splayed palms (fig. 54). The drive to register his own touch deposited onto the surface before him led Johns to the whole series called *Skin*, which could be called "Portrait of the Artist as a Cast Shadow" (fig. 55).

The trope of the shadow cast over the model to establish the artist's stance before her found its way into photography as well. In the 1950s Lee Friedlander stalked the streets of New York City and elsewhere, capturing its denizens with his own camera-bearing cast-shadow-merging photographer and prey (fig. 56).

Between 1937 and 1944 de Kooning's concern with the model tended toward single men, sometimes portraits, sometimes an anonymous seated man, sometimes himself as seen in a mirror, often stripped to the waist. The duplicated Women smeared onto the canvases either between the two models or behind them to summon forth what de Kooning saw as the all-important "negative space" gave way to increasingly abstract passages in the paintings of the 1950s, when de Kooning began to elaborate these formless smears and volumes into what would be called his "abstract urban landscapes": *Police Gazette* (1953), *Interchanged* (1955), *Gotham News* (1955), *The Time of the Fire* (1956), *Easter Monday* (1955–56; fig. 57), and *January 1st* (1956). Eventually these smeared, loosely brushed abstract passages were seen by de Kooning less as fragments of buildings than as glimpses of landscape.

The titles of *Woman as a Landscape* (1954–55) and *Two Women in the Country* (1954; fig. 42) make this transition more than clear. Another bridge to de Kooning's consideration of landscape emerges in the final monumental *Woman* painting: *Woman with Bicycle* (1952–53; fig. 9). Facing the viewer, the standing woman is flanked by heavily loaded brushwork. To her right the pale gray vertical strokes form a *V*, a visual trope that holds constant in the abstract highways to follow.

When the Guggenheim Museum hung the exhibition *Willem de Kooning in East Hampton*, half the work was from the series of landscapes begun in 1975, including *Whose Name Was Writ in Water*. The series was greeted with less than enthusiastic reviews. But de Kooning himself acknowledged its place in his art: "Then there is a time in life when you just take a walk: And you walk in your own landscape."[7]

While response to the landscapes and parkways was tepid in the 1970s, the 1959 Sidney Janis exhibition *Abstract Parkway Landscapes* stimulated the most enthusiasm of any show of the artist's work. De Kooning's oeuvre is articulated by sudden interruptions of his concentrated devotion to a given subject. The monumental Women thrust aside his opening preoccupation with abstract composition, just as the landscapes would in turn intervene abruptly in the development of Women. Some speculations on the importance of the Parkways have been convincingly made. Mine will see it as more of a return than a departure.

4

Through a Glass Darkly

These wildly inventive abstractions were soon known as "abstract landscapes." In a 1960 interview de Kooning enthused, "I love to be on those highways. And they are really not very pretty, but the big embankments and the shoulders of the roads and the curves are flawless—the lawning of it, the grass. . . .When I was working on this picture, this thing came to me; it's just like the Merritt Parkway [fig. 58]."[1]

The intense popularity of the Parkway abstractions in 1959 matched the general enthusiasm for this theme, as witnessed in *Nature in Abstraction*, which the Whitney Museum had mounted in 1958 with de Kooning's *February* juxtaposed to works by Phillip Guston, Alexander Calder, David Hare, and Mark Tobey.

An early example, *Door to the River* (1960; fig. 59), placed the parkway along the Hudson, just as the title of *Palisade* (1957) had done. The idea of the Parkway subsequently yielded to the long-distance implication of highways with names like *Montauk Highway* (1969), *Bolton Landing* (1957; fig. 36), and *Suburb in Havana* (1958; fig. 60). In his brilliant analysis of *Suburb in Havana*, Timothy Clark likens the ochre ground, dark horizon line, and converging orthogonal lines of the *V* in the picture to van Gogh's final painting, *Wheatfield with Crows* (1890; fig. 61), with the line of crows at the horizon of the field countered by the field's double pathways converging as a *V* into the body of the artist at his easel, that *V* hypothesized by some art historians to have produced the anxiety that might have triggered his suicide.[2] Imagining all the possibilities that the addition of the *V* at the end of de Kooning's labor on the Havana painting could signify, Clark suggests not only the *V* in Van Gogh but also Hemingway's suburban villa ten miles from Havana, which de Kooning had visited: Finca Vigía.

The *V* could also be windshield wipers, he adds, which would put de Kooning himself in the passenger seat of a car, with the smears at the upper left of the painting an indication of the driver. In relation to the highway pictures, de Kooning declared his love of country driving. "I'm crazy about weekend drives," he said, "even if I drive in the middle of the week. I'm just crazy about going over the roads and highways."[3] Describing his associations while passing various landscapes, he said, "I had a vast area of nature—a highway and the metamorphosis of passing things. A highway, when you sit in the car—removed . . . "[4] Such "remove" was that of sitting in the passenger seat; de Kooning, a nondriver, was regularly chauffeured by Wilfred Zogbaum in his Packard. Clark makes the association between the passenger-seat perspective of the road and the 1917 Matisse *The Windshield, On the Road to Villacoublay* (fig. 62), which de Kooning could have known from Alfred Barr's monograph on Matisse.

With their views outward toward a horizon in the distance, we could ask whether the highway paintings break with the triplex organization of the Women. But to sit in the front of a car—particularly at night—is to feel the white road markings rushing toward oneself, converging into a *V* that constantly disappears beneath the windshield and the hood of the car. The converging *V* in *Havana* is like the *V* in *Merritt Parkway*, which in turn is like the onward rushing *V* in *Bolton Landing*, presaged by the *V* flanking *Woman with Bicycle* (fig. 9). Once more de Kooning has put his overlapping figures in place with the landscape serving as his "model" (when he says "coming around roads . . . and having sensation of a piece of it"),[5] and the car's windshield his canvas, with the onrushing road markers instating the artist himself as tacit point of view.[6] "I still have it now," he says, "from some fleeting thing—like when one passes something, . . . and it makes an impression."[7]

"The painting," Clark says, "is all about wresting a viewpoint, a lookout, from a landscape where 'in fact' you never found one. There is a way in which once you have Matisse's view through the windshield . . . as key, *Suburb in Havana* can come to look naively literal about its view of things from the passenger seat. Is that the driver behind the wheel to the left? Are those smears of rain across the glass? About to be cleared by *the V of the wiper-blades*? Well no, not quite."[8]

The Parkway Landscapes would occupy de Kooning for seven years, an even longer time than his labor on the monumental phase of his Women. To account for such a fixation, the Parkways, with their automotive interiors, must have satisfied de Kooning's impulse toward the triplex composition. This can be plotted by understanding the windshield, with its plane of representation, as a kind of "canvas" onto which the model of the landscape seen through it is imprinted in turn.

If that accounts for two aspects of the tripartite template, the third—the artist himself—is included as the viewpoint at the nexus of the onrushing highway's *V*. Conrad Fried speaks of de Kooning's early concerns with these windshields: "Then there was an advertising campaign in which Ford asked for a dozen views of America through the windshield. So Bill carefully laid out a windshield. Then he painted this winding road ahead and cows off to the side."[9]

With the windshield playing the role of the canvas, it was there for de Kooning as something that always needed to be pierced. Like Picasso before him, de Kooning struggled to break with the two-dimensional aspect of painting. But as had been structured into his grasp of painting, the model's body organized this distanced view: *Woman I*, he said, reminded him of a landscape, "with arms like lanes and a body of hills and fields, all brought up close to the surface, like a panorama squeezed together."[10]

If the monumental Women entered in 1950 to interrupt the triumphant series of abstract paintings that culminated in *Excavation* (fig. 15), and continued from 1950 to 1964, the Parkway Landscapes would in turn intrude into the flow of the Women in 1957 and continue to 1963. The earliest of these was *Palisade* (1957), soon followed by *Door to the River* (1960).

The windshield as representational field is both transparent (like a window) and flat (like a picture plane). This makes the Parkway pictures a burgeoning forth of the important window/canvas's representational surface at the upper right corner of the monumental *Women*. Thus the formal condition for the women holds constant even in the unlikely Parkway pictures—the window/canvases playing their continuing duplicative role, and the road markers placing the artist/viewer "inside" the painting. De Kooning's grasp of the perspicuous role of Renaissance perspective never deserted him. It is what produces the mastery that so many observers and scholars have wanted to share with their readers.

But this formal constant is what some writers dismiss as "habit," something, they argue, de Kooning was compelled to break.[11] This constant, however, intuited from Ingres's *Comtesse d'Haussonville* (fig. 32) and even more from Matisse's windows flooding his studio with images that invade the interior surfaces to leave their representational imprints, was a formal conviction from which de Kooning would never withdraw.

I have raised the perplexing question why de Kooning couldn't desert the Woman as subject/object. This is the center of the problem of *Willem de Kooning Nonstop*. It is a *why*? that needs now to be pursued.

"I can't get away from the Woman," de Kooning admitted. "Wherever I look, I find her."[12] Ubiquitously finding her has the ring of a repetition-compulsion that might demand explanation in the dimension of the unconscious.

5

Totem and Taboo

Compulsively finding Woman "wherever he looks" makes it not inappropriate to say that *woman* had become de Kooning's fetish. De Kooning often described the uncontrollable transformation of the beautiful woman he had wanted to paint as the creation of a "monster."[1] Her aggressive mouth with its toothy smile (figs. 2, 10) is often identified as gynephobic. But in the literature on de Kooning this monstrous smile is reinterpreted: "*Woman I* is the depiction of a relationship. It suggests *two figures* locked in struggle. If the artist himself is not literally described, he is present nonetheless in the slashing and furious brushstroke. *The perspective is that of a child looking up at an adult.*"[2]

Freud's discussion of the development of the fetish takes place in the context of the uncanny, the triggering of tremendous dread as though at the threatening sight of death (the uncanny return of the protective double now turned into a threat to the child's ego). The menace within the uncanny's threat is castration, Freud argues, of which the child is in dread but which he can stave off until that fateful moment when he sees his mother's genitals and concludes that she has been castrated. The vantage point of this sight is that of lying down and looking up the mother's skirt, a revelatory glance upward from below. Freud says that the last thing the child sees before this fateful observation will become his fetish, his preservation from death by way of this penis-substitute, and thus the possibility of still believing in the wholeness of his mother's body. His example is from the analysis of a patient bilingual in German and English. His fetish, he told Freud, was a "shine on the nose." In German, this "shine" is *Glanz*, homophonic with English's *glance* so that German's *Glanz auf der Nase* would be English's "*glance* at the nose." Such a *glance* is, for Freud, from the vantage upward from below. Which makes it significant that de Kooning would organize his own vantage on the monumental Women upward from below.

Doubles have a role to play in the context of the uncanny. In childhood, doubles of the self (such as mirror images or one's shadow cast on the ground) are imagined as protective extensions of the ego. But there comes a moment, Freud says, that instead of guardians of the ego, doubles are seen as turning round against it and becoming a castrative peril. At this point in his analysis Freud outlines Otto Rank's theory of the double:

> an insurance against destruction to the ego, an "energetic denial of the power of death," as Rank says; and probably the "immortal" soul was the first "double'" of the body. This invention of doubling as a preservation against extinction has its counterpart in the language of dreams, which is fond of representing castration by a doubling or multiplication of the genital symbol. . . . Such ideas, however, have sprung from the soil of unbounded self-love, from the primary narcissism which holds sway in the mind of the child as in that of primitive man; and when this stage has been left behind the double takes on a different aspect. From having been an assurance of immortality, he becomes the ghastly harbinger of death.[3]

This double, this first narcissistic projection, is thus thought primitively through the agency of all doubles: shadows cast by the body as well as the body's mirrored reflections. The shadow is the earliest form through which the soul is imagined: projecting the persistence of the bodiless self after death in the form of a "shade." For many cultures the shadow is also the form in which the souls of the dead return, to haunt or take possession of the living.[4] What the fetish achieves, then, is denial; it persists because it remains a token of triumph over the threat of castration and a safeguard against it. For Freud, once the fetish is installed, it cannot but be repeated over and over, summoned back to its protective place.

Most of the monumental Women organize their vantage on the female body according to the fetish *Glanz auf der Nase*, upward from below. This is particularly prescient in *Woman IV*, where the blue hemispheres of knees and skirt rhyme with the heavy spherical breasts (fig. 6). In *Woman V* the yellow parallelogram of her lap reinforces the perspectival glance upward and the distance between legs and body (fig. 7). Perhaps this fetish character explains de Kooning's determination to encode that perspective on the Women which made it so difficult for him to "stop."

The premonition of de Kooning's Woman-as-fetish might explain both the monstrous and threatening character of her compulsively repeated representations and her exaggerated sexual attributes, such as her enormous breasts and splayed legs, as in *Woman III* (fig. 5). Between the legs of *Woman I* is a triangular patch, which may, of course, indicate the empty place of the woman's genitals (fig. 1). More significant is the way the neck and head surmount the prominent breasts to suggest the erect phallic form of castration denial. Thomas Hess speaks of the Women in these terms: "Face, breasts and sex, each pulled open to confront the viewer on a vertical axis suggesting a totem."[5]

De Kooning's Women began with his struggle to map a perspectival vantage on the body (something he felt he hadn't achieved until his talk with Schapiro); it developed that vantage into the onset of the fetish with the discovery of castration, from the trigger of which the woman swells into the fetish form of the phallus, with monstrous breasts and pubis. The surmounting breasts and head are found at the horizon of the perspectival thrust, combined as a Nose, glimpsed fleetingly from below.

The smeared representation of the woman on the strip of canvas added to the right side of *Woman I* also takes a phallic shape, performing the role Rank gives to the double.

The frequently twinned women pictured on the porch of the Castelli East Hampton house enact the protective doubling, explaining in part the compositional repetition within de Kooning's oeuvre, a repetition that the publicly declared end of abstract expressionism brought to a close.

6

"After Abstract Expressionism"

De Kooning had the misfortune to accede to a *posthumous life*. This began as early as 1953, when the boyish Robert Rauschenberg rang his doorbell and charmed him into a long talk. Soon the younger man explained his visit as a desire to have one of de Kooning's drawings—not to keep it but to *erase* it. De Kooning would eventually see from the change in Sidney Janis's gallery exhibitions, such as the Pop Art show of 1962, the rising interest the dealer was manifesting in the nascent movements of Pop and the New Realism. But even in 1953 he could turn to Rauschenberg and say of his request, "I know what you're doing."[1] He got out a portfolio of drawings and leafed through it. Finally he extracted a complex example made of charcoal, pencil, crayon, and ink. Settling on this over more minor ones, he told Rauschenberg, "I want to give you one that I'll miss."[2]

"He really made me suffer," Rauschenberg remembered; "It took me two months, and even then it wasn't completely erased. I wore out a lot of erasers"[3] (fig. 63).

The important MoMA exhibition *Sixteen Americans* definitively declared the obsolescence of Eighth Street's explosive smears and whiplash lines. It marked the debut appearances of the laconic Frank Stella and deadpan Ellsworth Kelly. But the biggest blow to de Kooning's self-esteem was the 1961 Guggenheim exhibition *The American Abstract Expressionists and Imagists* that H. H. Arnason mounted, in which color-field painting displaced abstract expressionism from every wall. It was at this juncture that Clement Greenberg delivered his definitive 1962 lecture "After Abstract Expressionism." The lecture repeated what Greenberg had been saying for the years during and since de Kooning's Woman series: figurative painting had been consigned to oblivion by abstraction and was now unremittingly *minor*. The swipes and smears of de Kooning's dragged paint, he said, unequivocally suggest the classical modeling that builds the illusion of three-dimensional forms. Any vestige of illusion, Greenberg insisted, destroys the ambitions of abstract art. This is because illusion per se is the womb primed to house nascent representational forms. The abstract expressionists might have turned away from traditional modeling and linear perspective, but their furtive continuation of the hills and valleys of illusionism nonetheless encouraged what Greenberg called "homeless representation."[4] The turbulence that gave rise to spatiality itself is what Heinrich Wölfflin had called the *painterly* (with respect to Tintoretto and Rembrandt), a painterliness to be seen in the case of abstract expressionism in the open webs of Pollock's art and the smeared brushstrokes of de Kooning's. "If the label 'Abstract Expressionism' means anything," Greenberg wrote, "it means painterliness: loose, rapid handling, or the look of it; masses that blotted and fused instead of shapes that stayed distinct; large and conspicuous rhythms; broken color; uneven saturations or densities of paint, exhibited brush, knife, or finger marks."[5] De Kooning's case was the one Greenberg turned to again and again, citing the tonal effects of shading and modeling as the artist's tendency to paint wet-into-wet graduated the smeared color from light to dark. "In itself, 'homeless representation' is neither good nor bad," Greenberg wrote, "and maybe some of the best results of Abstract Expressionism in the past were got by flirting with representation. Badness becomes endemic to a manner only when it hardens into mannerism. This is just what happened to 'homeless representation' in the mid-1950s, in de Kooning's art."[6]

Were it not enough to be consigned to a living death as a painter, de Kooning was even stripped by Greenberg of his preeminent touch. It was to the Pop artist Jasper Johns that Greenberg passed the torch of the de Kooning pictorial attack, writing of Johns that "his case is another exemplary one, for he brings de Kooning's influence to a head by suspending it clearly, as it were, between abstraction and representation"[7] (figs. 54–55). The wretched irony in this was that Greenberg was now describing de Kooning's "manner" as the desperate illusionism of "homeless representation," stripping it of all possibility of attaining to the abstraction that de Kooning had fought for in *Excavation* and his Urban Landscapes.

The "After" in Greenberg's title marked a watershed in the history of ambitious art, a past and future rotating around the contradiction between painterliness and color: "Unequal densities of paint become, as I have said, so many differences of light and dark, and these deprive color of its purity and its fullness . . . the slapdash application of paint ends by crowding the picture plane into a compact jumble."[8] At that juncture, what he called "the free flow of color-space" was the only way to achieve *major* art. For the painters who had broken through to this kind of handling, color "is more than chromatic intensity; it is rather one of an almost literal openness that embraces and absorbs color in the act of being created by it. Openness, and not only in painting, is the quality that seems most to exhilarate the attuned eyes of our time."[9] Of the abstract expressionists, only Newman, Rothko, and Clyfford Still were seen to have attained this openness, with their work now pointing to "the only way to high pictorial art in the near future."[10]

Greenberg's examples of the painters who had achieved the required openness were exactly those whose work had crowded Tenth Street painting from the galleries of Arnason's Guggenheim show: Morris Louis and Kenneth Noland. Color-field painting was thus the future that had developed in the aftermath of de Kooning's and Pollock's art.[11]

No matter how this massive repudiation must have stung de Kooning, he still had something to retrieve from openness as attained by Morris Louis. De Kooning was the artist who had wrestled with negative space and what was "between the lines" all his life. In Louis's series of *Unfurleds*, the large, unprimed white canvas ground burgeoned forth from a passive, negative underneath into an effulgent positivity (fig. 64). This promotion of the "empty" ground into a positive force became the basis of the last series of paintings de Kooning did until he stopped altogether, six years before his death in 1997. Sometimes called *Ribbon Paintings*, they were also referred to as "Alzheimer's Paintings," due to the dementia that debilitated him in his later years. Assessments of the "Alzheimer's Paintings" have generally been negative, seeing the in-between spaces as flaccid, empty. An example is Paul Brach, who wrote, "Consider the de Koonings from the early '80s to the present. The aged master, weak and near senility, cared for by his personal support system of assistants continues to paint."[12] That de Kooning might have vanquished negative space even while flirting with it has been ignored.

We remember de Kooning saying that his major problem was to puncture the surface of the canvas. We also remember his admiration for Miró's control of line so that one single stroke could weave its way through three dimensions: "He cut the Gordian knot . . . the idea of in and out, forward and backward."[13] This possibility of a single drawn line dispensing with negative space compensated for the "homeless representation" of de Kooning's turbulent surfaces. As Denby had reported: "De Kooning talked about how a masterpiece made the figures active and the voids around them active as well, as active as possible."[14] The *Ribbon Paintings* were de Kooning's way of voiding the painted spaces "between the edges" and taking up Miró's spatial control of line as he "cut the Gordian knot." Drawing had always been de Kooning's means of mastery, so much so that, as I have noted, Elaine de Kooning had called it the "facility . . . he was constantly struggling against."[15]

Untitled I (1985) dares to model line itself, using the edging brush of de Kooning's commercial background to produce line as bicolored contours (fig. 65). The pastel washes that tint the flanking areas between the lines achieve the look of layered planes, re-creating something of the triplex template of de Kooning's "habit." *Untitled I* "begins" at the lower left corner with the splayed *V* of the perspectival vantage point of *Woman, I*, encountering a bipart shape of the "model's" knees surmounted by her "torso"; to her left is a replication of this body, like the profile cast onto the canvas of Picasso's *Painter and Model* (fig. 24). Other ribbon paintings weave the space "in and out" through roller-coaster-like parallels (*The Cat's Meow* [1987; fig. 66]); still others suggest the spirals of a nautilus.

De Kooning's last hurrah was control of the negative space of the empty white interstitial fields. Perhaps it was Matisse, through his late cutouts (fig. 67), who gave permission for the *Ribbon Paintings*' translation of the triplex template. Given de Kooning's frequent visits to MoMA and his admiration for Matisse, it is tempting to imagine the late cutouts as a model for making white grounds into the force that will animate and activate the space between the lines.[16]

. . . Its Bad Name

7

With the 1949 revelatory article on Jackson Pollock—"Is He the Greatest Living Painter in the United States?"—*Life* magazine became the fount of information about the American avant-garde for a public aware that something new (and bewildering) was happening in the nation's art scene.[1]

The Pollock essay had been preceded in 1948 by a roundtable that *Life* convened in the penthouse of the Museum of Modern Art. (*Life*'s unusual attention to the American avant-garde was spearheaded by cultural editor Dorothy Seiberling, then married to critic and art historian Leo Steinberg.) "Fifteen distinguished critics and connoisseurs," wrote the editors, "undertake to clarify the strange art of today."[2] The panelists included Professor Meyer Schapiro, critic Clement Greenberg, and curator (first at MoMA and then at the Guggenheim) James Johnson Sweeney. *Life* also illustrated the work of what it called five "young American extremists," with de Kooning represented by *Painting* (fig. 14) and Jackson Pollock by *Cathedral*, in addition to works by Adolf Gottlieb, William Baziotes, and Theodore Stamos. *Life* singled out de Kooning by reporting that both Greenberg and Sweeney admired him:

> When the moderator inquired as to what Mr. de Kooning was trying to say, Mr. Greenberg replied that he thought Mr. de Kooning was wrestling with his fears, but that this overtone of foreboding and anxiety was not the most important aspect of the picture. "The emotion in that picture," continued Mr. Greenberg, "reminds me of all emotion. It is like a Beethoven quartet where you can't specify what the emotion is but are profoundly stirred nevertheless."[3]

This new avant-garde, so inexplicable to a wider public, fairly begged to be explained. Accordingly in 1951 Harold Rosenberg obliged with “The American Action Painters,” ballasting abstraction expressionism with a philosophical movement—existentialism.[4] This provoked a response from Mary McCarthy in *Partisan Review*, who called Rosenberg a “pirate” and puzzled over his point that the so-called Action Painter cared only about the “act” or “event” of painting and not about the finished product; her admonishment ended, “You cannot hang an event on the wall, only a picture.”[5] In response, Rosenberg penned “Critic within the Act,” in which he dismissed her objection by saying that events had so overtaken history as to obliterate the wall as such:

Perhaps you cannot hang an event on the wall, only a picture. But this is a problem for the picture more than it is for events. For a wall implies a space in which to stand next to it. This space is now lacking. The Bolshevik Revolution may have turned into a picture on the wall, but it was a picture that pulled the entire globe into it, and even outer space. No room was left for the spectator who merely looks, as there was in the days when the earth had empty spots and the heavens were full.[6]

In 1955 Clement Greenberg had anticipated McCarthy’s question with “‘American-Type’ Painting,” where he attended to the specific formal logic of each painter, beginning with de Kooning, moving to Pollock and Hofmann, and then to Still, Motherwell, and Newman.[7] At first Greenberg focused on the history of Western easel painting, which was structured by a strong contrast between lights and darks. It was only with the onset of impressionism, he argued, that a suppression of this contrast took hold and, by means of this suppression, paintings gained the power of all-over surfaces and greatly enlarged scale. Like impressionism’s own, the challenge that abstract expressionism mounted to easel painting came from the close-valued surfaces of Newman, Pollock, and Rothko, which, Greenberg explained, allowed them to magnify the size of their canvases as greatly as Monet in his Water Lily canvases had magnified his. Analytical cubism, in suppressing the depth achieved by value contrast, worked, as it needed to, in the mode of close value.

Within this formal logic, it is to cubism, then, that Greenberg looks for the understanding of de Kooning’s art:

De Kooning’s figurative paintings are haunted as much as his abstract ones are by the disembodied contours of Michelangelo’s, Ingres’s and even Rubens' nudes. Yet the dragged off-whites, the grays and the blacks in one phase, and the vermilions, yellows and mint greens in another, which insert these contours in shallow depth, continue to remind one of Picasso by their application and inflection. There is the same more or less surreptitious shading of every plane, and a similar insistence on sculptural firmness. No more than Picasso can de Kooning tear himself away from the figure and that modeling of it for which his sense of contour and chiaroscuro so well equip him.[8]

The complexity of this "explanation" by way of the shallow "Picassoid space" of analytical cubism could not prevail against the seductive idea of *action*, and Rosenberg's rubric—with its overtones of existentialist anxiety, despair, and absurdity—proved too fashionable to resist. De Kooning in particular had gotten the reputation of being a restless and implacable spirit. As the artist Louis Finkelstein said of him, "By the time I knew his name, he was already a kind of a legend.[9] Robert Rauschenberg echoes this assessment: "In the '50s and early '60s, to see Bill on the street downtown was to witness a vision whose aura eclipsed even his own shadow."[10]

Greenberg held his fire for nearly a decade before he savaged Rosenberg's "The American Action Painters" with the 1962 essay "How Art Writing Earns Its Bad Name."[11] Speaking of the unusually brilliant success of American abstract painting in Europe, he added, "It is as though a fatality dogged the success: a fatality of misinterpretation that was also a fatality of nonsense."[12] This fatality operated in American criticism as well. When *ARTnews* published "De Kooning Paints a Picture," its author, Tom Hess, was impelled to invoke the notion of existentialist *doubt*: "The result, like that of all works of art, can be compared to a *new map of the human sensibility*," he wrote.[13] Such a map then led Hess to speak of de Kooning's action in terms of a voyage: "the exploration for a constantly elusive vision" as a way of assuring his work's continuity. "He needs such *doubt*," Hess ended, "to keep off balance."[14] Hess's term *voyage* echoes Rosenberg's *action*, with its implications of risk on the way to self-discovery. Denying *Woman*'s status as "a progress or development," Hess corrected: "rather there was a voyage."[15]

Engaging with the existentialist argument of Rosenberg's "American Action Painters," Greenberg shrugged: "Transposing some notions from Heidegger's and Sartre's Existentialism, Mr. Rosenberg explained that these painters were not really seeking to arrive at art, but rather to discover their own identities through the unpremeditated and more or less uncontrolled acts by which they put paint to canvas."[16] "For them," he continued, "the picture surface was the 'arena' of a struggle waged outside the limits of art in which 'existence' strove as it were to become 'essence.'"[17]

Greenberg's 1962 refusal of an existentialist motive for de Kooning's work is somewhat complicated by his earlier remark, reported in the *Life* roundtable, that "de Kooning was wrestling with his fears, but that this overtone of foreboding and anxiety was not the most important aspect of the picture."[18]

The very idea of the "arena," from the 1951 "American Action Painters," had led Rosenberg to underscore action's precedence over final product. "Now, everything must have been in the tubes, in the painter's muscles," Rosenberg wrote. "If Lucrece should come out she will be among us for the first time—a surprise," stressing, "to the painter, she *must* be a surprise. In this mood there is no point to an act if you already know what it contains."[19] To underscore this surprise, Rosenberg stressed that the abstract expressionists had excluded sketches from their repertoire: "'B is not modern,' one of the leaders of this mode said to me. 'He works from sketches.'"[20]

Nonetheless, Hess's *ARTnews* essay had started by illustrating the enormous two-part sketch de Kooning had pinned up in his studio at the outset of *Woman I* (see fig. 16; "Lucretia" prefigured indeed!).[21] The deliberateness with which the artist worked was often reported, with Hess calling it "a method of a continuous series of drawings, which are cut apart, reversed, exchanged and otherwise manipulated on the painting."[22] As well, the disruptive action of scraping off the buildup of paint after every day's work had become notorious.

De Kooning's own description of his process belies the Rosenbergian "leap into the unknown." "I spend most of the time sitting there, studying the picture," he said in 1955, "and trying to figure out what to do next."[23] For Joop Sanders this time spent in front of the unfinished painting led to an existentialist kind of crisis: "I think the outstanding thing in his art is his doubt, his equivocating about it."[24]

De Kooning began to be made an existential hero because of his black-and-white pictures' famous ambiguity, *ambiguity* being one of the watchwords of the philosophical movement. Interviewed by Irving Sandler about his interest in existentialism, de Kooning remembered that the movement was "in the air. Without knowing too much about it, we were in touch with the mood. . . . I read the books, but if I hadn't I would probably be the same kind of painter. I live in my world."[25]

De Kooning's world may have been obsessed with Jean-Paul Sartre's 1945 lecture "Existentialism Is a Humanism," which was published in English in 1947, but de Kooning's resistance to action was supported by the systematic caution with which he worked.[26] Furthermore, his forty-year repetition of the tripartite template would suggest that essence, not action, preceded existence for him.

Yet no matter how tempting it is to agree with Greenberg and see *action* as the way art writing had indeed "earned its bad name," the record does not support this. Not only did de Kooning admit to Sandler that existentialism was "in the air," but in the context of Eighth Street circles, de Kooning began to be made an existential hero because of his inability to attain the end of doubt and thus to "stop."

In the postwar 1940s, writers, artists, and intellectuals in New York discussed Sartre's lecture, which fed their Cold War pessimism about the future. They identified Sartre's ideas about the impossibility of making a choice with de Kooning's inability to remove doubt. The avant-garde had become porous to existentialism. Sartre spoke of existentialism's conviction that God had abandoned mankind. Such abandonment means the disappearance of God as a calculus of *value* by which choices can be assessed. The absence of God commits man, then, to the radical choice of choosing not only for himself but for all men. Despair emerges from the inevitable realization that all choices are ambiguous. If this leaves man free to choose, no choice is free from doubt. From the triumphal lectures Sartre delivered in New York (in 1946 he spoke at Carnegie Hall), the watchwords of existentialist thought were *alienation*, *anguish*, *ambiguity*, and *despair*.

Given that *despair* was one watchword of existentialism, it is significant that de Kooning chose to address his contemporaries at the Eighth Street Subjects of the Artist: A New School[27] with his 1949 lecture "A Desperate View." De Kooning's lecture expressed the idea of desperation most consistently with the metaphor of "trembling": "If one takes the idea of trembling, for instance, all of a sudden most of art starts to tremble. Michelangelo starts to tremble. . . . All the Impressionists start to tremble. The Egyptians are trembling invisibly and so do Vermeer and Giacometti. . . . Cézanne was always trembling but very precisely."[28] It is hard to hear *trembling* in this context without thinking of Søren Kierkegaard's "Fear and Trembling." Pat Passlof reports that Elaine de Kooning read passages of Kierkegaard to Willem de Kooning in the evening, "and the ordinariness of Kierkegaard's heroes, or anti-heroes, appealed to Bill."[29]

Kierkegaard's concept of dread and despair—"the dizziness of freedom"—arose from the Genesis story of Abraham's command from God to sacrifice his son Isaac. God had told Abraham that his seed would multiply and populate the Promised Land, but, paradoxically, he now demanded that Abraham murder what he loved best. Having received no explanation, Abraham was then caught between his duty to God and the admonition to commit murder. He was forced to choose between the contradictions of belief and morality, a choice that can be made only in fear and trembling.

De Kooning's lecture on desperation was given, significantly, after the September 1949 issue of *Partisan Review* had published a translation of Maurice Merleau-Ponty's essay "Cézanne's Doubt." The essay begins with a strange, phenomenological kind of "Cézanne Nonstop": "He needed 100 working sessions for a still life, 500 sittings for a portrait. What we call his work was, for him, only an essay, an approach to painting."[30] Merleau-Ponty stresses Cézanne's determination to paint himself inside each picture as witness to the spectacle in the course of its becoming form:

> He wanted to depict matter as it takes on form, the birth of order through spontaneous organization. Cézanne wanted to paint this primordial world, and his pictures therefore seem to show nature pure, while photographs of the same landscapes suggest man's works, conveniences, and imminent presence. . . . Cézanne's paintings give the impression of an emerging order, of an object in the act of appearing, organizing itself before our eyes.[31]

What must have struck de Kooning most forcefully in this exposition is the description of Cézanne's registration of his own point of view, the crucial vantage as de Kooning had described it in "The Renaissance and Order":

> It was more intriguing to imagine himself busy on that floor of his—to *be*, so to speak, on the inside of his picture. He took it for granted that he could only measure things subjectively, and it was logical therefore that the best way was from the inside. It was the only way he could eventually project all the happenings on the frontmost plane. He became, in a way, the idea, the center, and the vanishing point himself—and all at the same time.[32]

In his 1972 interview with Harold Rosenberg, de Kooning introduced Merleau-Ponty's notion of Cézanne's paintings giving "the impression of an emerging order" by saying, "Cézanne said that every brushstroke has its own perspective. He didn't mean it in the sense of Renaissance perspective, but that every brush-stoke has its own point of view."[33]

In 1948, a year preceding the publication of "Cézanne's Doubt" and just after Sartre's pronouncement "Existentialism is a Humanism," Sartre turned his attention to Alberto Giacometti by publishing an introductory essay on the artist's sculpture for the catalogue of a 1948 exhibition at the Pierre Matisse Gallery (fig. 68). In "The Search for the Absolute," published in English as it was, de Kooning would have noted Sartre's stress on the multiple points of view: "[Giacometti] has to write movement into the total immobility, unity into the infinite multiplicity" rhymed with the infinite testing of Cézanne's doubt. In addition, the philosopher's attention to Giacometti's sculpture may have stimulated de Kooning's own.[34] The relationship became more emphatic when de Kooning entered the sculptural medium in 1969. Invited to Spoleto, Italy, to participate in the Festival of Two Worlds, de Kooning ran into his old 10th Street friend Herzl Emanuel in Rome. Emanuel had a small foundry in Trastevere, to which he invited de Kooning. Accepting gratefully, since he had no studio abroad, de Kooning soon asked Emanuel for clay. Piling the wet medium onto armatures made of found objects, de Kooning kneaded and pulled the earthen mass in the manner of his work with oil, as in his *Woman on a Sign* series of 1967. Emanuel, struck by this beginner's efforts made with his eyes closed, said, "To me the figures were in the spirit of his blind drawings."[35] This was all the truer in view of de Kooning's thumb and fingerprints as reminders of the famous 10th Street touch. In contrast to the smooth and anonymous surfaces of much modern sculpture, as well as the slick facades of the minimalist painting that had spelled de Kooning's own obsolescence, de Kooning's hand was always insistently present. Surprisingly satisfied with his output, de Kooning asked Emanuel if the figures could be cast. The process involved firing the pieces, made of water clay, in a kiln, after which a mold could be made for casting the sculptures in bronze.

Returning in 1969 to his studio in Springs, de Kooning continued to work in clay, writing to Emanuel that he "was really taking it [sculpture] serious enough."[36] But de Kooning's dealer, Xavier Fourcade, was not encouraging. "Look, they're not good," he told de Kooning. Without any possessiveness, de Kooning replied, "Of course, I don't know why you're making such a fuss. It's nothing."[37]

But de Kooning had already become committed to sculpture, comparing his work in wet clay favorably to his experience with oil. In 1972 he explained this:

> In some ways, clay is even better than oil. You can work and work on a painting but you can't start over again with the canvas like it was before you put that first stroke down. And sometimes, in the end, it's no good, no matter what you do. But with clay, I cover it with a wet cloth and come back to it the next morning and if I don't like what I did, or I changed my mind, I can break it down and start over. It's always fresh.[38]

In 1970 Henry Moore, visiting New York, saw de Kooning's Italian sculpture and told Fourcade he liked them. Moore's one reservation concerned the scale. They would be stronger enlarged, he thought, perhaps even to the monumental proportions of his own work. Revisiting his opinion about the quality of the sculpture, Fourcade acted on Moore's suggestion and commissioned an enlargement of *Untitled #12* (1969). The enlargement was titled *Seated Woman*. Another figure from the same series, *Untitled #2*, subsequently enlarged to become *Standing Figure* (fig. 69), repeats the model de Kooning used for most of his Italian bronzes: his 1964 charcoal drawing *Woman in a Rowboat*, a spread-eagled figure at the bottom of a boat whose upper edge contains her as if enclosed by a mandorla (fig. 70).

This doubling of a model as though her twin-half were her mirrored representation carries the tripartite composition into de Kooning's sculpture. It was the influence of Giacometti, whose *Nose* and *Man Pointing* (both 1947) de Kooning could have seen in New York in 1948, with their incorporation of the sculptor's point of view both in their rugged surfaces and in the barely compatible difference between the linear effect of the frontal view and the breadth of the silhouette that inscribed the first member of the triumvirate—artist, model, representation. It was in the difference between front view and silhouette that Giacometti inscribed his point of view on the work, just as Merleau-Ponty described Cézanne's doubt: "He wanted to depict matter as it takes on form, the birth of order through spontaneous organization."[39]

De Kooning's own *Head #3* (1973; fig. 71), with its rugged surface and incompatible points of view echoes what Sartre had written about the presence of the sculptor as the ambient point of view, at the point when frontal ridge line gives way to broadened profile: "[Giacometti] has to write movement into the total immobility, unity into the infinite multiplicity."[40] We can hear in this de Kooning's analysis of the Renaissance painter, as "he became, in a way, the idea, the center, and the vanishing point himself—and all at the same time."[41]

De Kooning probably drew his mid-1960s studies of *Woman in a Rowboat* with his eyes closed.[42] The vellum paper he used for some drawings suspends the woman over the surface's splotches of light and dark to make the woman appear to float in the water. The spread-eagled posture in boat or water, with one leg the mirrored twin of the other, opens the vulva and pudendum to view as the center and focus of the figure.

All the Women, and particularly the 1964 painting group loosely called *Sag Harbor* (fig. 12), express the genitals atop the supporting legs. The suggestion has been made above that Woman had become de Kooning's fetish, the registration of the uncanny opening onto an impossible doubt that forced endless repetition. On its vellum support, the sun-struck *Woman in a Rowboat* seems to be *trembling*, caught between Kierkegaard's uncanny belief and refusal. Beginning in Rome, de Kooning's cast sculptures prolong this structure of doubt into his last major phase of production. Sexual ambiguity reflected de Kooning's sense that existentialism was what was "in the air." And de Kooning would prolong that conviction until his death.

8

De Kooning's Doubt

After moving to Springs, the Long Island town where he had built a studio, in 1963, de Kooning began a new group, *Clam Diggers* (fig. 13), resulting in many paintings and drawings of figures standing in water and of their reflections and the reflections of those reflections. The shimmer he was after was inscribed on a 1963 drawing: "no fear but a lot of trembling" (fig. 72). The figure depicted above the inscription is like one of his women in a rowboat, but seen in profile. De Kooning said of his *Clam Diggers* (fig. 13):

> I try to free myself from the notion of top and bottom, left and right, from realism! Everything should float. When I go down to the water's edge on my daily bicycle ride I see the clam diggers bending over, up to their ankles in the surf, their shadows quite unreal, as if floating. This is what gave me the idea. . . . The whole secret is to free yourself of gravity![1]

Clam Diggers (1963) achieves this very freedom and effect of floating by leaving out the women's feet, both allowing the reading that they are standing in water and untethering them from the earth. The presence of reflections in the series suggests the topic of optical illusions to Rosenberg. Denying such an effect, Rosenberg shrugs: "That business of putting a stick in water so that it looks as if it's broken . . . " But just as adamantly defending the effect, de Kooning replies, "Well it is. That's the way you see it."

> ROSENBERG: What do you mean, it is broken? If you pull it out of the water, it's not broken.
> DE KOONING: I know. But it's broken while it's in the water.
> ROSENBERG: The break is an illusion.
> DE KOONING: That's what I am saying. All painting is an illusion. Mondrian gives you one kind of illusion, whatever you call it, tension . . .[2]

The figure standing in the water up to her waist is like the stick reflected so as to seem broken. And it is the effect of the illusion of breakage that causes the image to tremble.

In their effect of trembling, the *Clam Diggers* enter the world of Cézanne's doubt. As noted earlier, in developing this doubt, Merleau-Ponty wrote, "he wanted to depict matter as it takes on form, the birth of order through spontaneous organization. Cézanne wanted to paint this primordial world, and his pictures therefore seem to show nature pure, while photographs of the same landscapes suggest man's works, conveniences, and imminent presence."[3] Similarly, the *Clam Diggers*, emerging from the water as a trembling bent stick, give, like Cézanne's paintings, "the impression of an emerging order, of an object in the act of appearing, organizing itself before our eyes."[4] In Merleau-Ponty's view, this was the source of Cézanne's doubt, and as a parallel, the trembling stick in the water can be seen as de Kooning's portrait of Cézanne in his "Desperate View" lecture: "Cézanne was always trembling, but very precisely."[5]

The *Clam Diggers* are mostly paired figures of women, but the *Sag Harbor* or *Accabonac* paintings that de Kooning painted on the hollow-core doors (fig. 73) delivered to the building site of his studio in Springs were single, like the *Women* of the 1950s. The elongated door format would seem to preclude the tripartite template of the early *Women*, leaving no room for the canvas-bound, displaced representation of the model, or no place in the excited brushstrokes for the artist's inclusion as viewer. Yet, squeezed as they would have to be, the smears on the right side of the field indicate a burgeoning place of representation, just as the eight inches added to the right of *Woman I* (fig. 3) do.

In *Woman, Sag Harbor* (1964), however, the tapering of the body from anus to tiny head and the single "juicy swipe" that bridges the bottom edge of the door with the figure's buttocks re-creates the artist's presence before the model (fig. 12). De Kooning had admired Cézanne's insight by quoting the artist's saying that "every brushstroke has its own perspective." Cézanne "didn't mean it in the sense of Renaissance perspective," de Kooning emphasized, "but that every brushstroke has its own point of view."[6]

Acknowledgments

It was in the midst of John Elderfield's inspired 2011 Willem de Kooning exhibition at the Museum of Modern Art that my convictions about this book took form. My friend Karen Kennerly had insisted that we visit it together, I more or less as her guide, Karen having known that my senior thesis at Wellesley College had been on de Kooning. Fixing on the repetitive formats of the Women paintings along with an explanation of the pictorial intelligence behind them, I realized that my improvised exposition was developing a series of explanatory tropes nowhere to be found in the de Kooning literature. I revisited the show many times, two of them to try out my observations on friends and colleagues: with my Columbia University associate Noam Elcott, with whom we focused on the presence of Picasso in de Kooning's work; and with my friend and collaborator (on *October* magazine and for the *l'Informe* exhibition at the Centre Pompidou, Paris) Yve-Alain Bois.

There is an empty gesture made in many acknowledgments at the outset of academic books that gratefully names readers of the book in draft form and then ritualistically exonerates them from any blame for mistakes or lapses in the text. Here, then, are the readers who have helped and encouraged me, with or without responsibility for errors of fact or judgment, listed without exoneration: Denis Hollier, Julia Garretson Strand, Susan Crile, Yve-Alain Bois, Noam Elcott, Anne Hollander, Lauren Sedofsky, and of course Karen Kennerly.

Timothy Clark was not a reader of my draft but an exemplar for it. His masterly essay on *Suburb in Havana* set the standard for writing about de Kooning's important series of landscapes.

The production of this book would not have been possible without meticulous work on the illustrations by my Columbia University research assistant, Tina Rivers Ryan. In addition, this project has been reinforced by the essential cooperation of the de Kooning Foundation.

To Susan Bielstein, the Press's executive editor for art, architecture, and classical studies, my gratitude is endless. From the very first she believed in the value and freshness of this work, and during the course of the editing she pressed me to expand and refine my descriptive analyses of the works. No thanks here are enough.

Notes

CHAPTER ONE

1. Willem de Kooning, in David Sylvester, *Interviews with American Artists* (New Haven, CT: Yale University Press, 2001), 57.

2. In his 1948 "The Crisis of the Easel Picture," Clement Greenberg described this genre as subordinating "decorative to dramatic effect. It cuts the illusion of a box-like cavity into the wall behind it, and within this, as a unity, it organizes three-dimensional semblances" ("The Crisis of the Easel Picture," in *Arrogant Purpose, 1945–1949*, vol. 2 of *Clement Greenberg: The Collected Essays and Criticism*, ed. John O'Brian [Chicago: University of Chicago Press, 1988], 221).

3. This is the argument made by Richard Shiff in the "Stop" section of *Between Sense and de Kooning* (London: Reakton Books, 2011).

4. This story is told in Thomas B. Hess, "De Kooning Paints a Picture," *ARTnews* 52, no. 1 (March 1953): 30–33, 64–67.

5. The *Clam Diggers* are mostly paired figures of women, but the series of *Woman Sag Harbor*, or *Acabonic* (fig. 73), or *Montauk*, some of which de Kooning painted on the hollow-core doors he ordered for his new studio in Springs, or on door-sized sheets of vellum, were single, like the Women of the 1950s. Thomas B. Hess, "De Kooning's New Women," *ARTnews* 64 (March 1965): 36.

6. Alfred H. Barr Jr., "Gorky, De Kooning, Pollock," *ARTnews* 49 (June-August 1950).

7. Mark Stevens and Annalyn Swan, *De Kooning, an American Master* (New York: Alfred A. Knopf, 2004), 309. Stevens and Swan note, "There are numerous accounts of de Kooning's struggle with *Woman I* and the technical processes he employed to make the picture. Most rely upon Thomas B. Hess, 'De Kooning Paints a Picture,' *ArtNews* (March 1953), 30–33, 64–67. See also E. A. Carmean, *American Art at Mid-Century: The Subjects of the Artist*, exhibition catalog (Washington: National Gallery of Art, 1978)."

8. Barr Jr., "Gorky, De Kooning, Pollock."

9. Stevens and Swan, *De Kooning*, 294.

10. Edwin Denby, *Willem de Kooning*, ed. Raymon Foye and Francesco Clemente (Madras: Hanuman Books, 1988), 50.

11. Willem de Kooning, quoted by David Sylvester in Sylvester, Richard Shiff, and Marla Prather, *Willem de Kooning: Paintings* (Washington, DC: National Gallery of Art, 1994), 16.

12. Stevens and Swan, *De Kooning*, 105.

13. Dore Ashton, *The New York School: A Cultural Reckoning* (New York: Viking, 1973), 81.

14. Stevens and Swan, *De Kooning*, 130–31.
15. Ashton, *New York School*, 79.
16. Stevens and Swan, *De Kooning*, 131.
17. Ibid., 105.
18. Edwin Denby, "The Thirties," in *Dance Writings and Poetry* (New Haven, CT: Yale University Press, 1998), 3. This essay originally appeared under the same title in *The 30s: Painting in New York* (New York: Poindexter Gallery, 1956).
19. Steven and Swan, *De Kooning*, 310. Stevens and Swan are here drawing from Willem de Kooning, interview by Selden Rodman, in *Conversations with Artists* (New York: Capricorn, 1957), 105. Edwin Denby, "My Friend de Kooning," *ARTnews Annual* 29 (1964): 91.
20. Denby, "My Friend de Kooning," 91.
21. Joan Mitchell, quoted in Eleanor Munro, *Originals: American Women Artists* (New York: Simon and Schuster, 1979), 245.
22. E.A. Carmean Jr., "Willem de Kooning: The Women," in E. A. Carmean Jr. and Eliza E. Rathbone with Thomas B. Hess, *American Art at Mid-century: The Subjects of the Artist*, exh. cat. (Washington, DC: National Gallery of Art, 1978), 154.
23. De Kooning in Sylvester, *Interviews*, 49–50.
24. Denby, "My Friend de Kooning," 91–92.
25. Willem de Kooning, "The Renaissance and Order," in Thomas B. Hess, *Willem de Kooning*, exh. cat. (New York: Museum of Modern Art, 1968), 141 (italics for "subjectively" are mine). "The Renaissance and Order," written for a lecture series at Studio 35 on Eighth Street in New York, was originally published in *Trans/formation* 1, no. 2 (1951): 85–87.
26. Willem de Kooning, interview by Harold Rosenberg, *ARTnews* 71 (September 1972): 55.
27. Stevens and Swan, *De Kooning*, 98, includes a photograph of the two painters with *Organization* hanging behind them.
28. Ibid., 104, 139.
29. Pat Passlof, "1948," in "Willem de Kooning, on His Eighty-Fifth Birthday," special issue, *Art Journal* 48, no. 3 (Autumn 1989): 229.
30. Thomas B. Hess, *Willem de Kooning* (New York: George Braziller, 1959), 29.
31. Paul Brach, "De Kooning's Changes of Climate," *Art in America* 83, no. 1 (January 1995): 74.
32. Joan Levy, interviews by Mark Stevens and Annalyn Swan, February 6 and June 13, 1995, quoted in Stevens and Swan, *De Kooning*, 297.
33. Passlof, "1948," 229.
34. In his state-by-state account of *Woman, I*'s development, E. A. Carmean does not mention the window/canvas ambiguity (Carmean, "Willem de Kooning: The Women"). Elderfield similarly ignores the window/canvas of *Woman I*. The only recognition he gives to the model's twinning by the inclusion of her depiction appears in his account of *Woman V*: describing a tilted rectangle seemingly collaged onto the painting's surface, he notices vertical and horizontal struts flanking it that imply a tilted representational surface (Elderfield et al., *De Kooning*, 274).
35. Hess, "De Kooning Paints a Picture," 65.
36. Ashton, *New York School*, 166–67.
37. Denby, "My Friend de Kooning," 88. Rudy Burckhardt, "Long Ago with Wil-

lem de Kooning," in "Willem de Kooning, on His Eighty-Fifth Birthday," special issue, *Art Journal* 48, no. 3 (Autumn 1989): 87.

38. Denby, "The Thirties."

39. In his discussion of the Woman series, Elderfield speaks of "the artist's struggles with foreshortening," made more complicated by "his practice of extensive revision" (Elderfield et al., *De Kooning*, 199).

40. Denby, *Willem de Kooning*, 24.

41. De Kooning, *Time*, unpublished interview by Welch, "An Analysis of Abstract Expressionism, Its Meaning, the Major Figures," background file, July 20, 1958, quoted in Stevens and Swan, *De Kooning*, 136–37.

42. Conrad Fried, interviews by Mark Stevens and Annalyn Swan, May 31 and June 1, 1995, quoted in Stevens and Swan, *De Kooning*, 182.

43. De Kooning in Sylvester, *Interviews*, 104.

44. Pat Passlof, interview by Mark Stevens and Annalyn Swan, July 18, 1990, quoted in Stevens and Swan, *De Kooning*, 270.

45. De Kooning, in Margaret Staats and Lucas Mathiessen, "The Genetics of Art," *Quest* 1 (March-April 1977): 70; as quoted in Judith Zilczer, *Willem de Kooning: From the Hirshhorn Museum Collection* (Washington, DC: Hirshhorn Museum and Sculpture Garden, Smithsonian Institution, and Rizzoli, 1993), 47n87.

46. Ibid.

47. Gregory Battcock, "Big Splash," *Time*, May 18, 1959, 72.

48. Jasper Johns (January 1983), in Stedelijk Museum, *Willem de Kooning: Het Noordatlantisch Licht / The North Atlantic Light, 1960–1983* (Amsterdam: Stedelijk Museum, 1983), 83.

49. Lou Rosenthal, interview by Mark Stevens and Annalyn Swan, October 23, 1991, quoted in Stevens and Swan, *De Kooning*, 493.

50. Ibid.

51. Denby, "My Friend de Kooning," 91.

52. Edwin Denby, "Notes on Nijinsky Photographs" (1943), in *Dance Writings*, ed. Robert Cornfield and William Kackay (London: Dance Books, 1986), 496.

53. Tom Ferrara, multiple interviews by Mark Stevens and Annalyn Swan, July 8, 1992, to February 16, 1996, quoted in Stevens and Swan, *De Kooning*, 562.

54. This is the title of the fourth section of Harold Rosenberg's *The Tradition of the New* (New York: McGraw-Hill, 1965).

55. Stevens and Swan, *De Kooning*, 367.

56. Clement Greenberg, unpublished interview for *Willem de Kooning*, exh. cat. (Paris: Centre George Pompidou, Musée national d'art moderne, 1984), as quoted in Stevens and Swan, *De Kooning*, 367. New York School painting was often identified as "10th Street" in reference to the district where many abstract expressionists lived.

57. Hilton Kramer, "De Kooning's Pompier Expressionism," *New York Times*, November 19, 1967.

58. Shiff, *Between Sense and de Kooning*, 81.

59. Manny Farber, "Art," *The Nation* 171 (November 11, 1950): 445.

60. Fried, interviews by Stevens and Swan, quoted in Stevens and Swan, *De Kooning*, 591.

61. Farber, "Art," 445.

62. Elaine de Kooning, "On the Work of Willem de Kooning" (1983–84), in *The Spirit of Abstract Expressionism: Selected Writings*, ed. Rose Slivka and Marjorie Luyckx (New York: George Braziller, 1994), 228.
63. Shiff, *Between Sense and de Kooning*, 82.
64. Denby, "My Friend de Kooning," 87–88.
65. Hess, *Willem de Kooning*, 47.
66. Joop Sanders, interviews by Mark Stevens and Annalyn Swan, October 31, 1990, to March 13, 1993, quoted in Stevens and Swan, *De Kooning*, 249.
67. Ibid.
68. Ibid.
69. Carmean, "Willem de Kooning: The Women."
70. See n. 22 above. Carmean, "Willem De Kooning: The Women," 154.
71. Hess, "De Kooning Paints a Picture," 30.
72. De Kooning quoted in Robert Goodnough, ed., "Artists' Sessions at Studio 35" (1950), in *Modern Artists in America*, ed. Robert Motherwell, Ad Reinhardt, and Bernard Karpel (New York: Wittenborn Shultz, 1951), 12.
73. Carmean, "Willem de Kooning: The Women," 162.
74. "De Kooning's Woman of the 1950s was soaked in his concepts of a New York light and space. She was throned in an artist's white-washed loft-studio, the panes of a window or panels of a door materialized at her shoulders." Hess, "De Kooning's New Women," 37.
75. Willem de Kooning, *Newsweek*, unpublished interview by Ann Ray Martin, background file, November 1, 1967, quoted in Stevens and Swan, *De Kooning*, 498.
76. De Kooning, "Renaissance and Order," 141.
77. De Kooning, interview by Rosenberg, 55.
78. Stevens and Swan, *De Kooning*, 108.
79. De Kooning, "Renaissance and Order," 142.
80. De Kooning, *Newsweek*, interview by Martin, as quoted in Stevens and Swan, *De Kooning*, 580.
81. De Kooning, "Renaissance and Order," 141.
82. Leo Steinberg, "The Philosophical Brothel," *October* 44 (Spring 1988): 64, italics added.
83. I thank Yve-Alain Bois for this suggestion about the circumnavigation of Matisse's windows. Matisse speaks about this effect in "Statement to Tériade: On Fauvism and Color, 1929," in *Matisse on Art*, ed. Jack Flam (Berkeley: University of California Press, 1995), 86.
84. De Kooning himself admitted this reverence for Matisse. "Lately I've been thinking," he said in 1980, "that it would be nice to be influenced by Matisse. I mean, he's so lighthearted. I have a book about how he was old and he cut out colored patterns and he made it so joyous. I would like to do that too—not *like* him, but joyous, more or less" (Willem de Kooning in Amei Wallach, "At 79, de Kooning Seeks Simplicity," *Newsday*, December 4, 1983, 7).
85. Rosenberg, "The American Action Painters," in *Tradition of the New*, 25.
86. Denby, "My Friend de Kooning," 88.

CHAPTER TWO

1. *Father, Mother, Sister, Brother* (1937) is one of the many versions of the triplex composition. See John Elderfield et al., *De Kooning: A Retrospective*, exh. cat., ed. David Frankel (New York: Museum of Modern Art, 2012), 72, plate 8.

CHAPTER THREE

1. See Willem de Kooning, "The Renaissance and Order," in Thomas B. Hess, *Willem de Kooning*, exh. cat. (New York: Museum of Modern Art, 1968).
2. This is brilliantly argued in Denis Hollier, "Pablo Picasso: The Painter without His Model," *Raritan* 9, no. 1 (Summer 1989): 1–26.
3. Willem de Kooning, in David Sylvester, *Interviews with American Artists* (New Haven, CT: Yale University Press, 2001), 48.
4. Ibid., 51–52.
5. Willem de Kooning, *Newsweek*, unpublished interview by Ann Ray Martin, background file, November 1, 1967, quoted in Mark Stevens and Annalyn Swan, *De Kooning, an American Master* (New York: Alfred A. Knopf, 2004), 498.
6. Thomas B. Hess, "De Kooning Paints a Picture," *ARTnews* 52, no. 1 (March 1953).
7. Willem de Kooning, from *Sketchbook No. 1: Three Americans*, a film produced and directed by Robert Snyder (1960).

CHAPTER FOUR

1. John Elderfield et al., *De Kooning: A Retrospective*, exh. cat., ed. David Frankel (New York: Museum of Modern Art, 2012), 317. Willem de Kooning, interview by David Sylvester, "Content Is a Glimpse," 1960, available at http://www.dekooning.org/documentation/words/content-is-a-glimpse.
2. T. J. Clark, "De Kooning's *Suburb in Havana*," lecture at Columbia University, December 6, 1995.
3. Willem de Kooning, in David Sylvester, *Interviews with American Artists* (New Haven, CT: Yale University Press, 2001), 53.
4. Willem de Kooning, interview by Harold Rosenberg, *ARTnews* 71 (September 1972): 55.
5. Willem de Kooning, in "Inner Monologue," unpublished typed transcript by Marie-Anne Sichère of a 1959 conversation between de Kooning, Michael Sonnabend, and Kenneth Snelson for Robert Snyder's "Masters & Masterworks" film. Courtesy the archives of The Willem de Kooning Foundation.
6. Clark, "De Kooning's *Suburb in Havana*."
7. De Kooning in Sylvester, *Interviews*, 51.
8. Clark, "De Kooning's *Suburb in Havana*."
9. Conrad Fried, interviews with Mark Stevens and Annalyn Swan, May 31 and June 1, 1995, quoted in Stevens and Swan, *De Kooning*, 183.
10. De Kooning, as paraphrased in Thomas B. Hess, "De Kooning Paints a Picture," *ARTnews* 52, no. 1 (March 1953): 67.

11. Shiff, *Between Sense and de Kooning*, 64.
12. Douglas Davis, "De Kooning on the Upswing," *Newsweek*, September 4, 1972, 70.

CHAPTER FIVE

1. Mark Stevens and Annalyn Swan, *De Kooning, an American Master* (New York: Alfred A. Knopf, 2004), 339.
2. Ibid., 339, italics added.
3. Sigmund Freud, "The Uncanny," in *The Standard Edition of the Complete Psychological Works of Sigmund Freud*, trans. James Strachey (London: Hogarth and the Institute of Psycho-analysis, 1953–74), 17:234–35. See also Otto Rank, *The Double*, trans. Harry Tucker Jr. (Chapel Hill: University of North Carolina Press, 1971).
4. Freud, "Uncanny." See also Rosalind Krauss, "Corpus Delicti," *October* 33 (Summer 1985): 31–72.
5. Thomas B. Hess, "De Kooning's New Women," *ARTnews* 64 (March 1965): 64.

CHAPTER SIX

1. Mark Stevens and Annalyn Swan, *De Kooning, an American Master* (New York: Alfred A. Knopf, 2004), 359. Stevens and Swan note that "the account given . . . is based on: Robert Rauschenberg, unpublished interview for *Willem de Kooning*, exh. cat. (Paris: Centre Georges Pompidou, Musée national d'art moderne, 1948); Leo Steinberg, *Encounters with Rauschenberg (A Lavishly Illustrated Lecture)* (Chicago: University of Chicago Press, 2000); and a conversation with Rauschenberg in Sept. 1997."
2. Ibid., 360.
3. Ibid.
4. Clement Greenberg, "After Abstract Expressionism," in *Modernism with a Vengeance, 1957–1969*, vol. 4 of *Clement Greenberg: The Collected Essays and Criticism*, ed. John O'Brian (Chicago: University of Chicago Press, 1993), 124.
5. Ibid., 123.
6. Ibid., 124.
7. Ibid., 126.
8. Ibid., 129.
9. Ibid., 131.
10. Ibid.
11. For Greenberg the desire for openness even leaped across the divide between painting and sculpture: in 1948, some years before "After Abstract Expressionism" he characterized contemporary sculpture as rejecting the dense, monolithic materiality of traditional sculpture in favor of an opticality that could make the three-dimensional medium a function of "eyesight alone," concluding: "To render substance entirely optical, and form, whether pictorial, sculptural or architectural, as an integral part of ambient space—this brings anti-illusionism full circle. Instead of the illusion of things, we are now offered the illusion of modali-

ties; namely, that matter is incorporeal, weightless, and exists only optically like a mirage" (Greenberg, "The New Sculpture" [1948/1958], in *Art and Culture: Critical Essays* [Boston: Beacon, 1961], 144).

12. Paul Brach, "Auditioning for Posterity," *Art in America* 79 (January 1991): 153.

13. De Kooning, *Time*, unpublished interview with Welch, "An analysis of Abstract Expressionism, its meaning, the major figures," background file, July 20, 1958, quoted in Stevens and Swan, *De Kooning*, 136–37.

14. Edwin Denby, *Willem de Kooning* (Madras: Hanuman Books, 1988), 24.

15. See Richard Shiff, *Between Sense and de Kooning* (London: Reaktion Books, 2011), 78; Elaine de Kooning, "On the Work of Willem de Kooning" (1983–84), in *The Spirit of Abstract Expressionism: Selected Writings*, ed. Rose Slivka and Marjorie Luyckx (New York: George Braziller, 1994), 228.

16. My thanks to Susan Crile for this observation.

CHAPTER SEVEN

1. Dorothy Seiberling, "Jackson Pollock: Is He the Greatest Living Painter in the United States?," *Life* 27, no. 6 (August 8, 1949): 42–43, 45. Seiberling was the art editor of the magazine in the 1950s.

2. Russell W. Davenport with Winthrop Sargeant, "A *Life* Round Table on Modern Art: Fifteen Distinguished Critics and Connoisseurs Undertake to Clarify the Strange Art of Today," *Life* 25, no. 15 (October 11, 1948): 56–68, 70, 75–76, 78–79.

3. Ibid., 62.

4. Harold Rosenberg, "The American Action Painters," in *The Tradition of the New* (New York: McGraw-Hill, 1965).

5. Mary McCarthy, "An Academy of Risk," review of Harold Rosenberg, *The Tradition of the New*, *Partisan Review* 26, no. 3 (Summer 1959): 476, 480.

6. Harold Rosenberg, "Critic within the Act," *Encounter* 16, no. 1 (June 1961): 59. Also in *ARTnews* 59, no. 6 (October 1960), and as the preface (1960) to Rosenberg, *Tradition of the New*.

7. Clement Greenberg, "'American-Type' Painting," in *Art and Culture: Critical Essays* (Boston: Beacon, 1961), 208–29. Originally published in *Partisan Review* 22, no. 2 (Spring 1955): 179–96.

8. Ibid., 213–14.

9. Louis Finkelstein, interview by Mark Stevens and Annalyn Swan, March 14, 1990, quoted in Stevens and Swan, *De Kooning, an American Master* (New York: Alfred A. Knopf, 2004), 266.

10. Robert Rauschenberg, statement in "Willem de Kooning, on His Eighty-Fifth Birthday," special issue, *Art Journal* 48 (Autumn 1989): 232.

11. Clement Greenberg, "How Art Writing Earns Its Bad Name" (1962), in *Modernism with a Vengeance, 1957–1969*, vol. 4 of *Clement Greenberg: The Collected Essays and Criticism*, ed. John O'Brian (Chicago: University of Chicago Press, 1993), 135–44.

12. Ibid., 135–36.

13. Thomas B. Hess, "De Kooning Paints a Picture," *ARTnews* 52, no. 1 (March 1953): 31, italics added.

14. Ibid., italics added.

15. Ibid., 135–36.

16. Greenberg, "How Art Writing Earns," 136.

17. Ibid.

18. Clement Greenberg in "*Life* Round Table on Modern Art."

19. Rosenberg, "American Action Painters," 25.

20. Ibid., 25.

21. Hess, "De Kooning Paints a Picture," 30.

22. Ibid., 31.

23. De Kooning, quoted in Irving Sandler, *A Sweeper-Up after Artists: A Memoir* (New York: Thames and Hudson, 2003), 53.

24. Joop Sanders, interviews by Mark Stevens and Annalyn Swan, October 31, 1990, to March 13, 1993, quoted in Stevens and Swan, *De Kooning*, 268.

25. De Kooning, quoted in Irving Sandler, "Conversations with de Kooning," in "Willem de Kooning, on His Eighty-Fifth Birthday," special issue, *Art Journal* 48, no. 3 (Autumn 1989): 217.

26. Jean-Paul Sartre, *Existentialism*, trans. Bernard Frechtman (New York: Philosophical Library, 1947). Note that though the text has been published under different titles, the proper translation of the French title is "Existentialism Is a Humanism."

27. The school was founded by Robert Motherwell, David Hare, Mark Rothko, and William Baziotes.

28. Willem de Kooning, "A Desperate View," in *The Collected Writings of Willem de Kooning* (Madras: Hanuman Books, 1988), 10–11.

29. Pat Passlof, interview by Mark Stevens and Annalyn Swan, July 18, 1990, quoted in Stevens and Swan, *De Kooning*, 277.

30. Maurice Merleau-Ponty, "Cézanne's Doubt," in *Sense and Non-sense*, trans. Hubert Dreyfuss (Evanston, IL: Northwestern University Press, 1964), 9; originally published in the September 1949 issue of *Partisan Review*.

31. Ibid., 13–14.

32. Willem de Kooning, "The Renaissance and Order," in Thomas B. Hess, *Willem de Kooning*, exh. cat. (New York: Museum of Modern Art, 1968), 141. Talk delivered at Studio 35, Eighth Street, New York, February 1950. First published in *Trans/formation* 1, no. 2 (1951): 85–87.

33. Willem de Kooning, interview by Harold Rosenberg, *ARTnews* 71 (September 1972): 55.

34. Sartre stressed Giacometti's constant striving to impose his point of view on obdurate matter: "[Giacometti] has to write movement into the total immobility, unity into the infinite multiplicity, the absolute into the purely relative" (Jean-Paul Sartre, "The Search for the Absolute," in *Alberto Giacometti: Exhibition of Sculptures Paintings Drawings*, exh. cat. [New York: Pierre Matisse Gallery, 1948], 2–22).

35. Herzl Emanuel, interviews by Mark Stevens and Annalyn Swan, February 25 and October 22, 1992, quoted in Stevens and Swan, *De Kooning*, 525.

36. Willem de Kooning, letter to Herzl Emanuel, unpublished, quoted in Stevens and Swan, *De Kooning*, 528.

37. Xavier Fourcade, in Laura de Coppet and Alan Jones, *The Art Dealers*, rev. and exp. ed. (New York: Cooper Square, 2002 [orig. 1984]), 183.
38. De Kooning, quoted in Stella Rosemarch, "De Kooning on Clay," *Craft Horizons* 32, no. 6 (December 1972): 35.
39. Merleau-Ponty, "Cézanne's Doubt," 13.
40. Jean-Paul Sartre, "The Search for the Absolute," as excerpted in *Theories and Documents of Contemporary Art: A Sourcebook*, ed. Kristine Stiles and Peter Selz (Berkeley: University of California Press, 1996), 185. First published as "La recherche de l'absolut," *Le Temps Moderne* 3, no. 28 (1948): 153–63. Reprinted as "The Search for the Absolute," trans. Lionel Abel, in *Alberto Giacometti* (New York: Pierre Matisse Gallery, 1948).
41. De Kooning, "Renaissance and Order," 141.
42. Douglas Davis, "De Kooning on the Upswing," *Newsweek*, September 4, 1972.

CHAPTER EIGHT

1. De Kooning quoted in Daniel Frasnay, *The Artist's World* (New York: Viking, 1969), 21.
2. Willem de Kooning, interview by Harold Rosenberg, *ARTnews* 71 (September 1972): 56.
3. Maurice Merleau-Ponty, "Cézanne's Doubt," in *Sense and Non-sense*, trans. Hubert Dreyfuss (Evanston, IL: Northwestern University Press, 1964), 13.
4. Ibid., 14.
5. Willem de Kooning, "A Desperate View," in *The Collected Writings of Willem de Kooning* (Madras: Hanuman Books, 1988), 11.
6. De Kooning, interview by Rosenberg, 55.

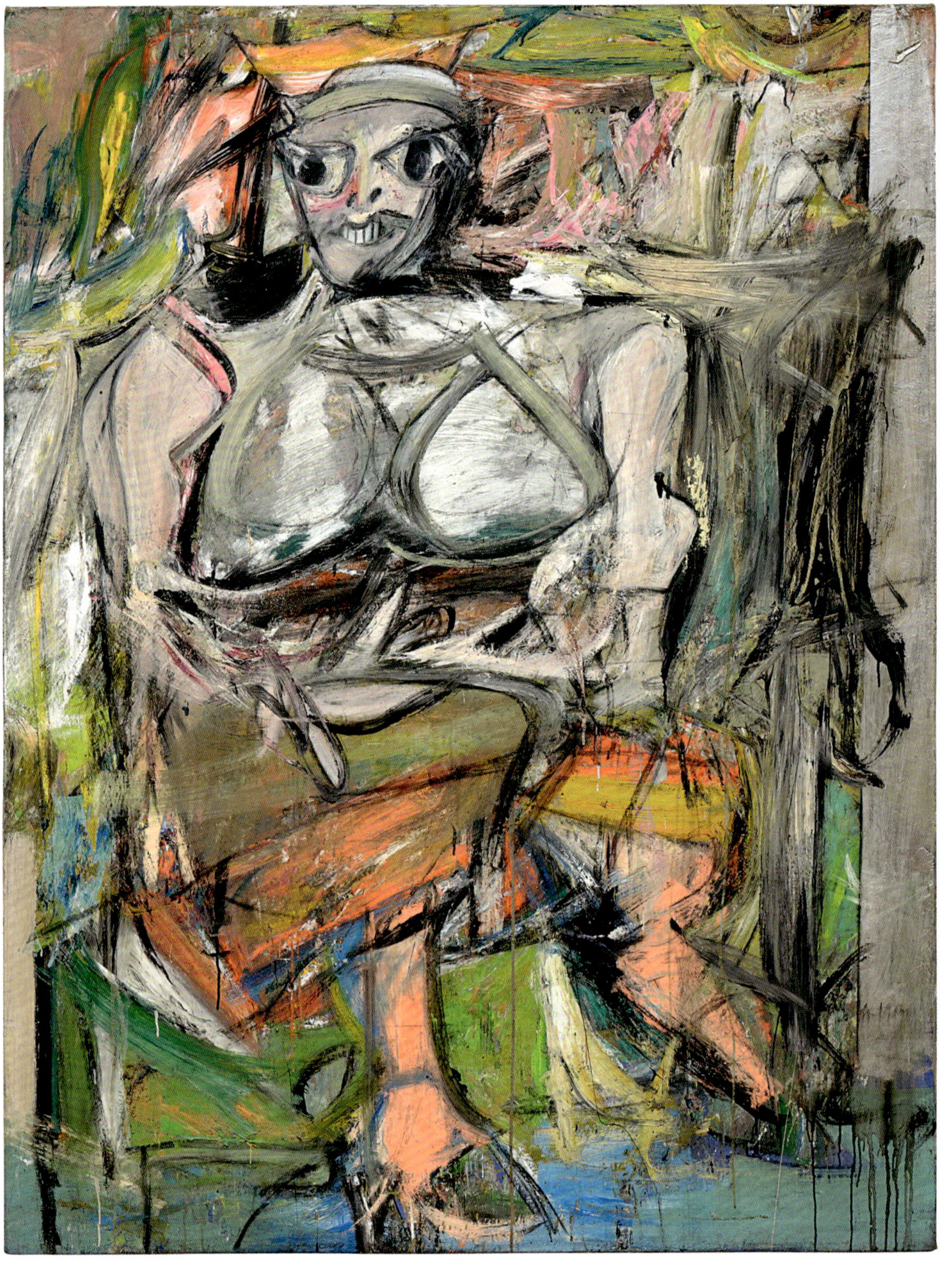

Figure 1. Willem de Kooning, *Woman I*, 1950–52. Oil on canvas, 6′3⅞″ × 58″ (192.7 × 147.3 cm). Purchase. Digital image © The Museum of Modern Art / Licensed by SCALA / Art Resource, NY. © 2014 The Willem de Kooning Foundation / Artists Rights Society (ARS), New York.

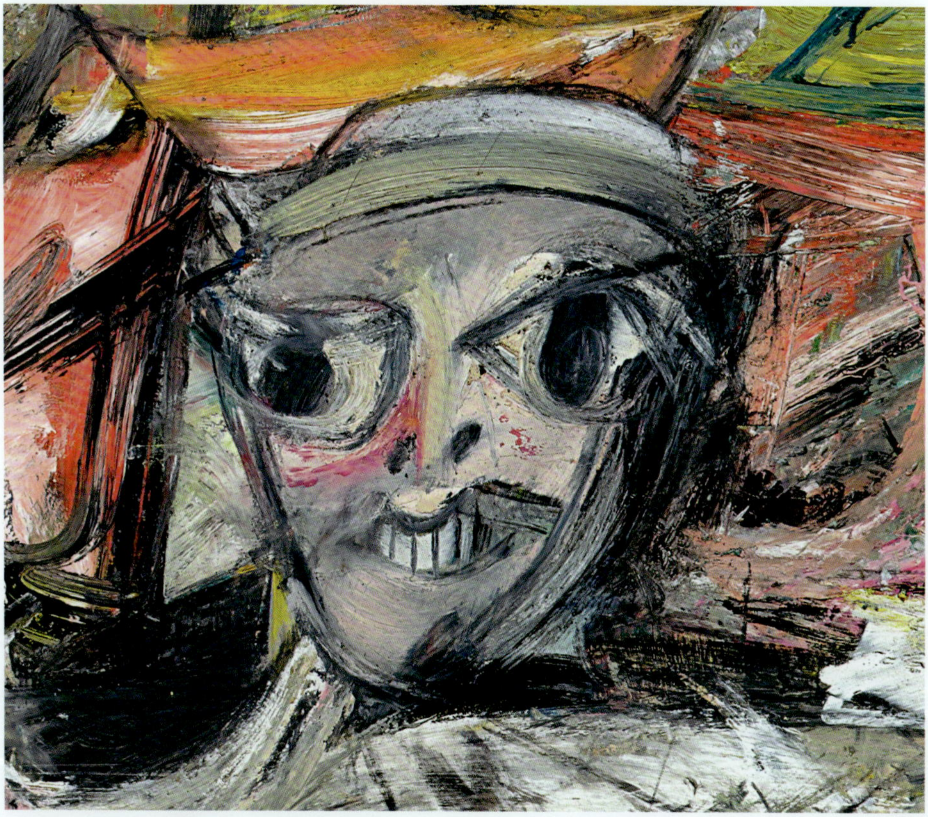

Figure 2. Willem de Kooning, detail, *Woman I* (mouth). Oil on canvas. 6′3⅞″ × 58″ (192.7 × 147.3 cm). Purchase. Digital image © The Museum of Modern Art / Licensed by SCALA / Art Resource, NY. © 2014 The Willem de Kooning Foundation / Artists Rights Society (ARS), New York.

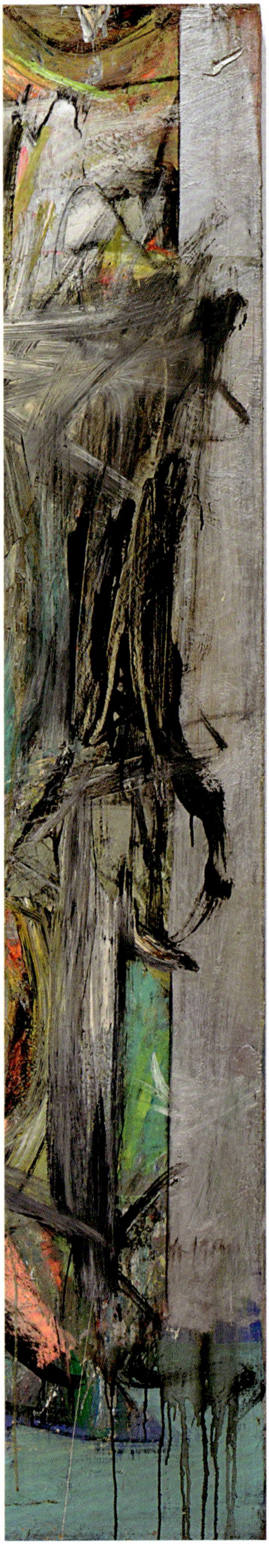

Figure 3. Willem de Kooning, detail, *Woman I* (side). Oil on canvas. 6′3⅞″ × 58″ (192.7 × 147.3 cm). Purchase. Digital image © The Museum of Modern Art / Licensed by SCALA / Art Resource, NY. © 2014 The Willem de Kooning Foundation / Artists Rights Society (ARS), New York.

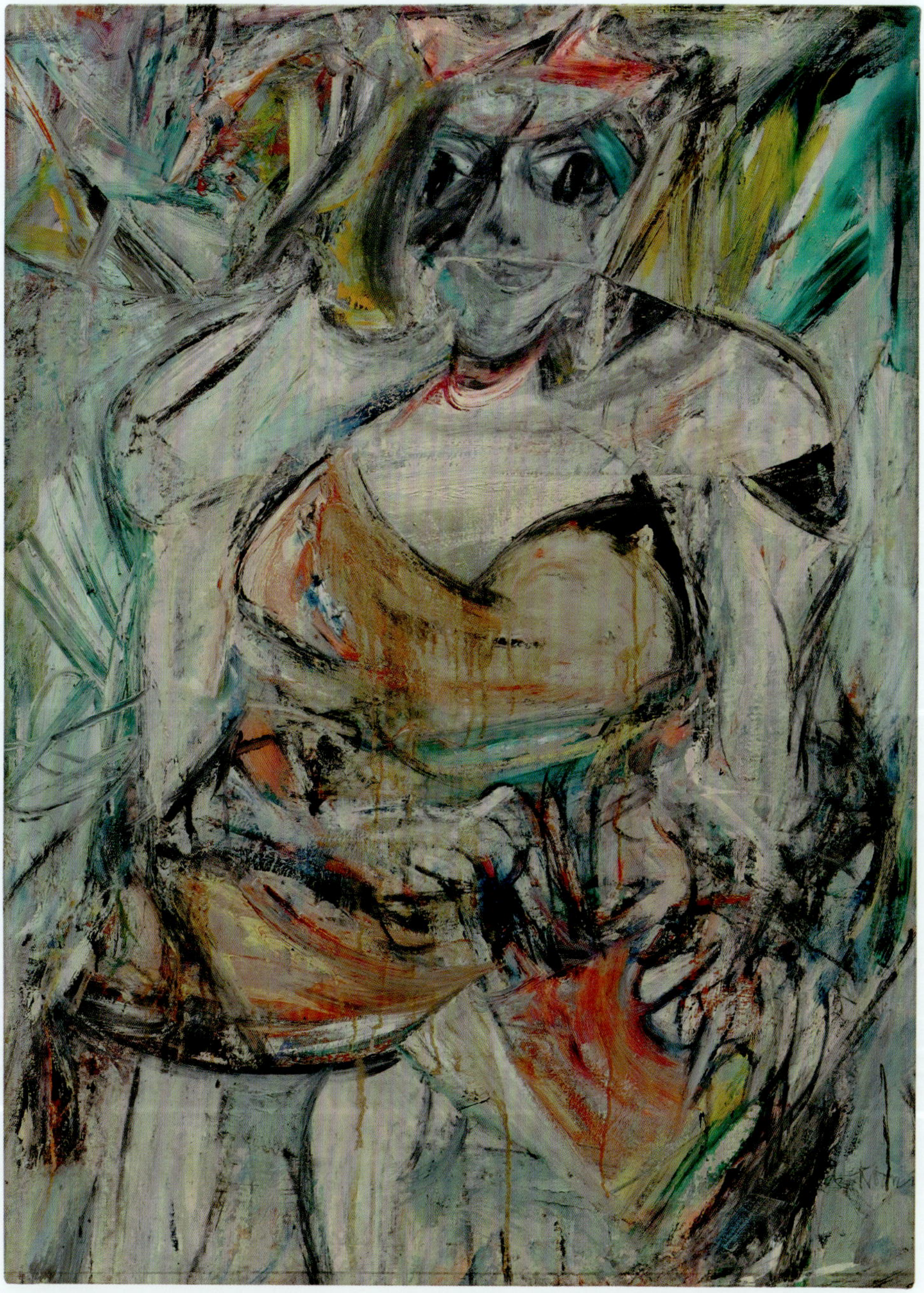

Figure 4. Willem de Kooning, *Woman II*, 1952. Oil on canvas. 59″ × 43″ (149.9 × 109.3 cm). Gift of Blanchette Hooker Rockefeller. Digital image © The Museum of Modern Art / Licensed by SCALA / Art Resource, NY. © 2014 The Willem de Kooning Foundation / Artists Rights Society (ARS), New York.

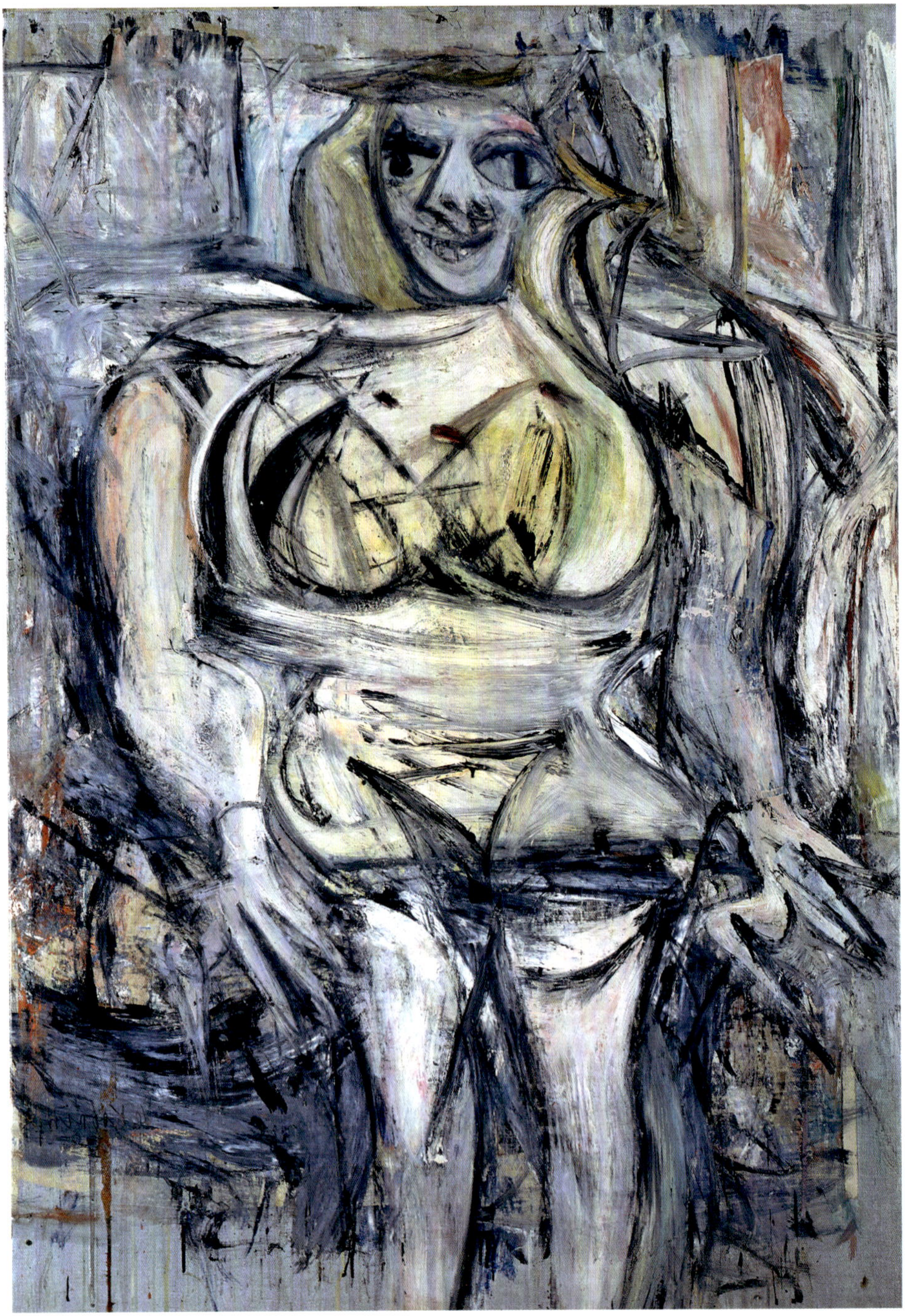

Figure 5. Willem de Kooning, *Woman III*, 1952–53. Oil on canvas. 68″ × 48½″ (172.7 × 123.2 cm). Courtesy Gagosian Gallery. © 2014 The Willem de Kooning Foundation / Artists Rights Society (ARS), New York.

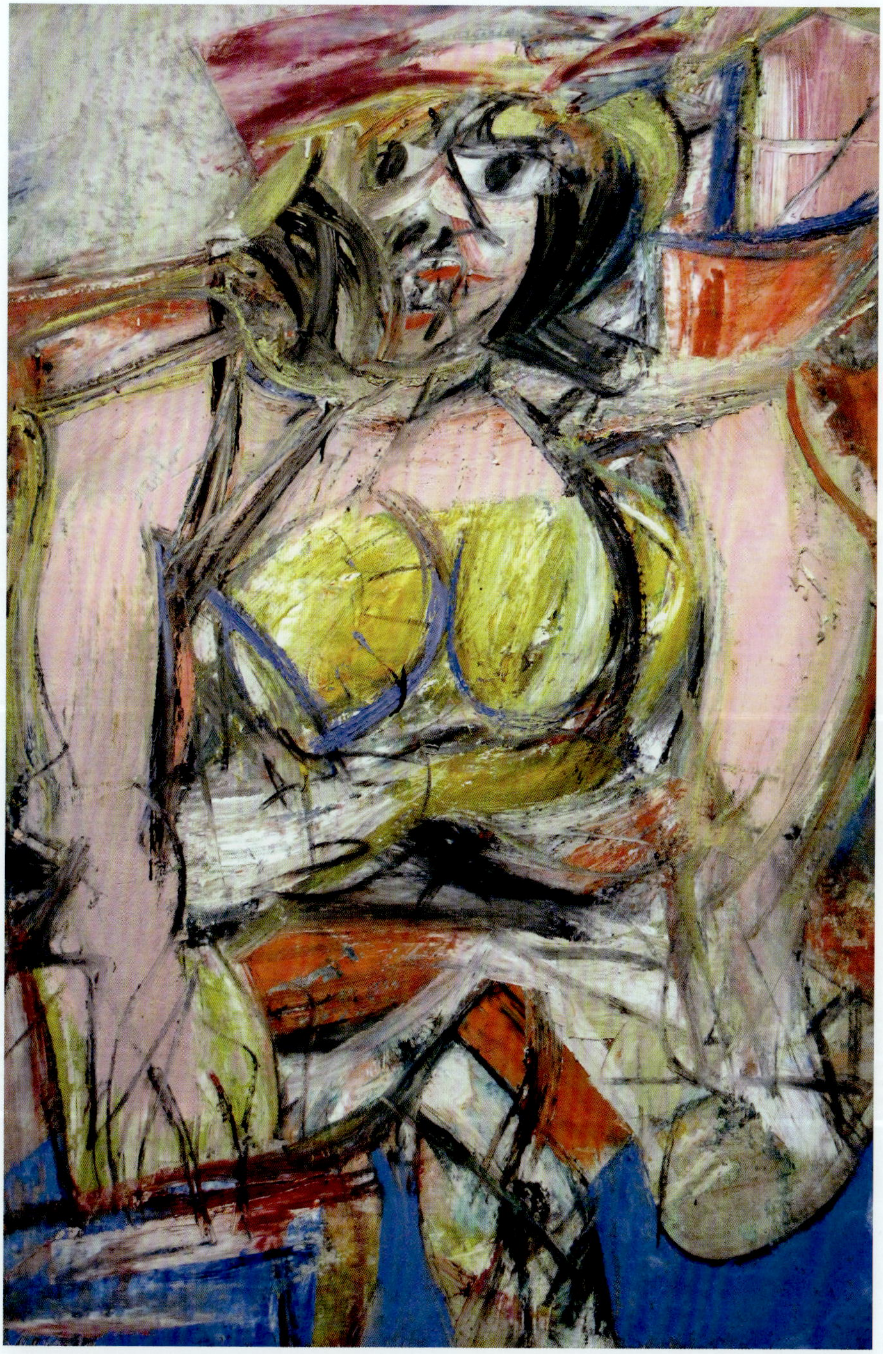

Figure 6. Willem de Kooning, *Woman IV*, 1952–53. Oil, enamel, and charcoal on canvas. 4′11″ × 46¼″ (149.86 × 117.48 cm). Album / Art Resource, NY. © 2014 The Willem de Kooning Foundation / Artists Rights Society (ARS), New York.

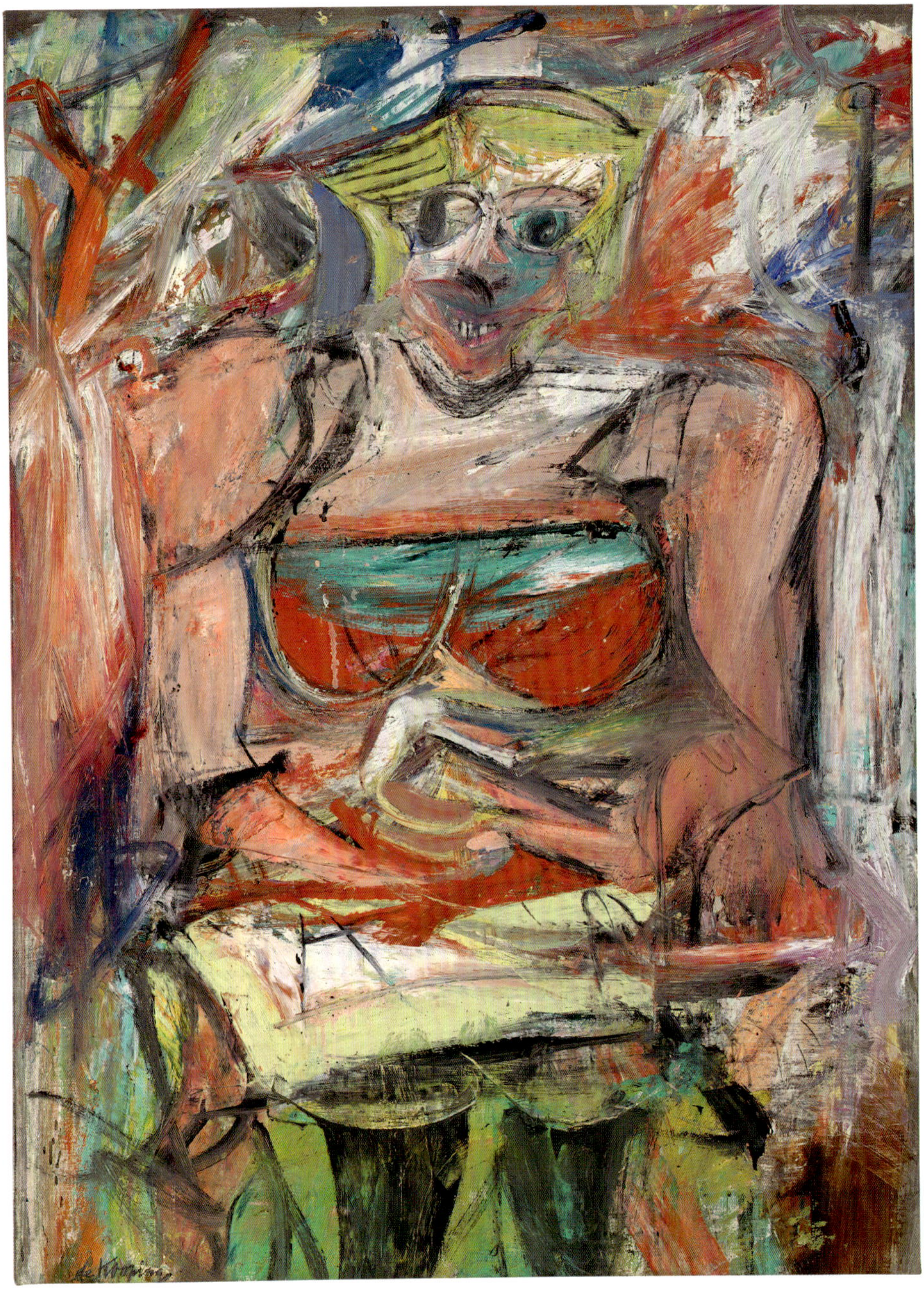

Figure 7. Willem de Kooning, *Woman V*, 1952–53. Oil and charcoal on canvas. 154.5 × 114.5 cm. National Gallery of Australia, Canberra, purchased 1974. © 2014 The Willem de Kooning Foundation / Artists Rights Society (ARS), New York.

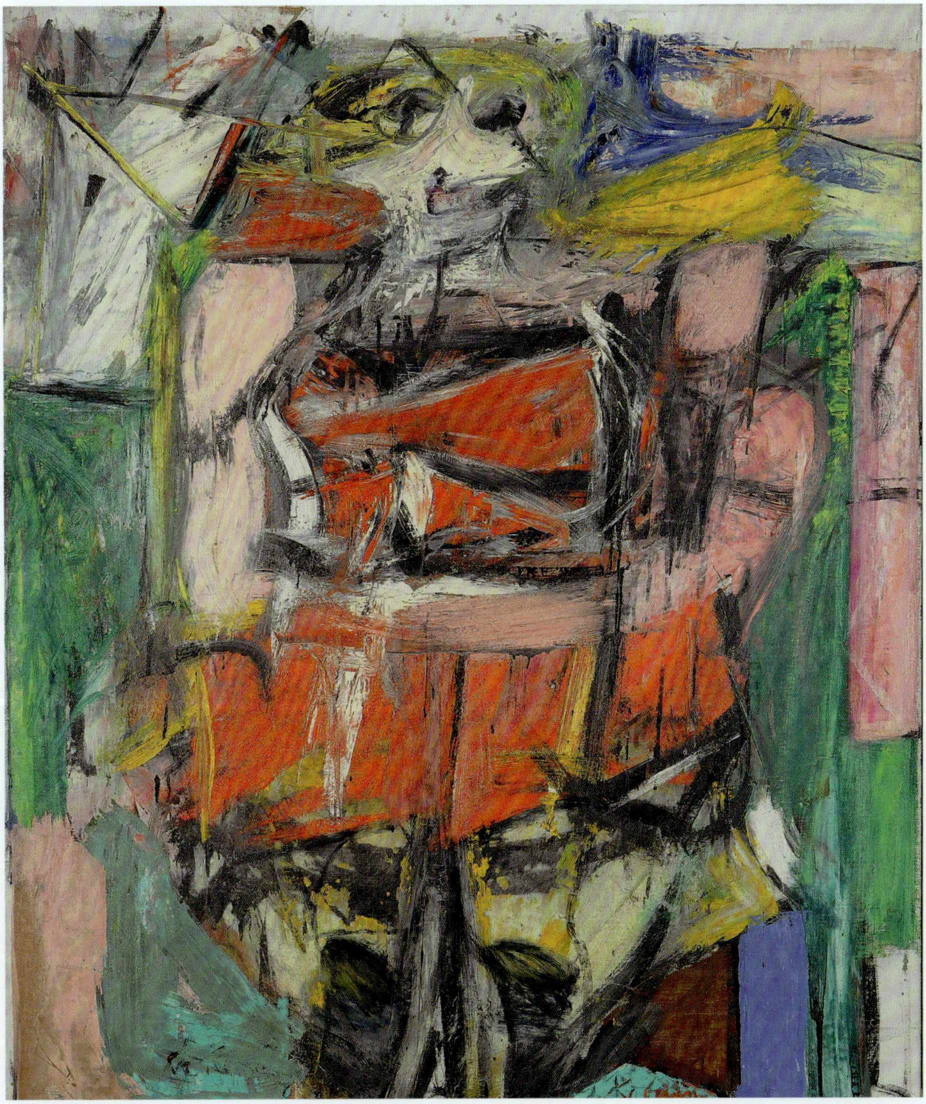

Figure 8. Willem de Kooning, *Woman VI*, 1953. Oil on canvas. 68½″ × 58½″. Carnegie Museum of Art, Pittsburgh: Gift of G. David Thompson, 55.24.4. © 2014 The Willem de Kooning Foundation / Artists Rights Society (ARS), New York.

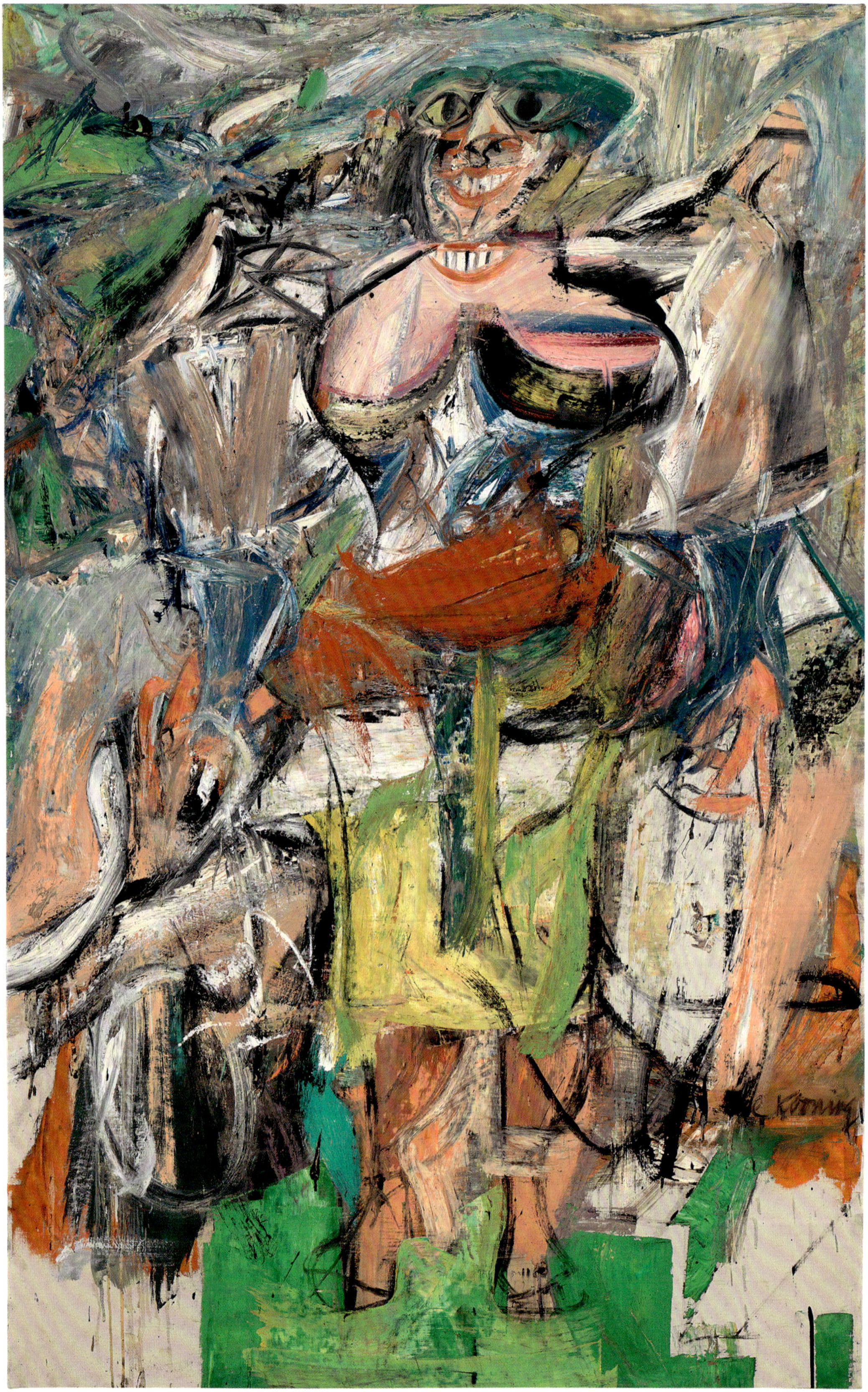

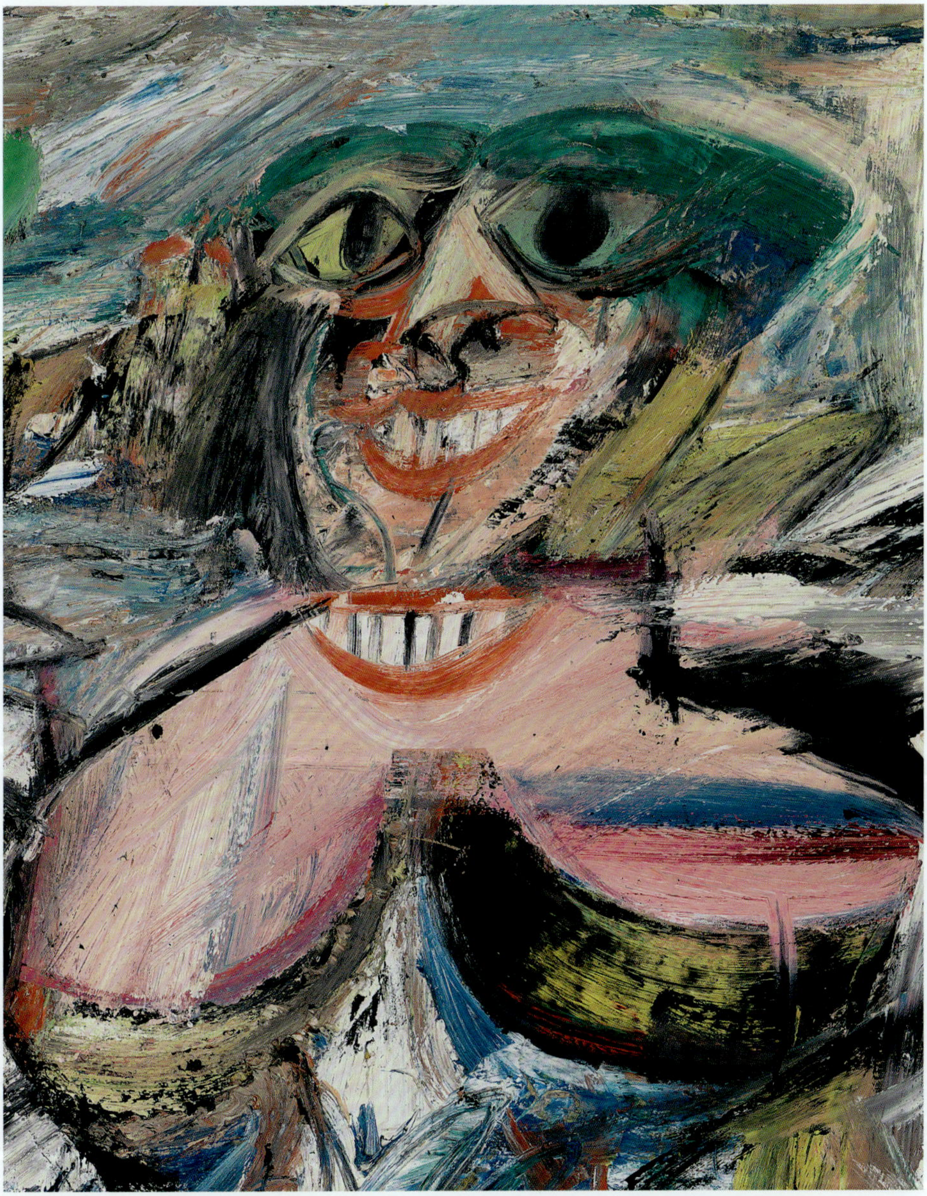

Figure 9. (facing) Willem de Kooning, *Woman with Bicycle*, 1952–53. Oil, enamel, and charcoal on linen. 76½″ × 49⅛″ (194.3 × 124.8 cm). Whitney Museum of American Art, New York; purchase 55.35. Digital image © Whitney Museum, New York. © 2014 The Willem de Kooning Foundation / Artists Rights Society (ARS), New York.

Figure 10. (above) Willem de Kooning, detail of *Woman with Bicycle* (mouth). Oil, enamel, and charcoal on linen. 76½″ × 49⅛″ (194.3 × 124.8 cm). Whitney Museum of American Art, New York; purchase 55.35. Digital image © Whitney Museum, New York. © 2014 The Willem de Kooning Foundation / Artists Rights Society (ARS), New York.

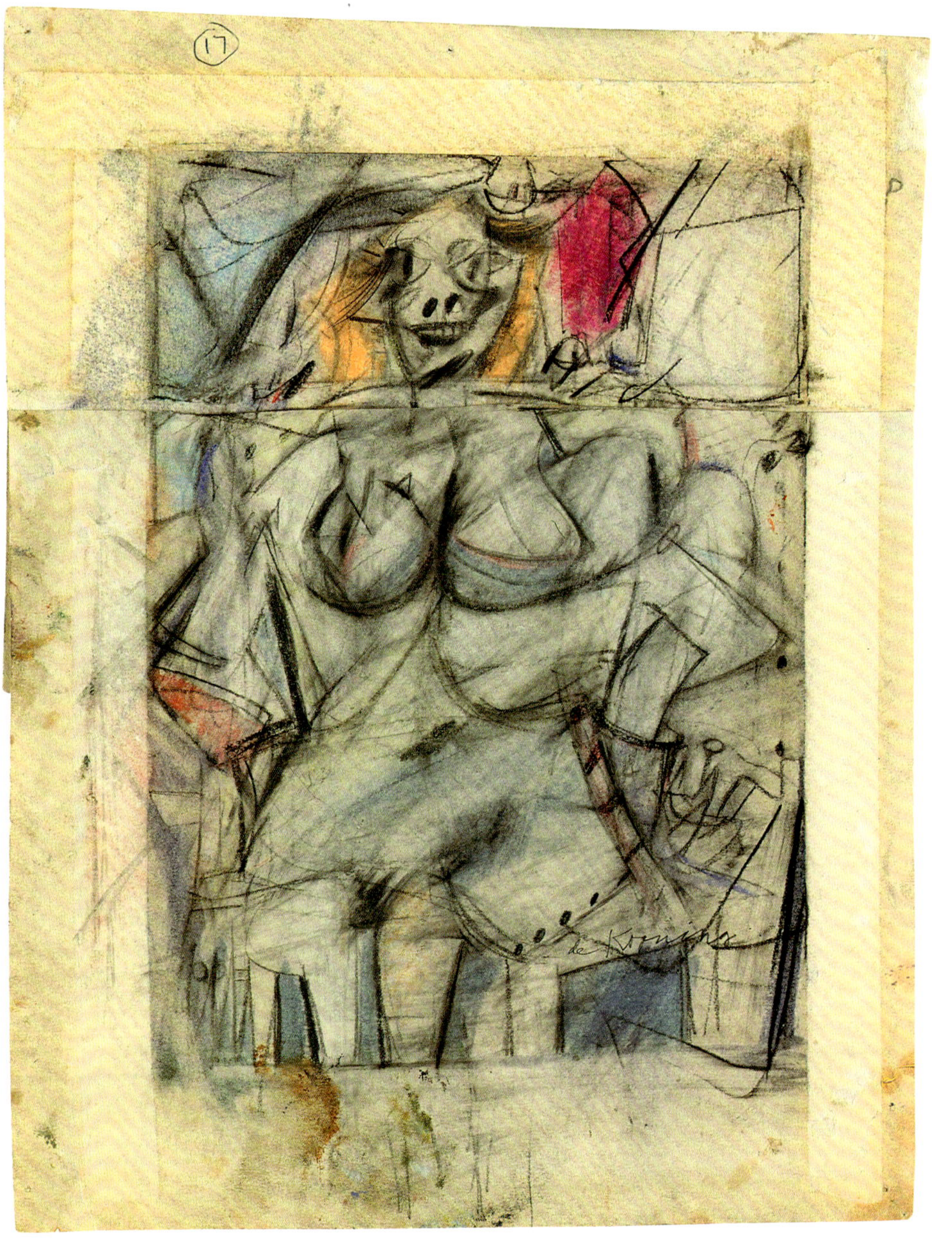

Figure 11. Willem de Kooning, *Seated Woman*, 1952. Pastel and pencil on cut and pasted paper. 12″ × 9½″. The Lauder Foundation Fund. Digital image © The Museum of Modern Art / Licensed by SCALA / Art Resource, NY. © 2014 The Willem de Kooning Foundation / Artists Rights Society (ARS), New York.

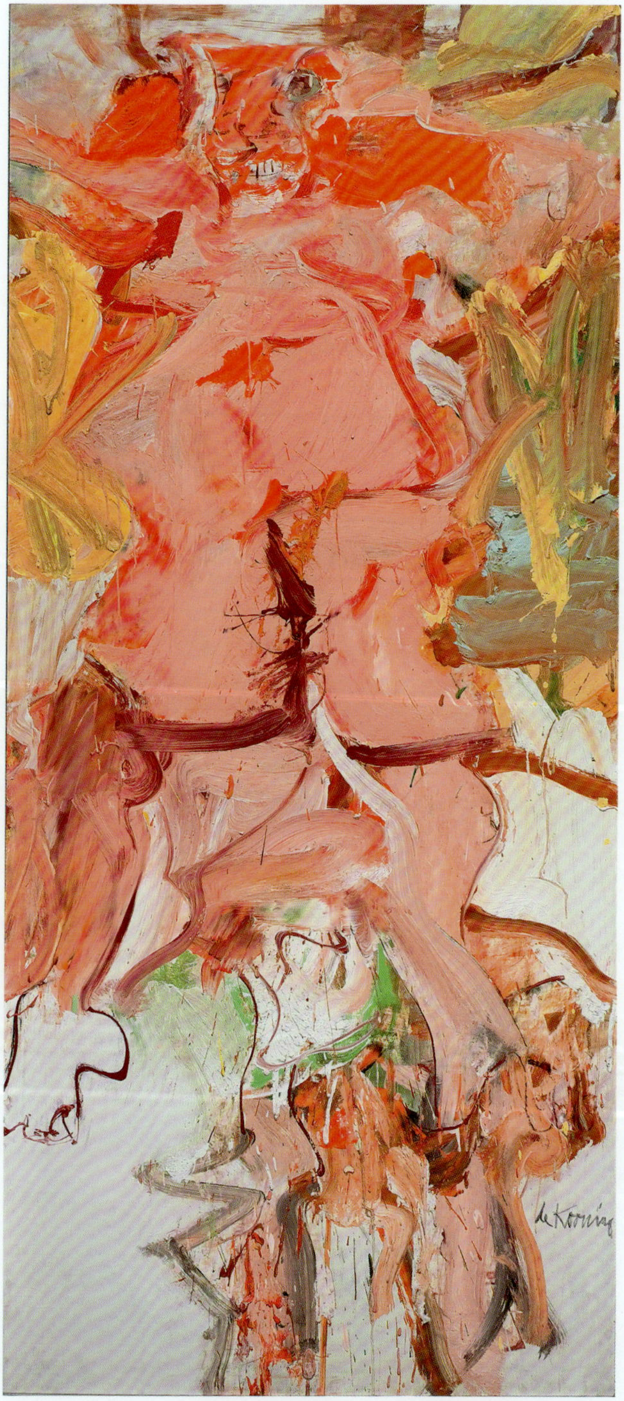

Figure 12.
Willem de Kooning, *Woman, Sag Harbor*, 1964. Oil and charcoal on wood. 80″ × 36″ (203.1 × 91.2 cm). Hirshhorn Museum and Sculpture Garden, Smithsonian Institution, Gift of Joseph H. Hirshhorn, 1966. Photography by Lee Stalsworth. © 2014 The Willem de Kooning Foundation / Artists Rights Society (ARS), New York.

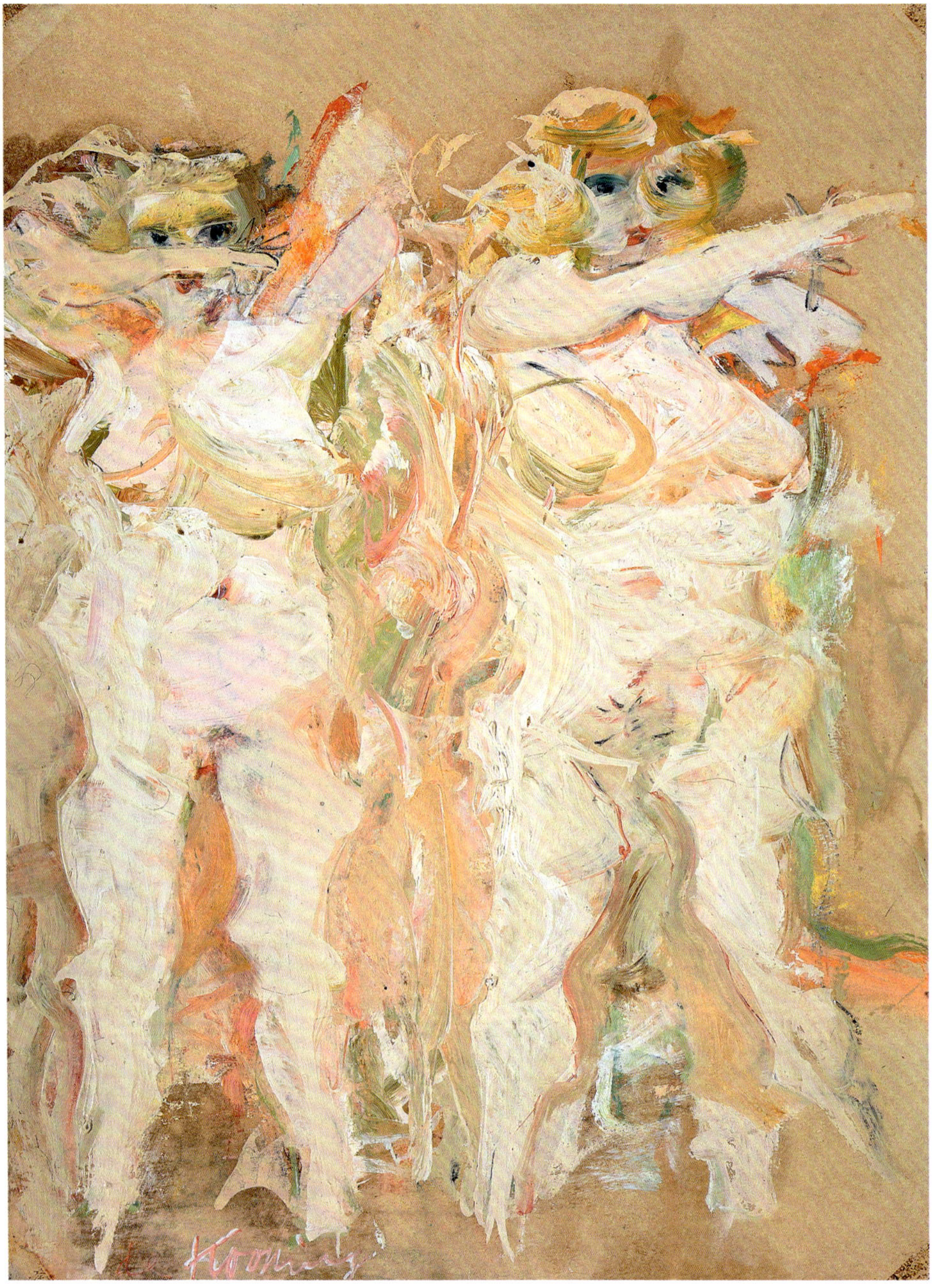

Figure 13. Willem de Kooning, *Clam Diggers*, 1964. Oil and graphite on paper on Masonite. 19 23/32″ × 14¾″ (50.1 × 37.5 cm). Private collection / Photo © Christie's Images / Bridgeman Images. © 2014 The Willem de Kooning Foundation / Artists Rights Society (ARS), New York.

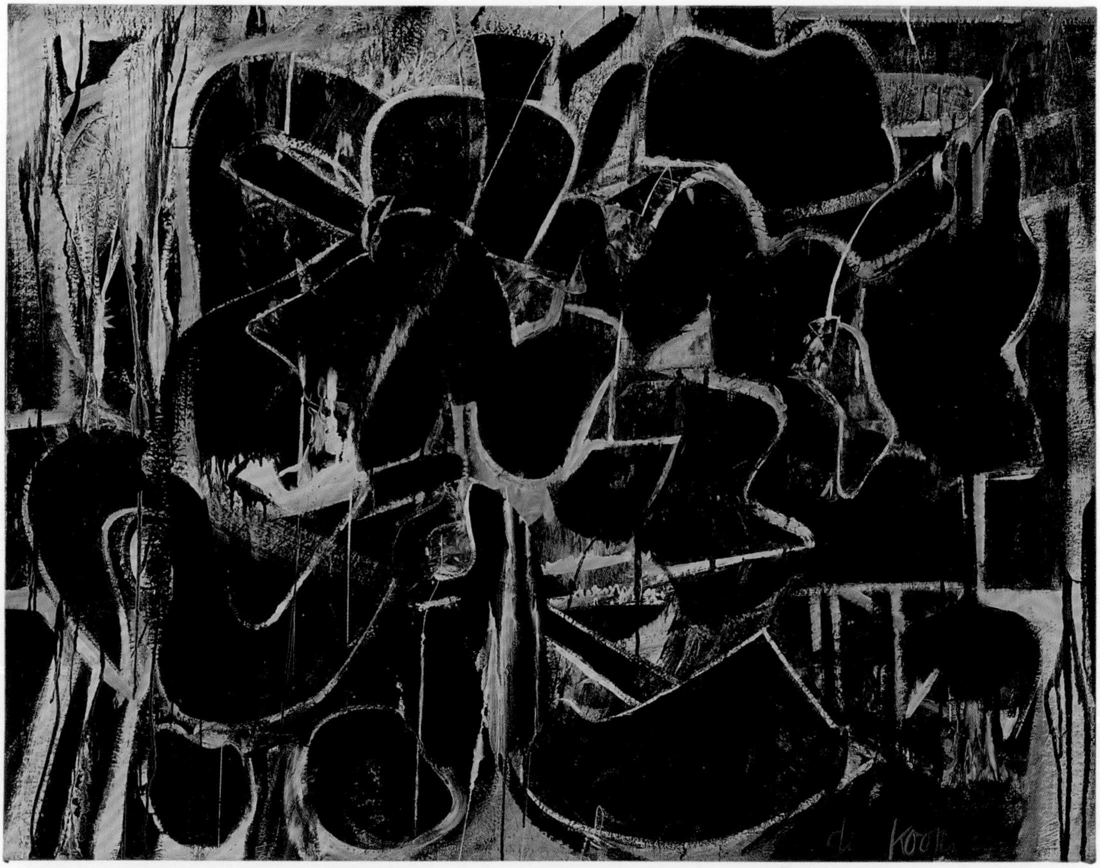

Figure 14. Willem de Kooning, *Painting*, 1948. Enamel and oil on canvas. 42⅝" × 56⅛". Purchase. Digital image © The Museum of Modern Art / Licensed by SCALA / Art Resource, NY. © 2014 The Willem de Kooning Foundation / Artists Rights Society (ARS), New York.

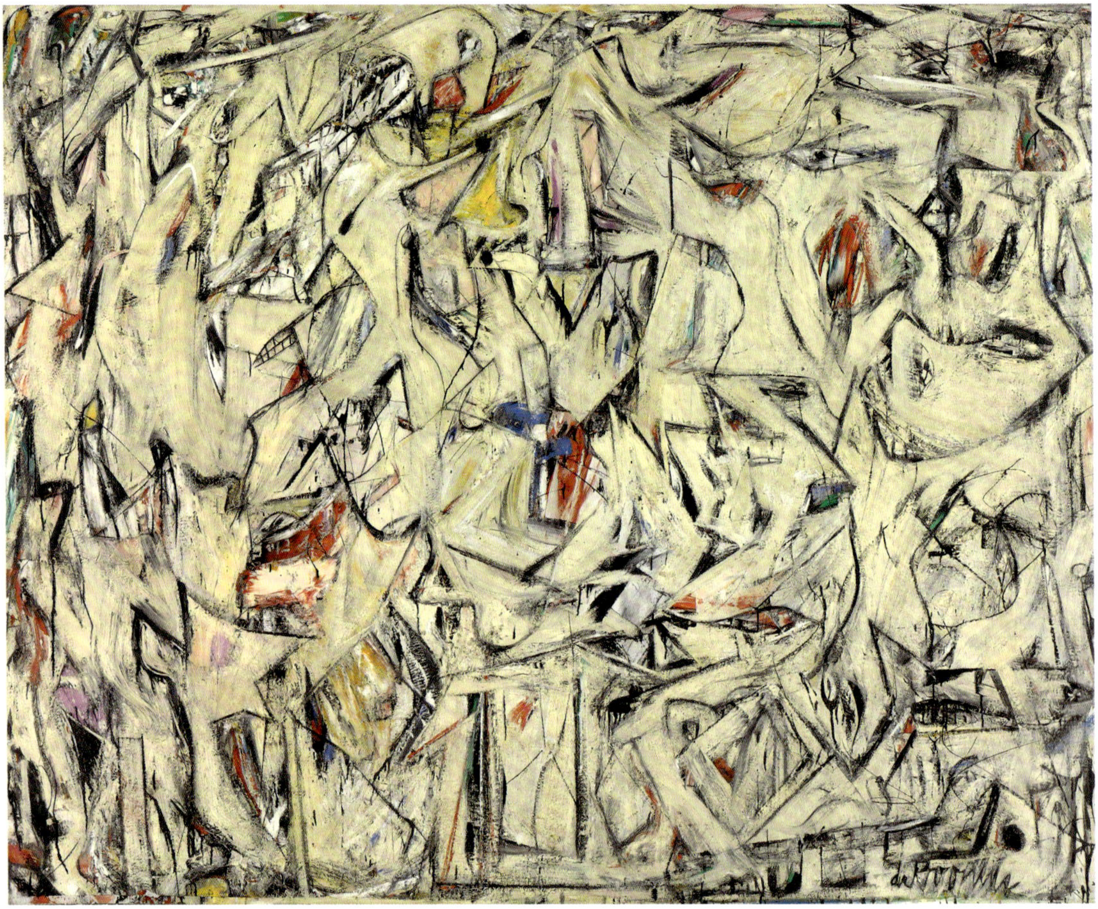

Figure 15. Willem de Kooning, *Excavation*, 1950. Oil on canvas, 205.7 × 254.6 cm (81″ × 100¼″), without frame. Mr. and Mrs. Frank G. Logan Purchase Prize Fund; restricted gifts of Edgar J. Kaufmann Jr. and Mr. and Mrs. Noah Goldowsky, 1952.1, The Art Institute of Chicago. Photography © The Art Institute of Chicago. © 2014 The Willem de Kooning Foundation / Artists Rights Society (ARS), New York.

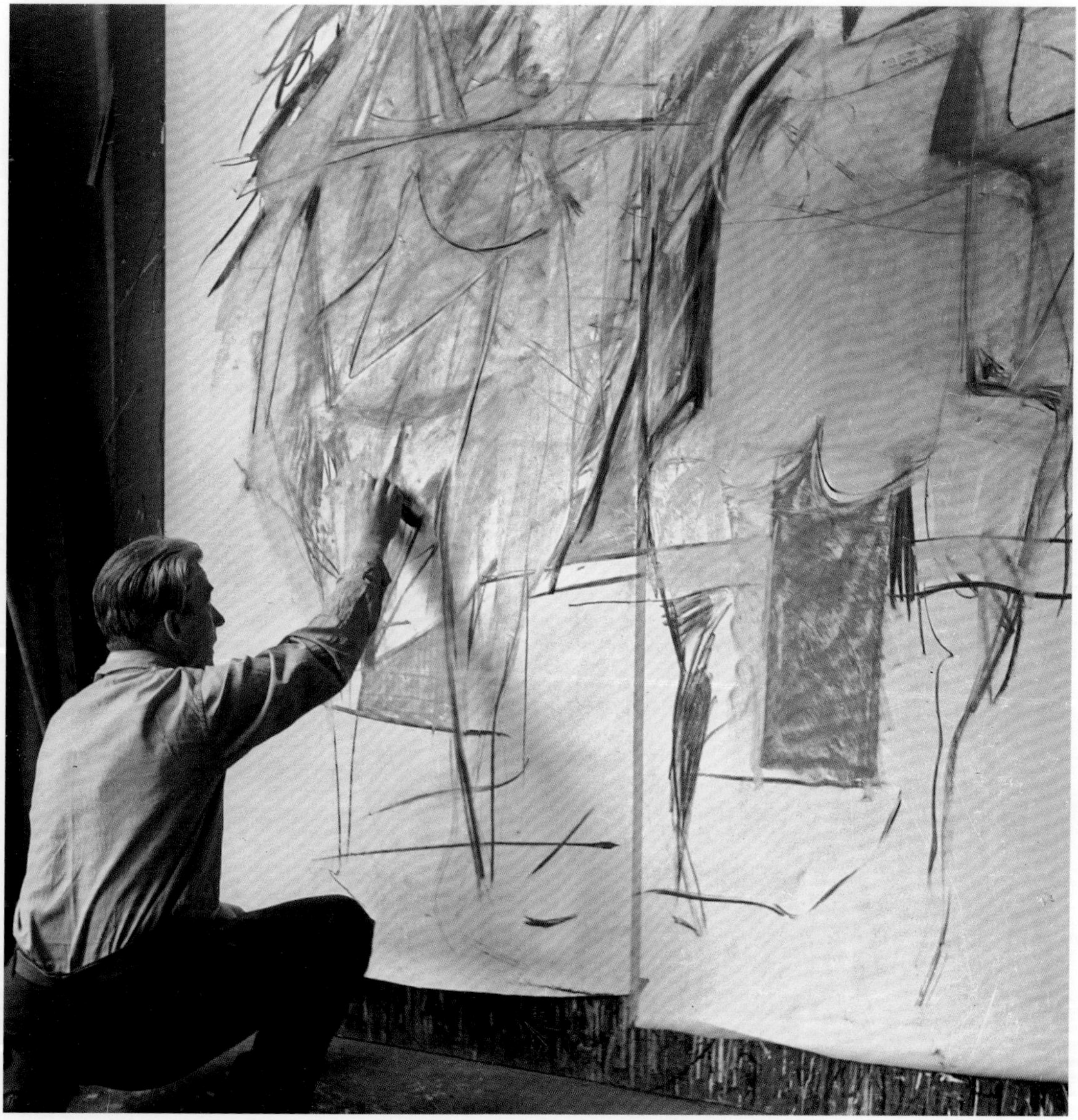

Figure 16. Rudolph (Rudy) Burckhardt, photograph of Willem de Kooning working on a two-part drawing preparatory to *Woman I*, June 1950. Photo courtesy Jacob Burckhardt and the Museum of Modern Art, New York. Photo © 2014 Estate of Rudy Burckhardt / Artists Rights Society (ARS), New York. Art © 2014 The Willem de Kooning Foundation / Artists Rights Society (ARS), New York.

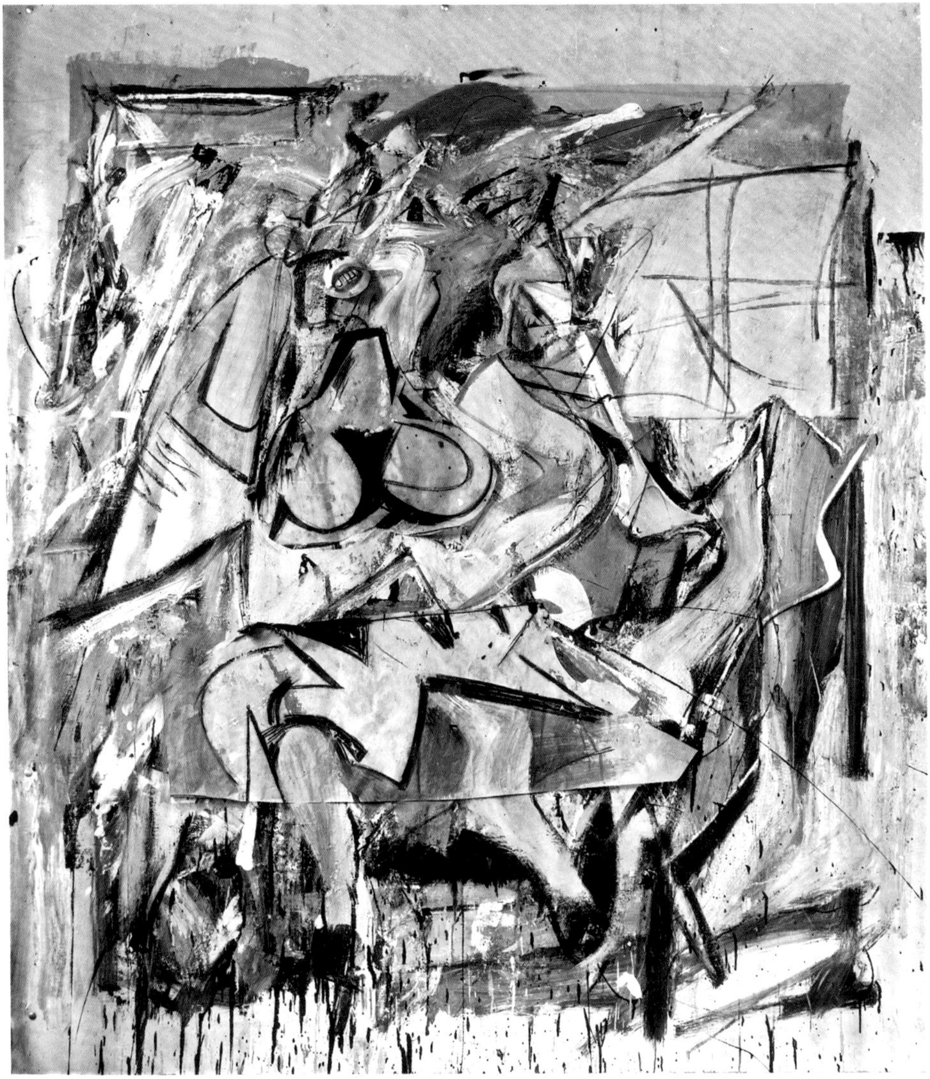

Figure 17. Burckhardt, photograph of State 1 of Willem de Kooning, *Woman I*, 1950. Photo courtesy the Museum of Modern Art, New York. Photo © 2014 Estate of Rudy Burckhardt / Artists Rights Society (ARS), New York. Art © 2014 The Willem de Kooning Foundation / Artists Rights Society (ARS), New York.

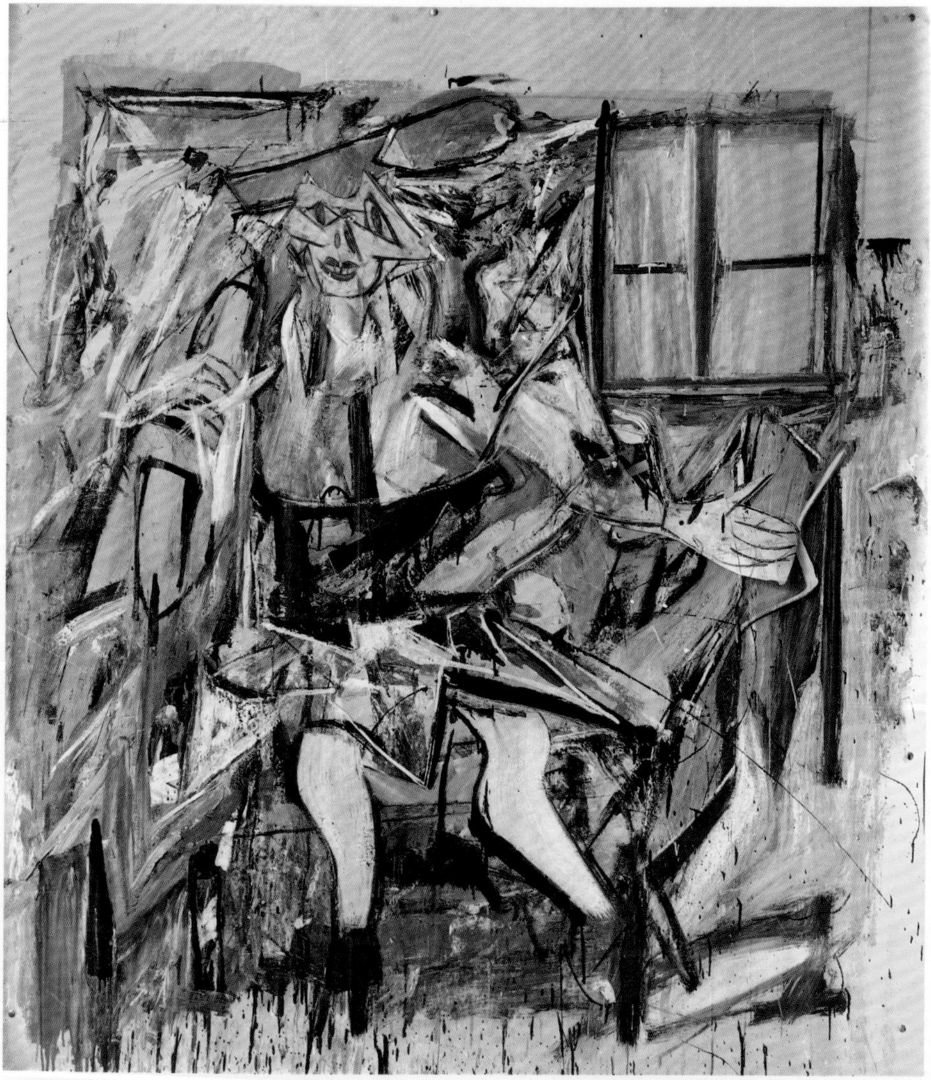

Figure 18. Burckhardt, photograph of State 2 of Willem de Kooning, *Woman I*, 1950. Photo courtesy the Museum of Modern Art, New York. Photo © 2014 Estate of Rudy Burckhardt / Artists Rights Society (ARS), New York. Art © 2014 The Willem de Kooning Foundation / Artists Rights Society (ARS), New York.

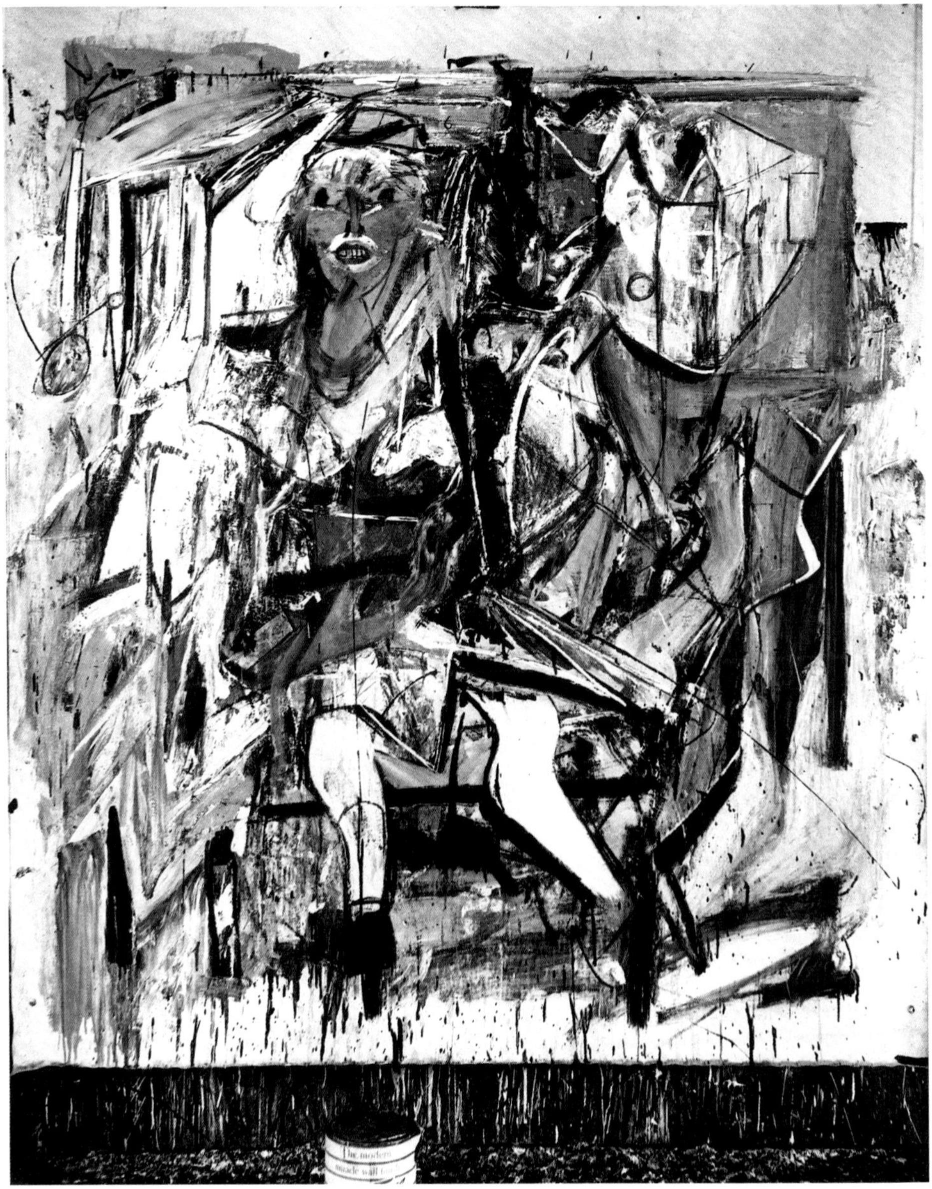

Figure 19. Walter Auerbach, photograph of State 3 of Willem de Kooning, *Woman I*, 1950. Photo Walter Auerbach. Courtesy the Museum of Modern Art, New York. Art © 2014 The Willem de Kooning Foundation / Artists Rights Society (ARS), New York.

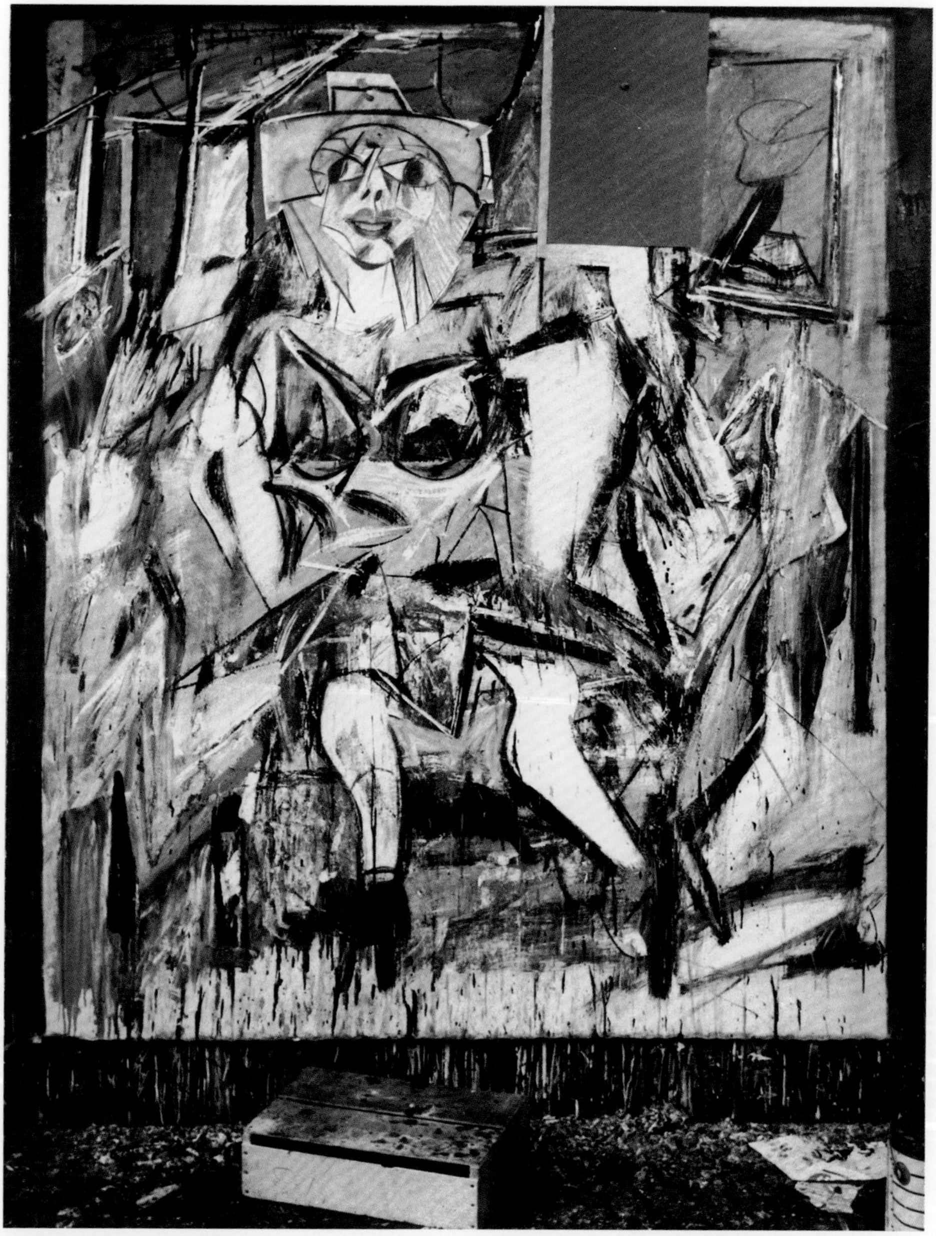

Figure 20. Auerbach, photograph of State 4 of Willem de Kooning, *Woman I*, 1950–52. Photo Walter Auerbach. Courtesy the Museum of Modern Art, New York. Art © 2014 The Willem de Kooning Foundation / Artists Rights Society (ARS), New York.

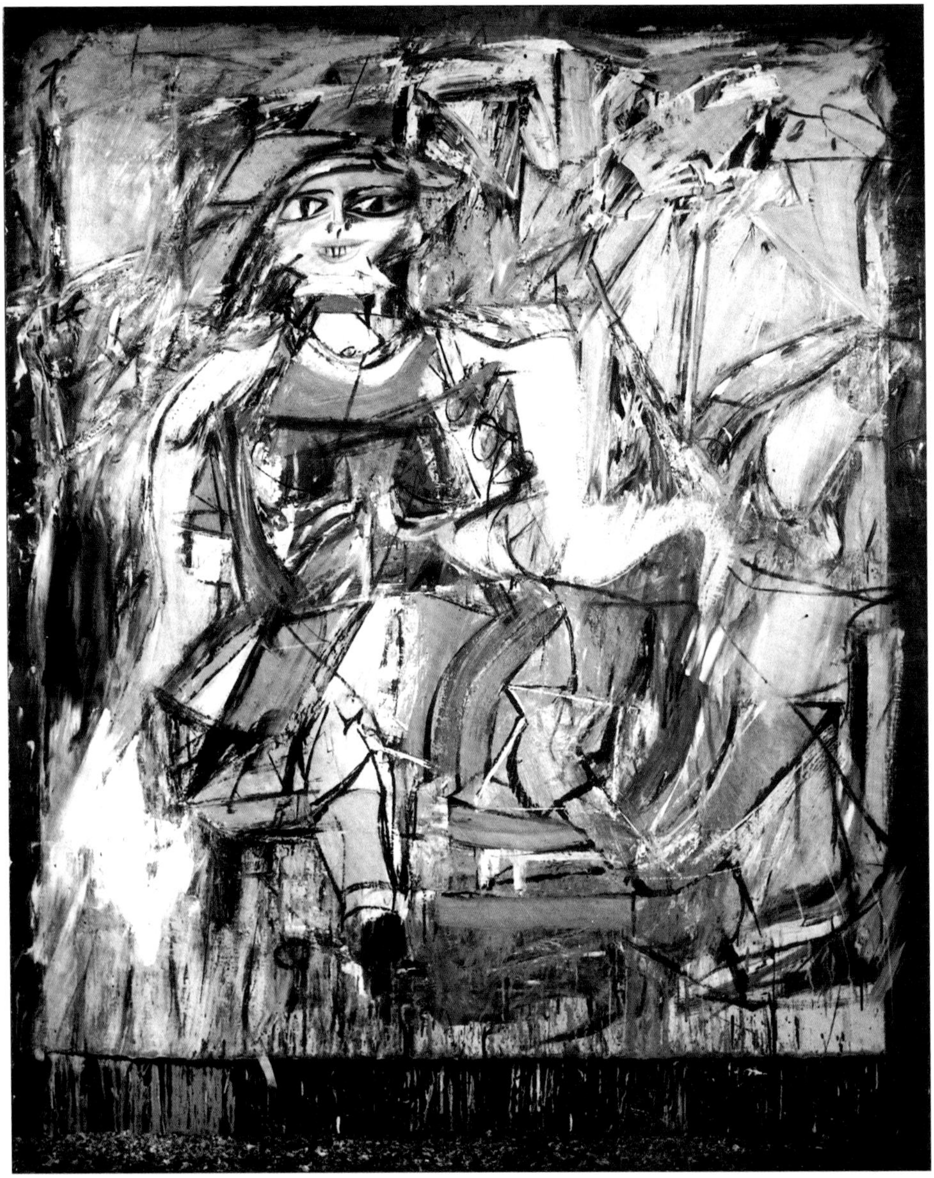

Figure 21. Auerbach, photograph of State 5 of Willem de Kooning, *Woman I*, 1950–52. Photo Walter Auerbach. Courtesy the Museum of Modern Art, New York. Art © 2014 The Willem de Kooning Foundation / Artists Rights Society (ARS), New York.

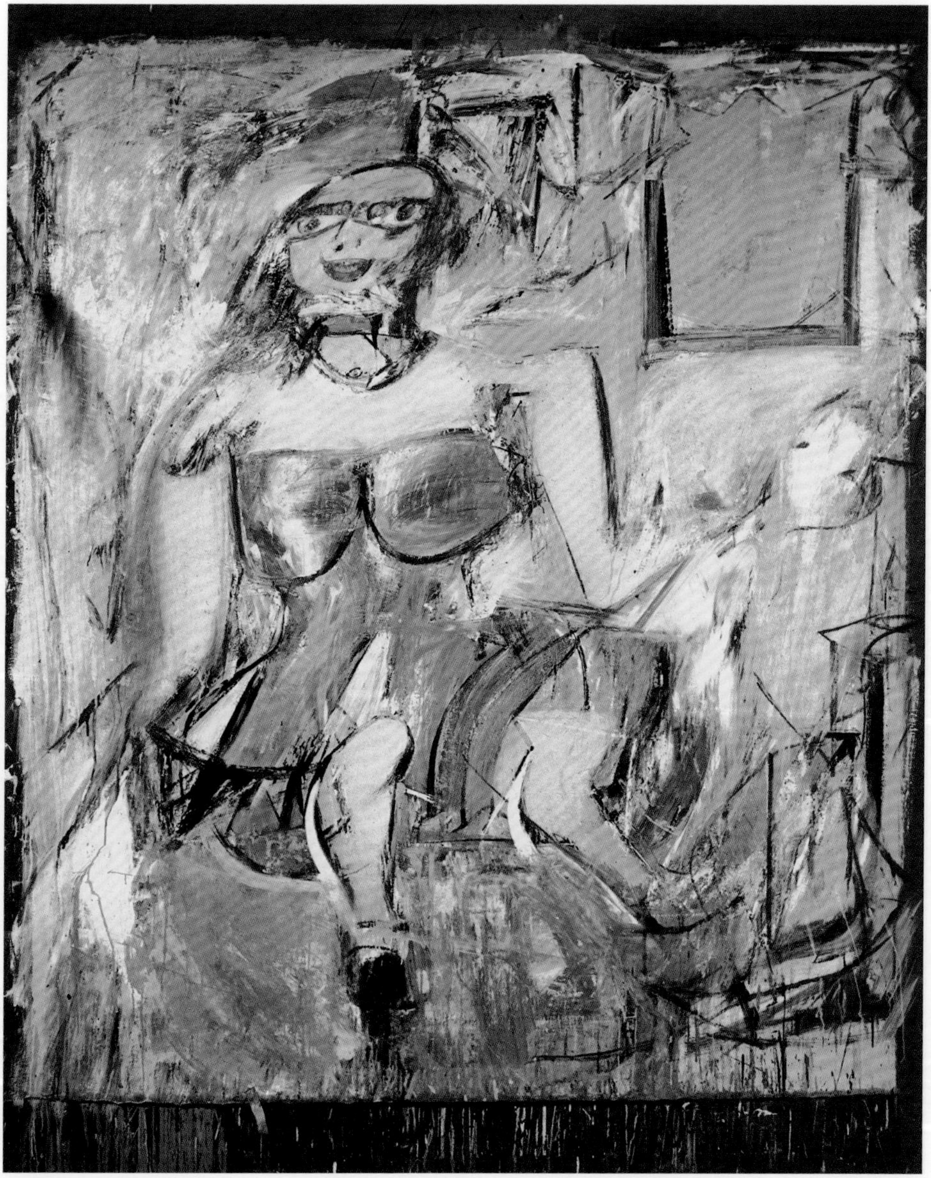

Figure 22. Walter Auerbach, photograph of State 6 of Willem de Kooning, *Woman I*, 1950–52. Courtesy the Museum of Modern Art, New York. Art © 2014 The Willem de Kooning Foundation / Artists Rights Society (ARS), New York.

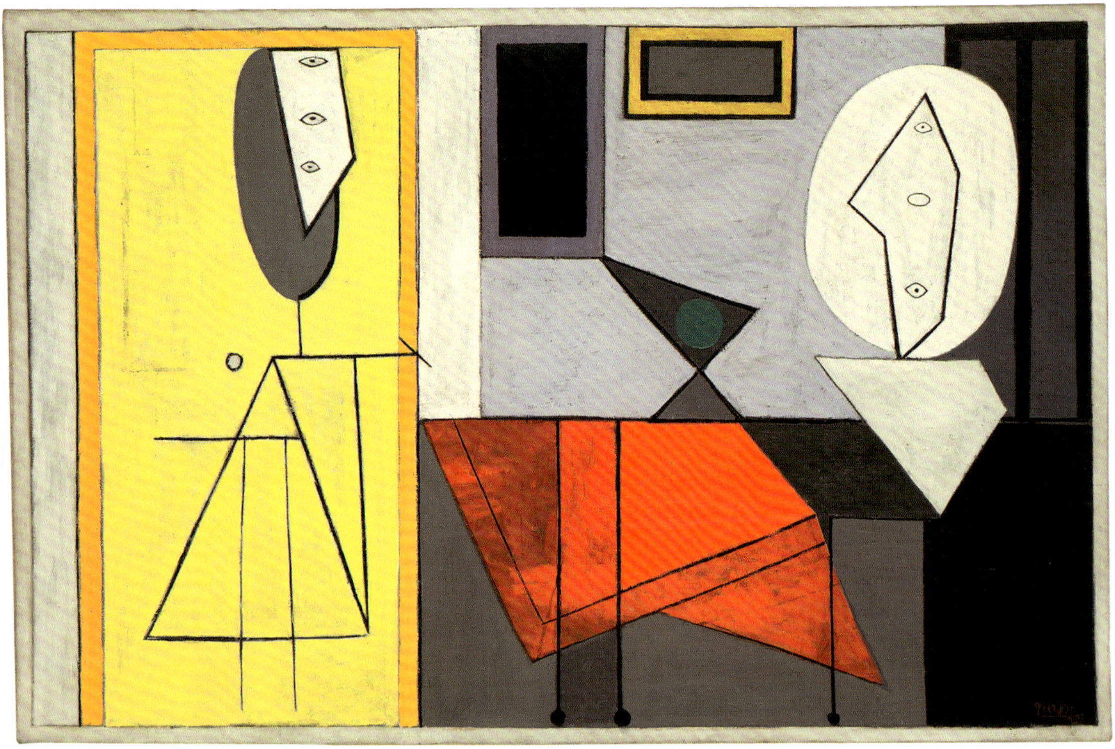

Figure 23. Pablo Picasso, *The Studio*, Paris, winter 1927–28. Oil on canvas. 59″ × 7′7″ (149.9 × 231.2 cm). Gift of Walter P. Chrysler Jr. Digital image © The Museum of Modern Art / Licensed by SCALA / Art Resource, NY. © 2014 Estate of Pablo Picasso / Artists Rights Society (ARS), New York.

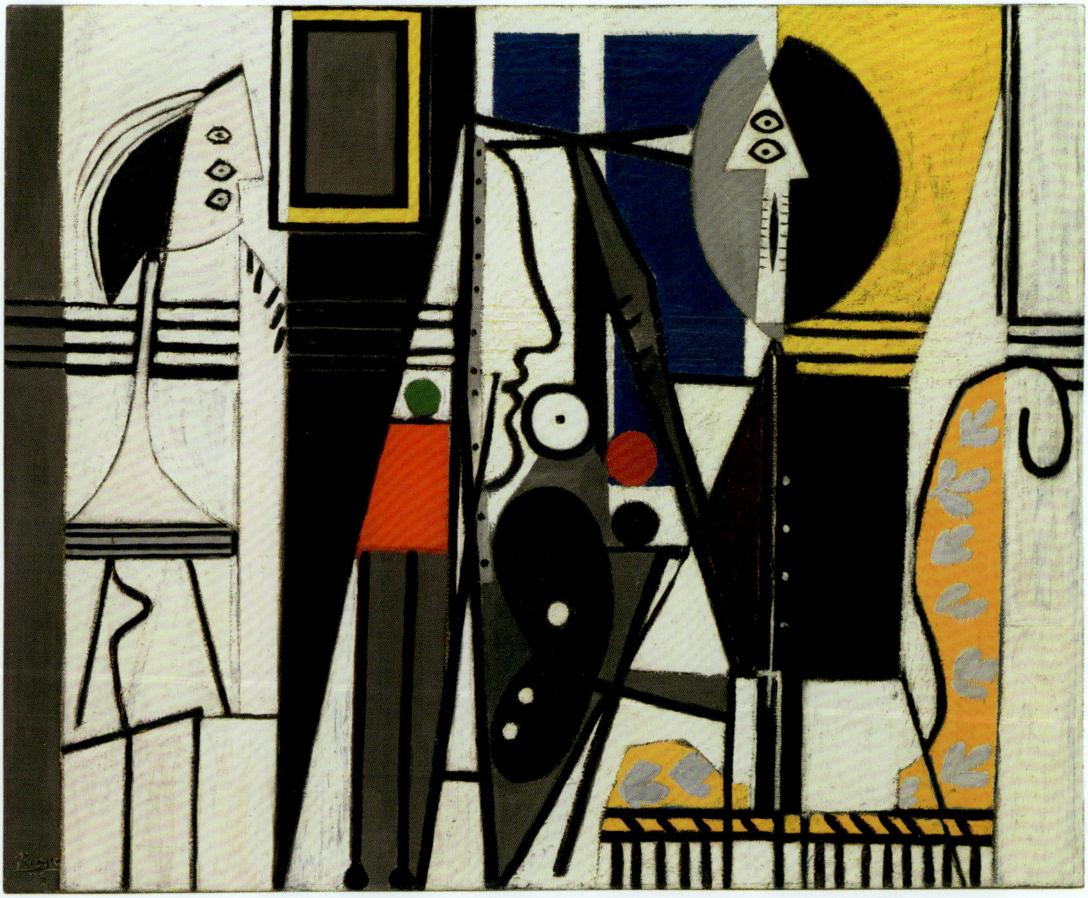

Figure 24. Picasso, *Painter and Model*, Paris, 1928. Oil on canvas. 51⅛″ × 64¼″ (129.8 × 163 cm). The Sidney and Harriet Janis Collection. Digital image © The Museum of Modern Art / Licensed by SCALA / Art Resource, NY. © 2014 Estate of Pablo Picasso / Artists Rights Society (ARS), New York.

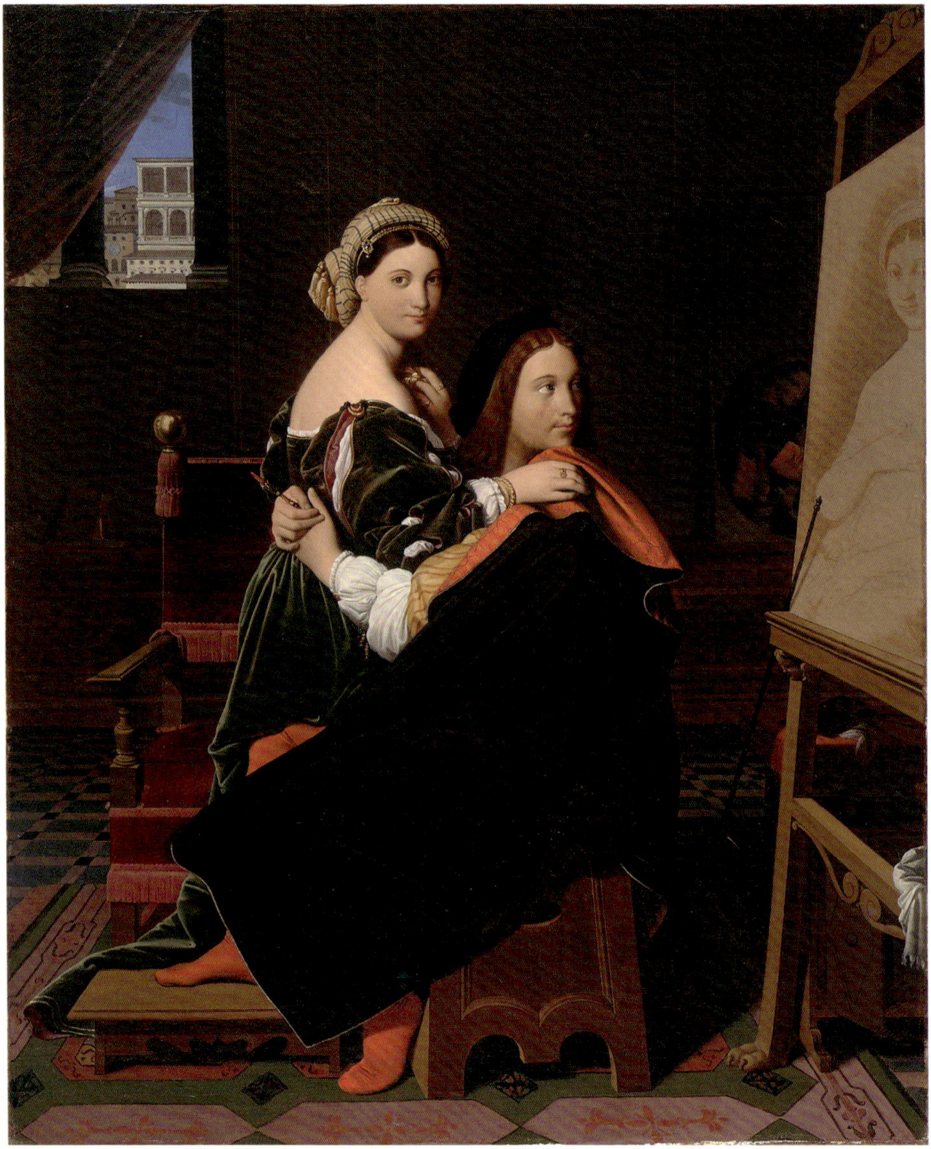

Figure 25. Jean-Auguste-Dominique Ingres, *Raphael and the Fornarina*, 1814. Oil on canvas. 64.8 × 53.3 cm (25½" × 21"). Frame: 88.6 × 76.8 × 9.5 cm (34⅞" × 30¼" × 3¾"). Harvard Art Museums / Fogg Museum, Bequest of Grenville L. Winthrop, 1943.252. Photo: Imaging Department © President and Fellows of Harvard College.

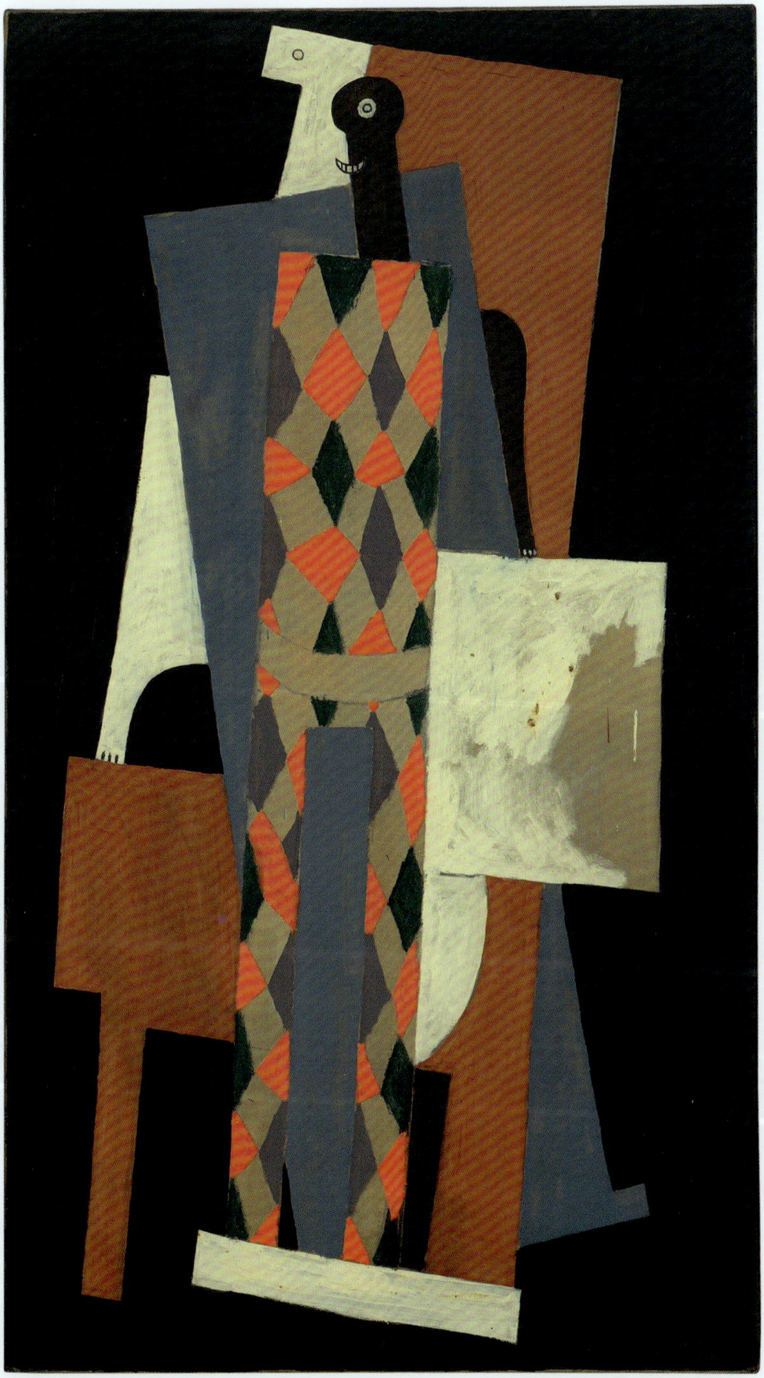

Figure 26.
Picasso, *Harlequin*, Paris, late 1915. Oil on canvas. 6′¼″ × 41⅜″ (183.5 × 105.1 cm). Acquired through the Lillie P. Bliss Bequest. Digital image © The Museum of Modern Art / Licensed by SCALA / Art Resource, NY. © 2014 Estate of Pablo Picasso / Artists Rights Society (ARS), New York.

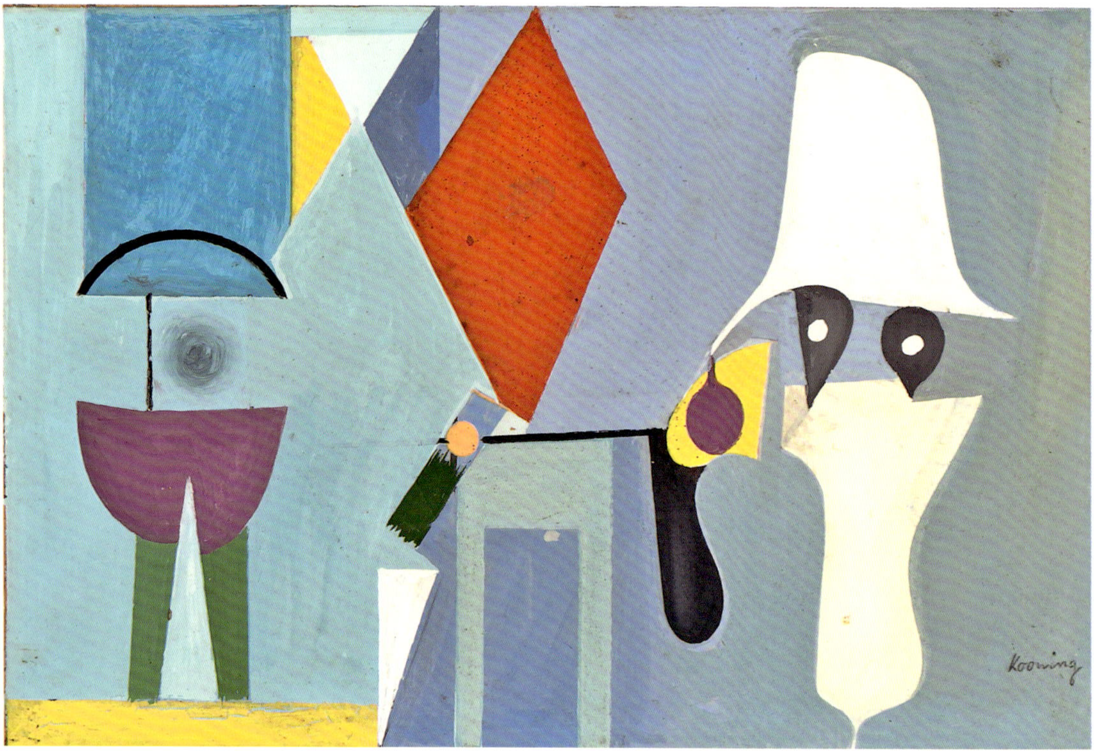

Figure 27. Willem de Kooning, *Untitled*, circa 1939. Oil on board. 8½" × 12¾" (21.6 × 32.4 cm). Picker Art Gallery, Colgate University, gift of Edwin J. Safford '58, 1991.48. © 2014 The Willem de Kooning Foundation / Artists Rights Society (ARS), New York.

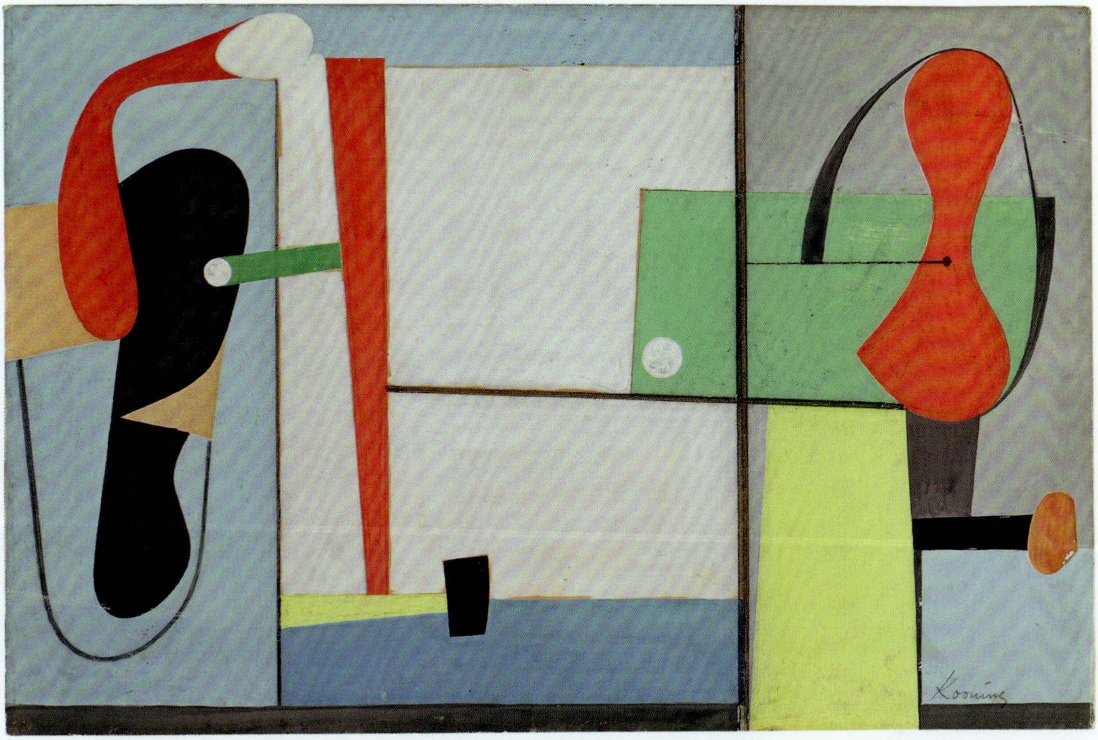

Figure 28. Willem de Kooning, *Study for the Williamsburg Project*, 1935. Gouache, pencil, and cardboard. 9⁵⁄₁₆" × 14⅜" (23.7 cm × 36.5 cm). Iris and B. Gerald Cantor Center for Visual Arts at Stanford University; bequest of Dr. and Mrs. Harold C. Torbert. © 2014 The Willem de Kooning Foundation / Artists Rights Society (ARS), New York.

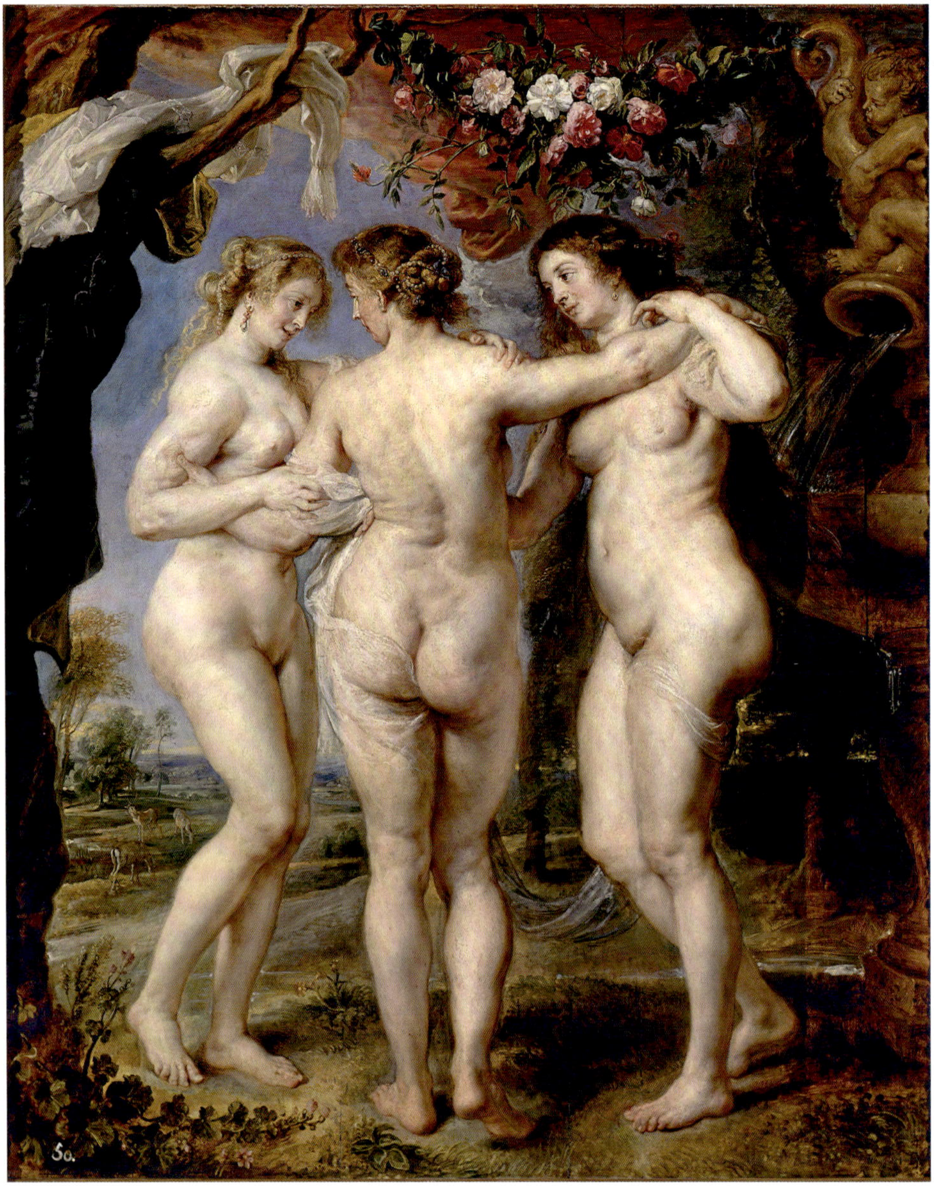

Figure 29. (above) Peter Paul Rubens, *The Three Graces*, circa 1635. Oil on canvas. 221 × 181 cm. Madrid, Prado Museum. Album / Art Resource, NY.

Figure 30. (facing) Picasso, *The Three Dancers* (*Les Trois Danseuses*), 1925. Oil on canvas. Support: 215.3 × 142.2 cm. Purchased with a special Grant-in-Aid and the Florence Fox Bequest with assistance from the Friends of the Tate Gallery and the Contemporary Art Society 1965. Tate, London / Art Resource, NY. © 2014 Estate of Pablo Picasso / Artists Rights Society (ARS), New York.

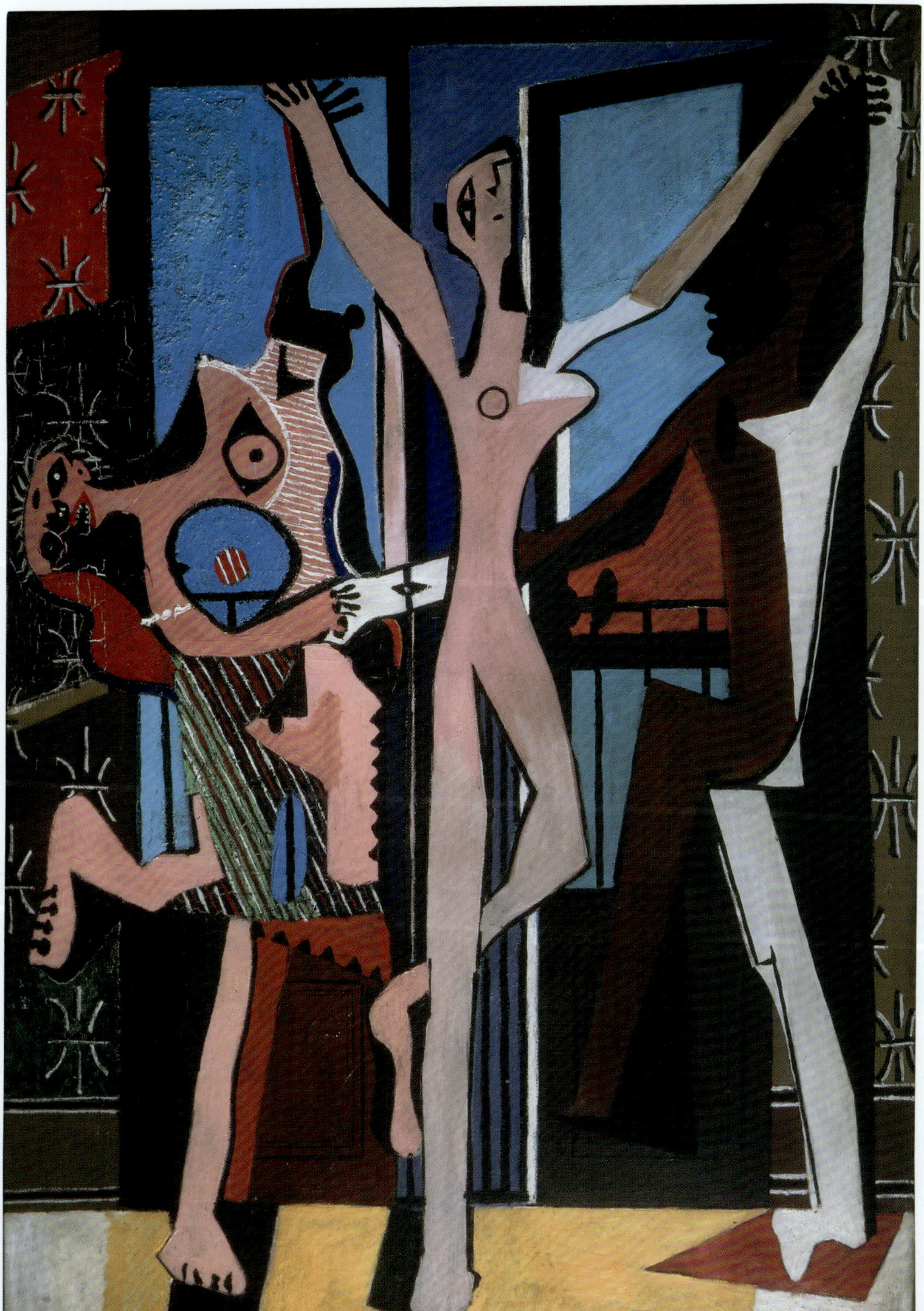

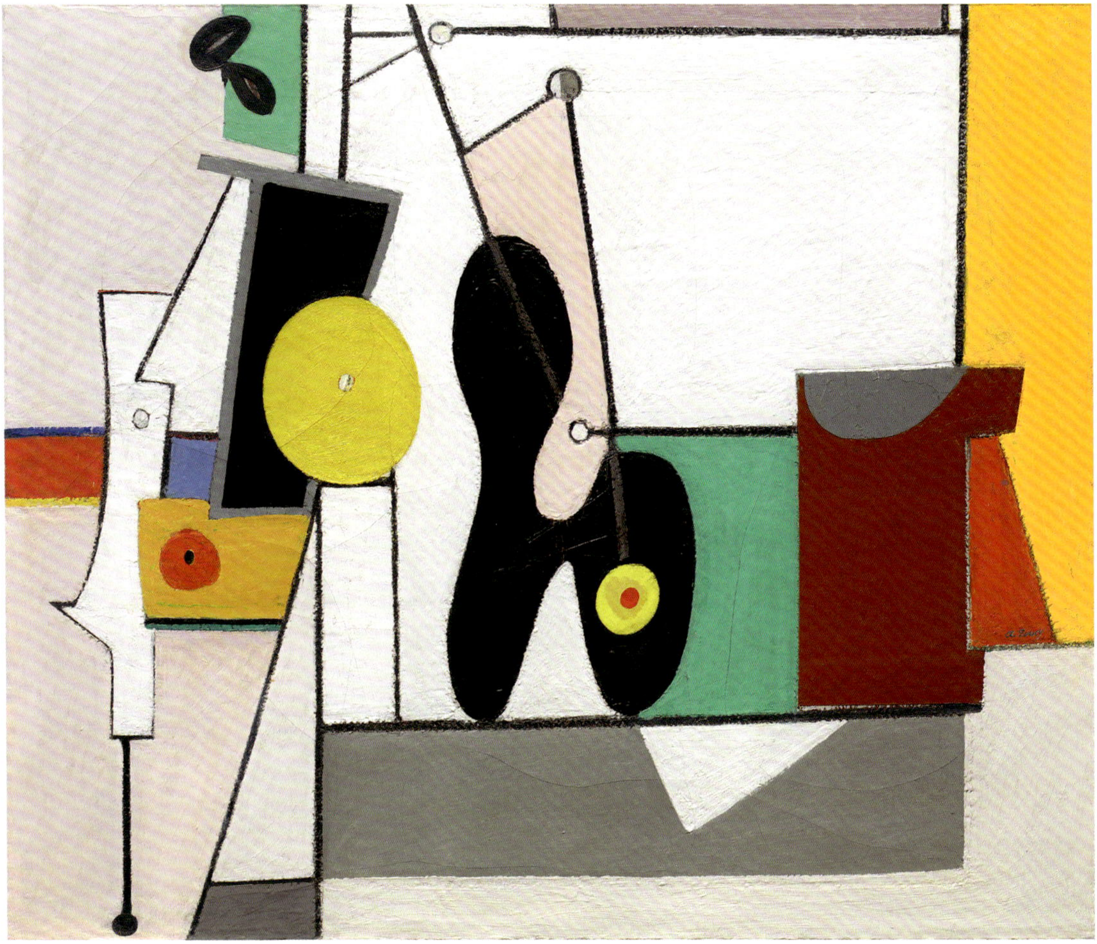

Figure 31. Arshile Gorky, *Organization*, 1933–36. Oil on canvas. Overall: 127 × 152 cm (50″ × 59$^{13}/_{16}$″); framed: 134.6 × 160 × 7 cm (53″ × 63″ × 2¾″). National Gallery of Art, Washington, DC, Ailsa Mellon Bruce Fund, 1979.13.3. © 2014 The Arshile Gorky Foundation / The Artists Rights Society (ARS), New York.

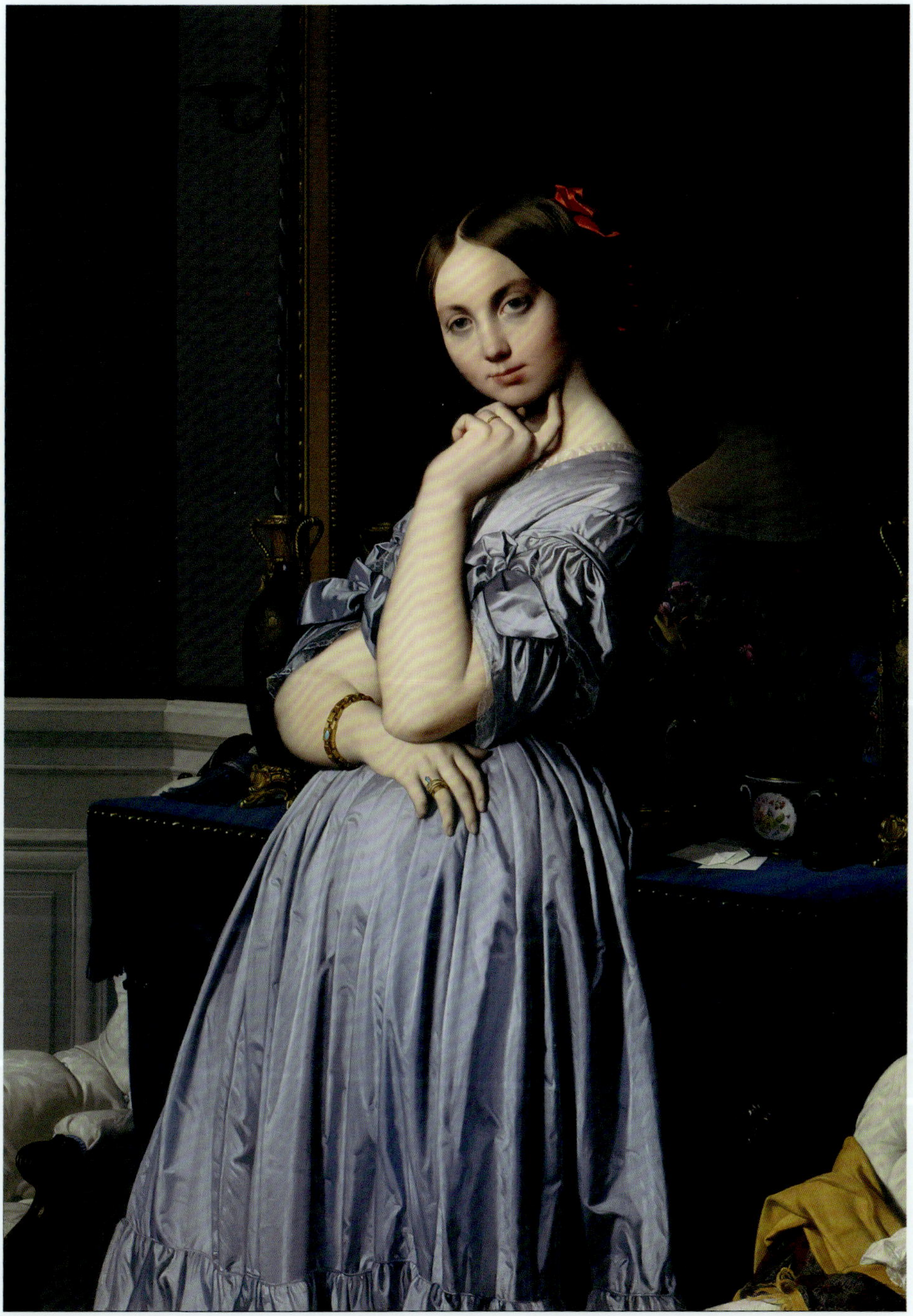

Figure 32. Ingres, *Comtesse d'Haussonville*, 1845. Oil on canvas. 51⅞″ × 36¼″ (131.8 × 92.1 cm). Framed: 66½″ × 51″ × 4¼″ (168.9 × 129.5 × 10.8 cm). © The Frick Collection, New York.

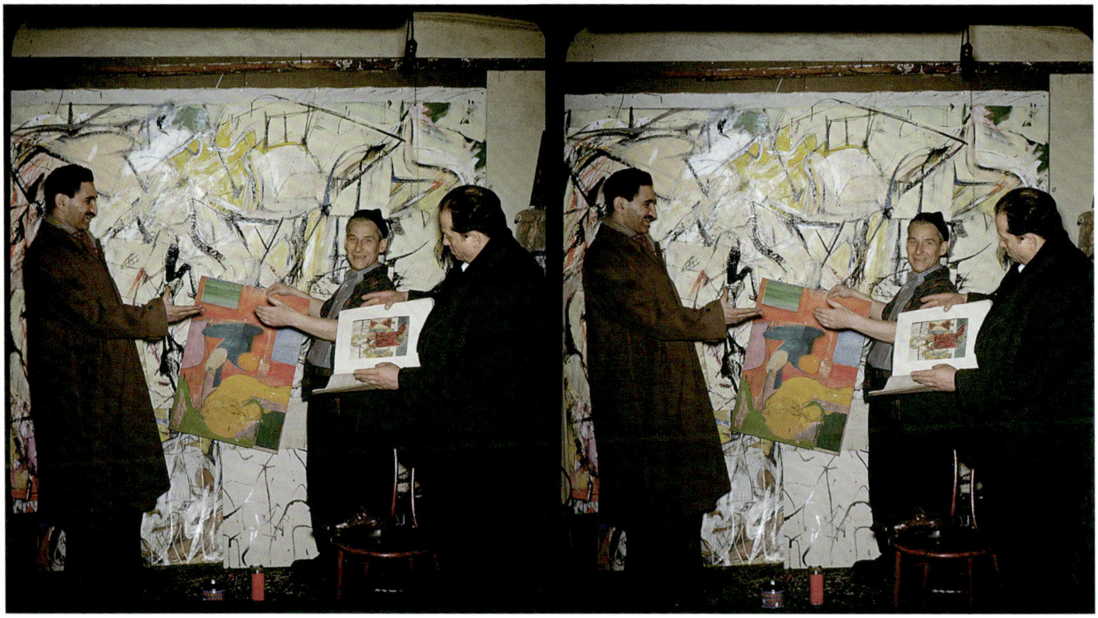

Figure 33. Max Margulis, stereoscopic photograph of (L to R) Harold Rosenberg, Willem de Kooning, and Landes Lewitin, March 22, 1950. 35mm Kodachrome slides. Courtesy of the Family of Max Margulis.

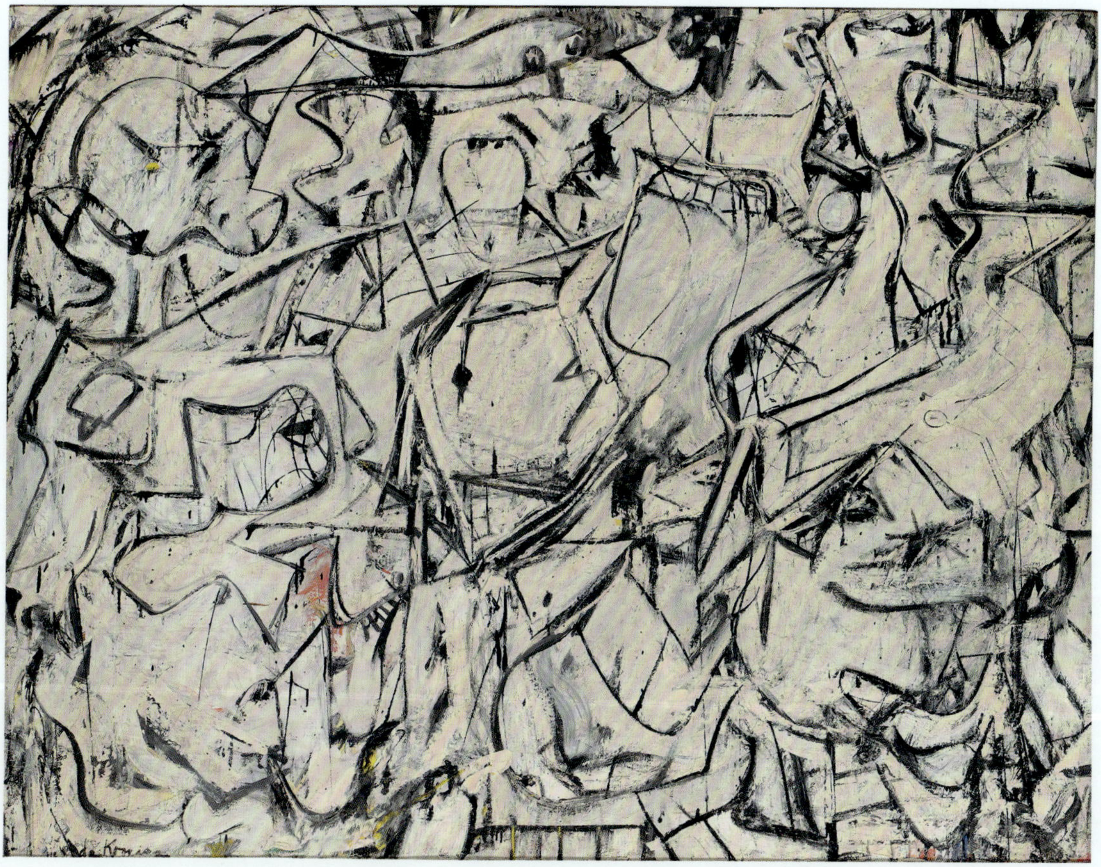

Figure 34. Willem de Kooning, *Attic*, 1949. Oil, enamel, and newspaper transfer on canvas. 61⅞" × 81" (157.2 × 205.7 cm). The Muriel Kallis Steinberg Newman Collection, gift of Muriel Kallis Newman, in honor of her son Glenn David Steinberg, 1982. Image copyright © The Metropolitan Museum of Art. Image source: Art Resource, NY. © 2014 The Willem de Kooning Foundation / Artists Rights Society (ARS), New York.

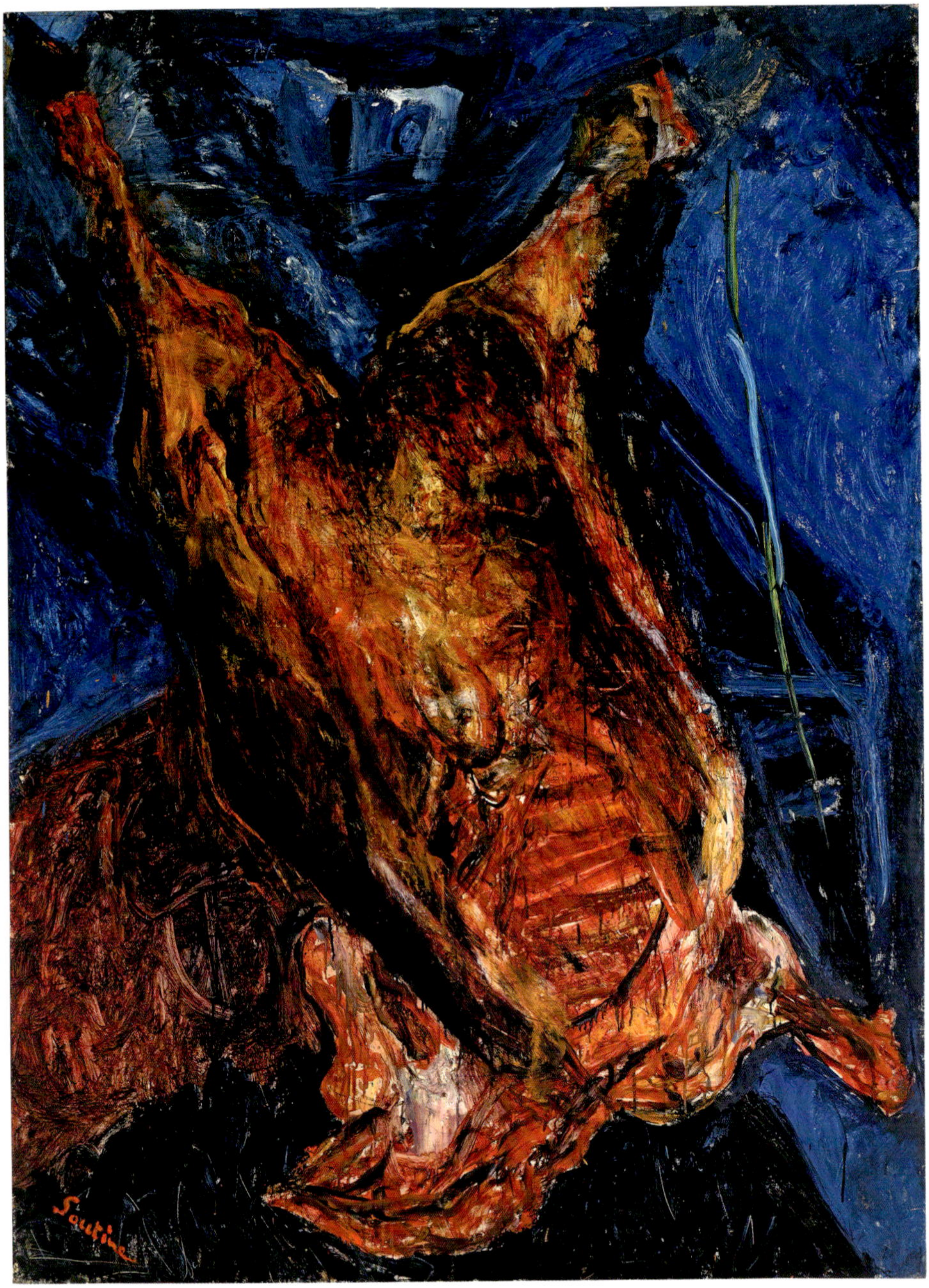

Figure 35. Chaim Soutine, *Carcass of Beef*, circa 1925. Oil on canvas. Support: 55¼″ × 42⅜″ (140.33 × 107.63 cm.); framed: 61½″ × 48¼″ × 5½″ (156.21 × 122.55 × 13.97 cm). Room of Contemporary Art Fund, 1939. Albright-Knox Art Gallery / Art Resource, NY. © 2014 Artists Rights Society (ARS), New York.

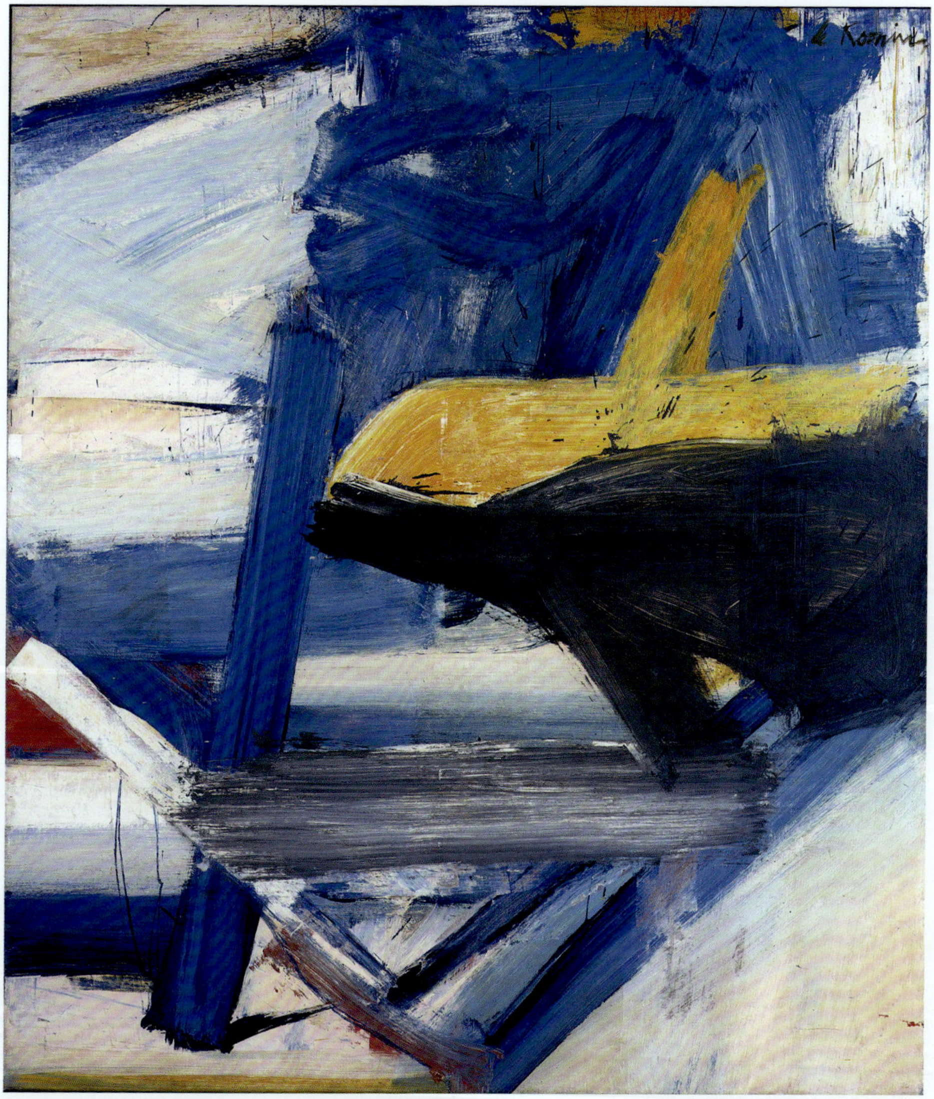

Figure 36. Willem de Kooning, *Bolton Landing*, 1957. Oil on canvas. 6′11¾″ × 6′2″ (212.7 × 188 cm). Image courtesy of Mitchell-Innes & Nash, New York. © 2014 The Willem de Kooning Foundation / Artists Rights Society (ARS), New York.

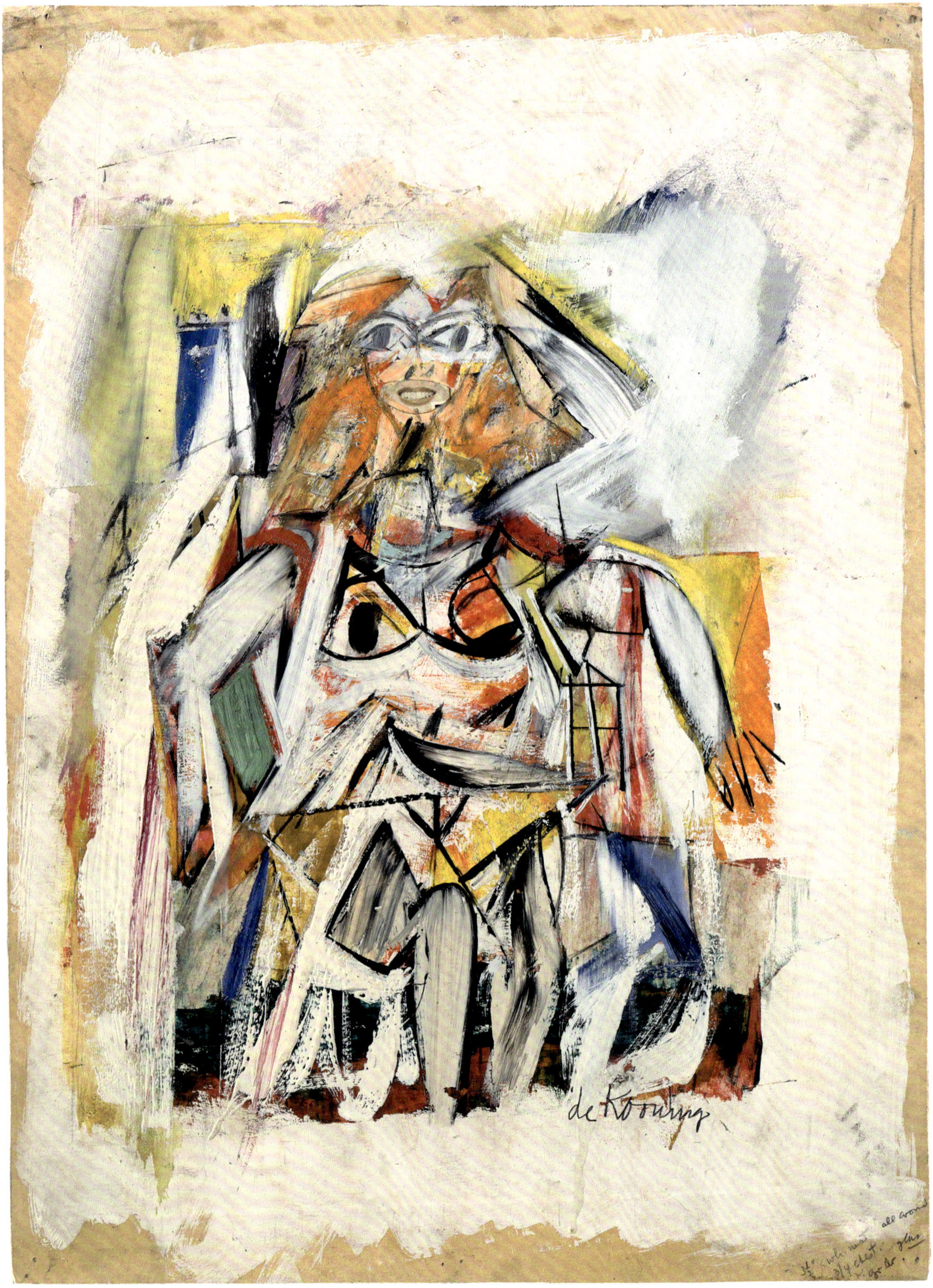
de Kooning

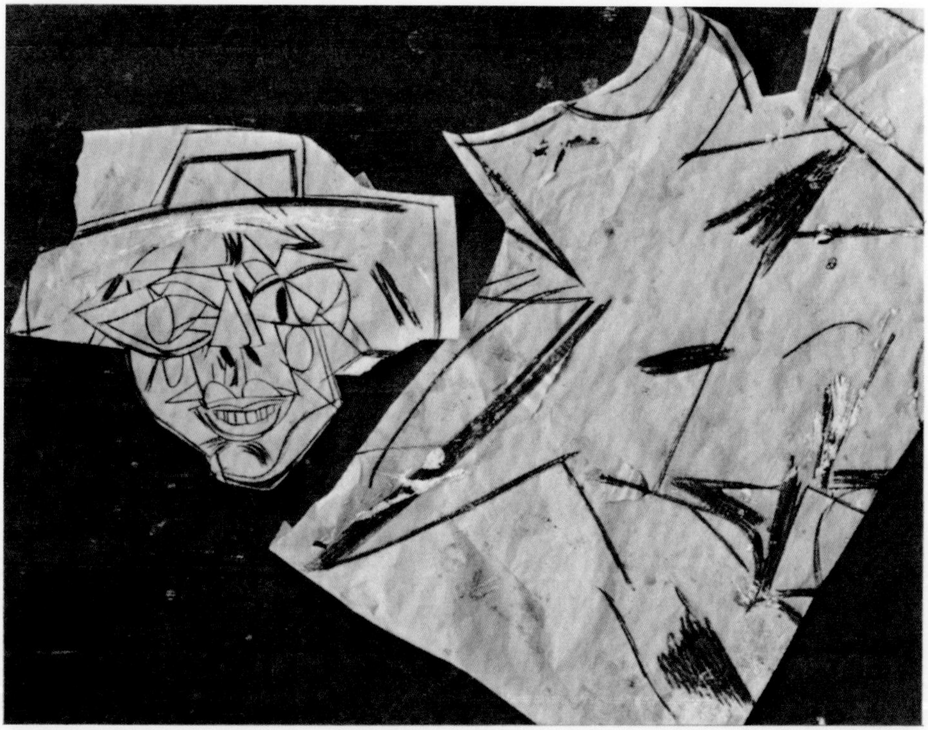

Figure 37. (facing) Willem de Kooning, *Woman*, 1950. Oil, cut and pasted paper on cardboard. 14¾" × 11⅝" (37.5 × 29.5 cm). From the Collection of Thomas B. Hess, gift of the heirs of Thomas B. Hess, 1984, 1984.613.6. Image copyright © The Metropolitan Museum of Art. Image source: Art Resource, NY. © 2014 The Willem de Kooning Foundation / Artists Rights Society (ARS), New York.

Figure 38. (above) Willem de Kooning, tracing of *Woman I*; destroyed. Charcoal on paper. Digital image © 2011 MoMA, NY. Photo © 2014 Estate of Rudy Burckhardt / Artists Rights Society (ARS), New York. Art © 2014 The Willem de Kooning Foundation / Artists Rights Society (ARS), New York.

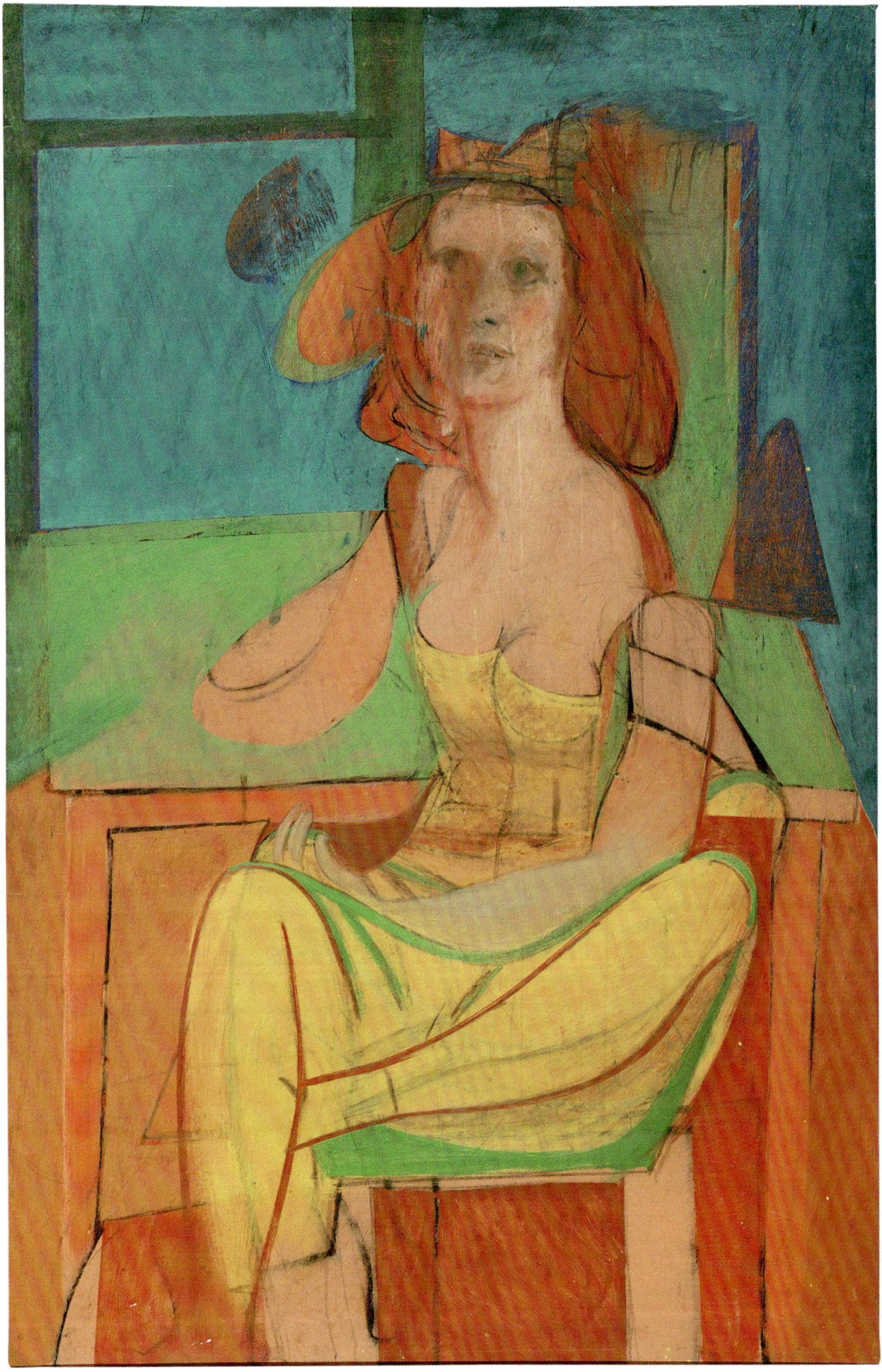

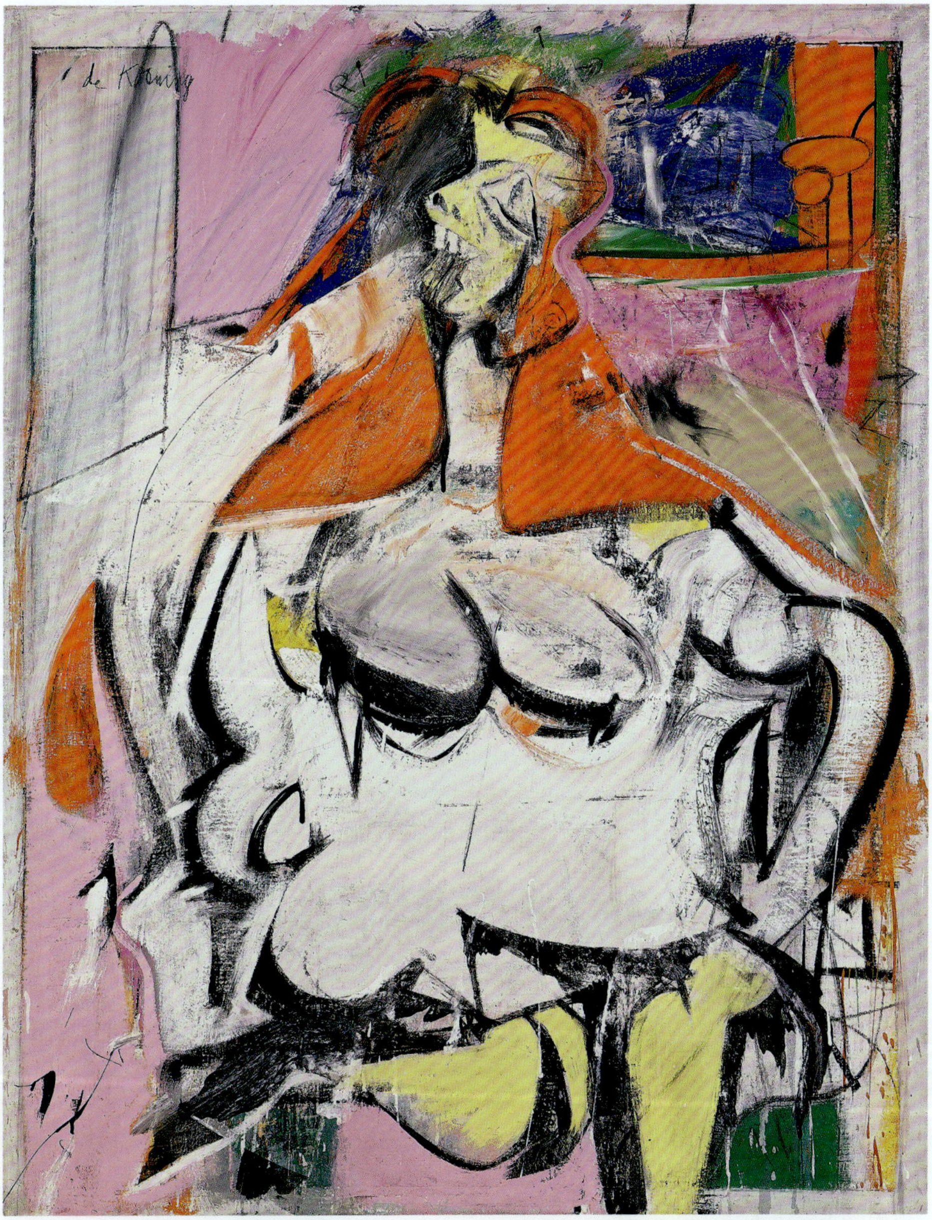

Figure 39. (facing) Willem de Kooning, *Seated Woman*, circa 1940. Oil and charcoal on Masonite. $54\frac{1}{16}$″ × 36″ (137.3 × 91.4 cm); framed: $54\frac{1}{16}$″ × $37\frac{3}{4}$″ × $2\frac{1}{2}$″ (137.3 × 95.9 × 6.4 cm). The Albert M. Greenfield and Elizabeth M. Greenfield Collection, 1974. The Philadelphia Museum of Art / Art Resource, NY. © 2014 The Willem de Kooning Foundation / Artists Rights Society (ARS), New York.

Figure 40. (above) Willem de Kooning, *Woman*, 1949. Oil, enamel and charcoal on canvas. 153.3 × 121.9 cm. Private collection / Photo © Christie's Images / Bridgeman Images. © 2014 The Willem de Kooning Foundation / Artists Rights Society (ARS), New York.

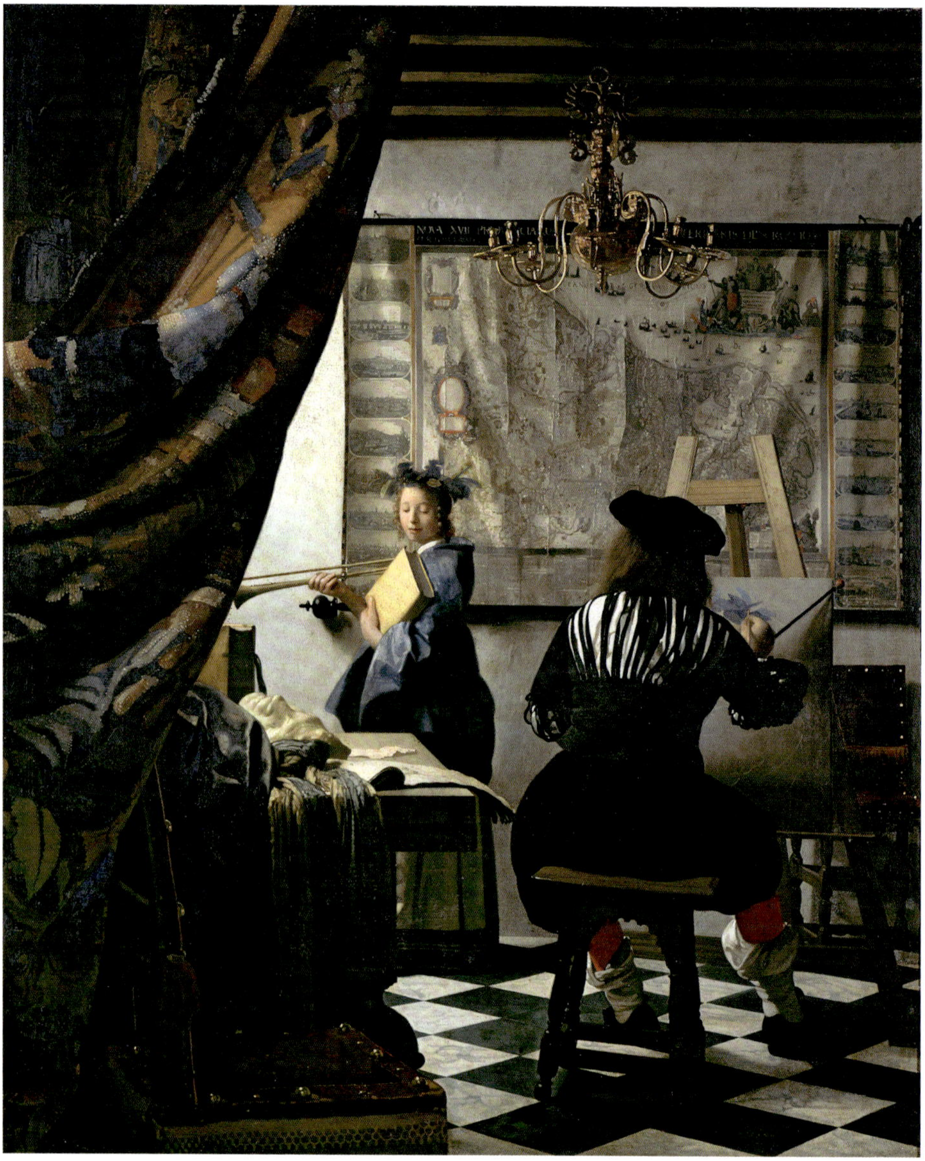

Figure 41. Jan Vermeer, *The Art of Painting*, also known as *Die Malkunst*, or *The Painter (Vermeer's Self-Portrait) and His Model as Klio*, 1665/66. Oil on canvas. 120 × 100 cm. Erich Lessing / Art Resource, NY.

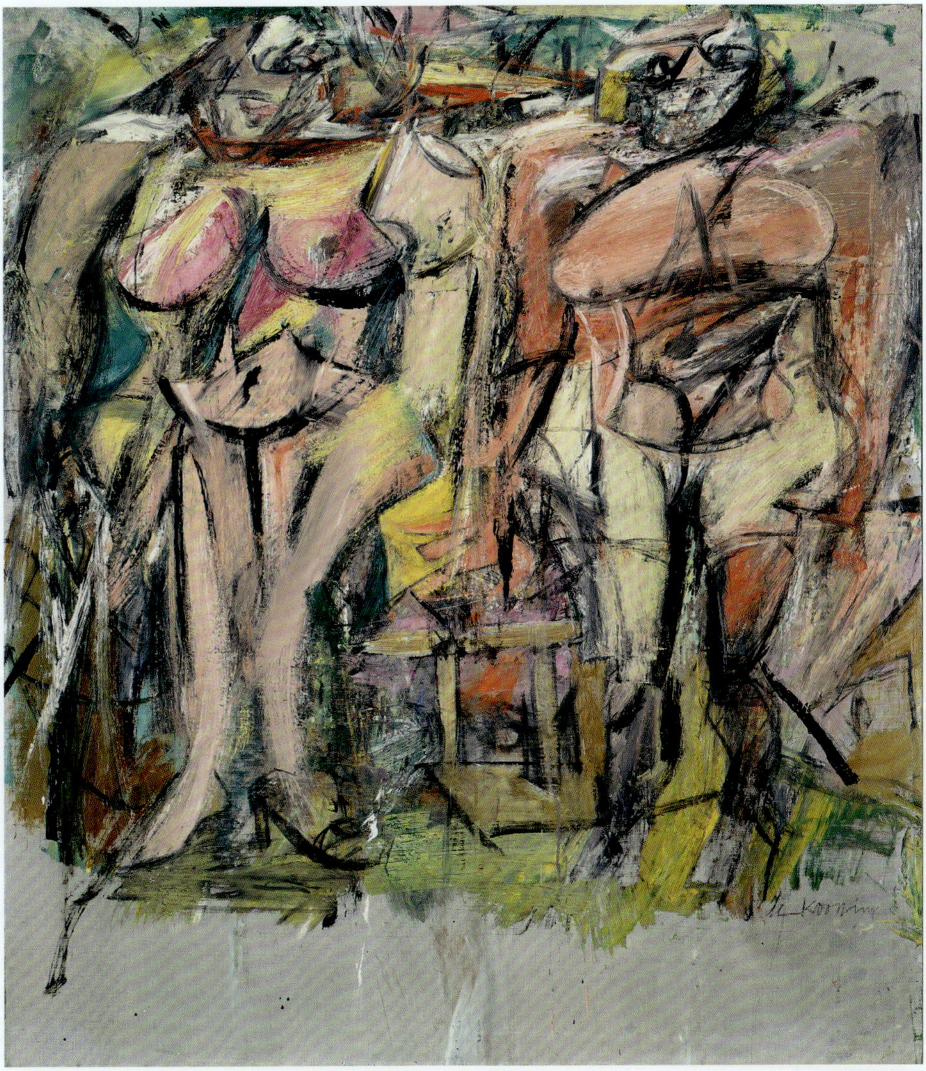

Figure 42. Willem de Kooning, *Two Women in the Country*, 1954. Oil, enamel, and charcoal on canvas. 46⅛" × 40¾" (117.1 × 103.5 cm). Hirshhorn Museum and Sculpture Garden, Smithsonian Institution, gift of Joseph H. Hirshhorn, 1966. Photography by Lee Stalsworth. © 2014 The Willem de Kooning Foundation / Artists Rights Society (ARS), New York.

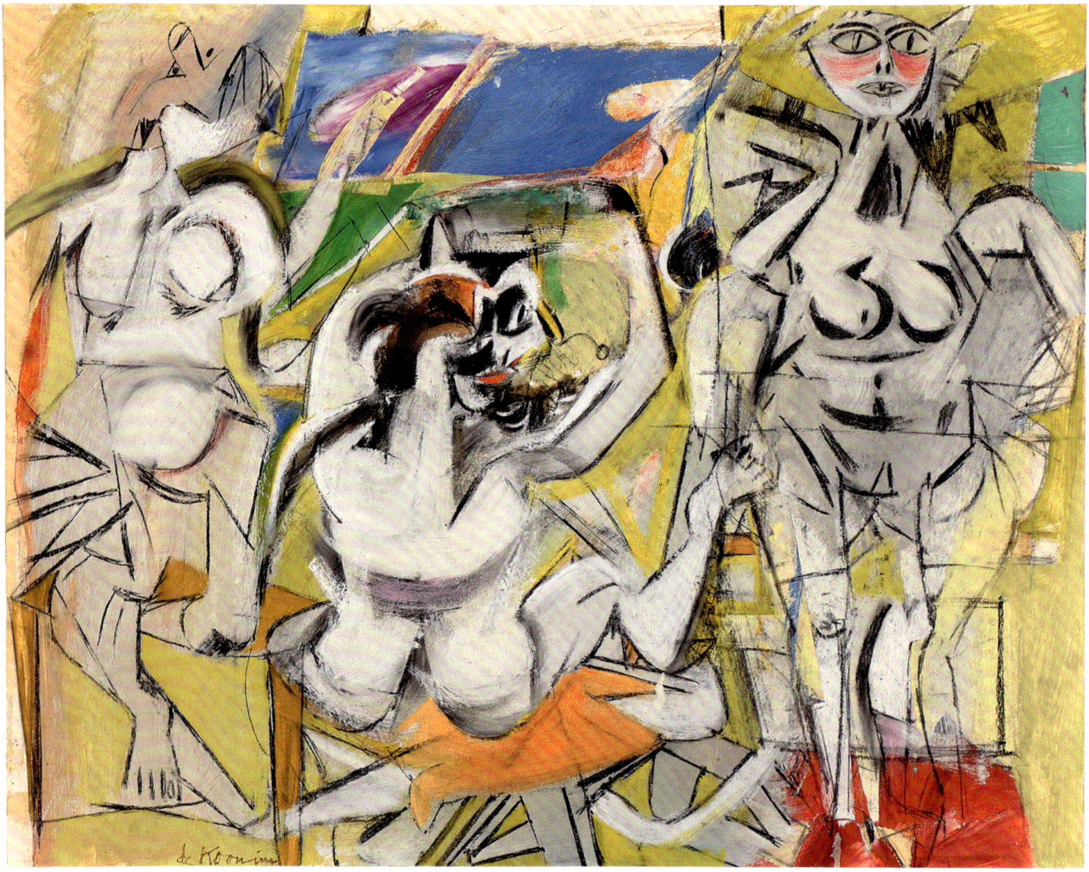

Figure 43. Willem de Kooning, *Untitled* (*Three Women*), circa 1948. Oil and crayon on thick white paper adhered to board. 20″ × 26⅜″ (50.8 × 67 cm). Frances Lehman Loeb Art Center, Vassar College, Poughkeepsie, New York. Gift of Mrs. Richard Deutsch (Katherine W. Sanford, Class of 1940). © 2014 The Willem de Kooning Foundation / Artists Rights Society (ARS), New York.

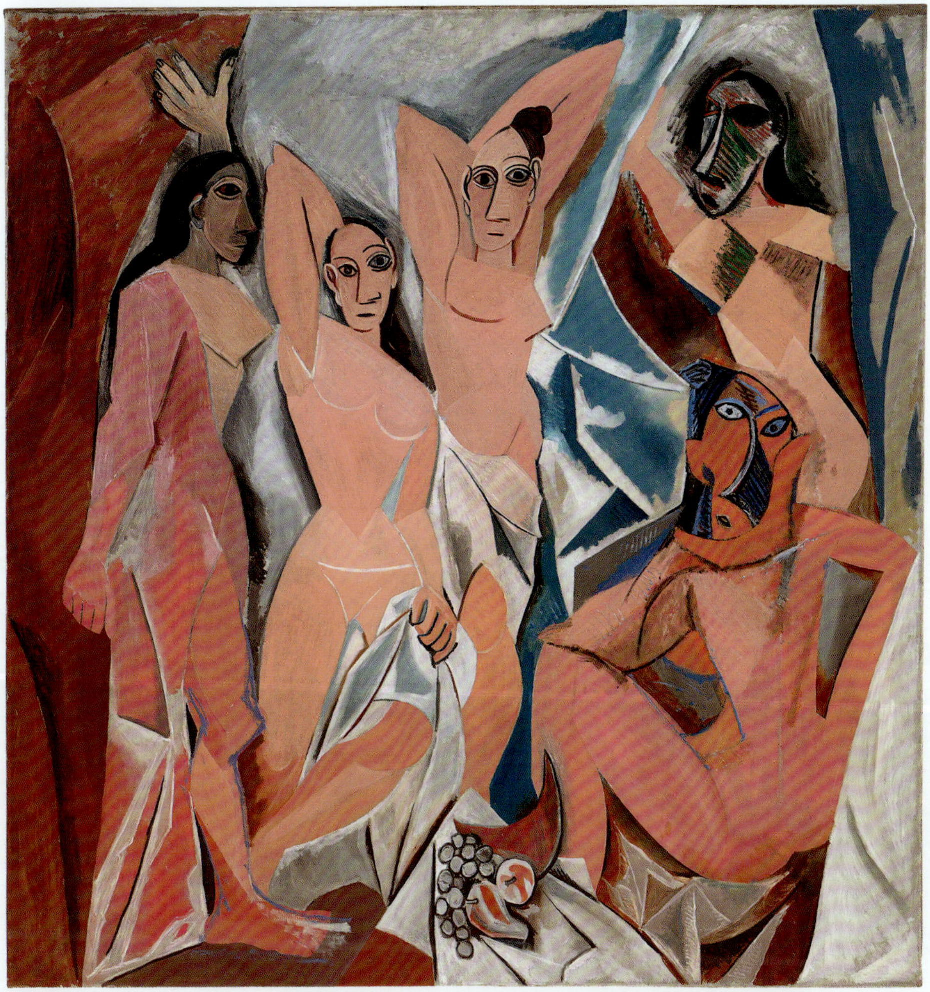

Figure 44. Picasso, *Les Demoiselles d'Avignon*, Paris, June-July 1907. Oil on canvas. 8′ × 7′8″ (243.9 × 233.7 cm). Acquired through the Lillie P. Bliss Bequest. Digital image © The Museum of Modern Art / Licensed by SCALA / Art Resource, NY. © 2014 Estate of Pablo Picasso / Artists Rights Society (ARS), New York.

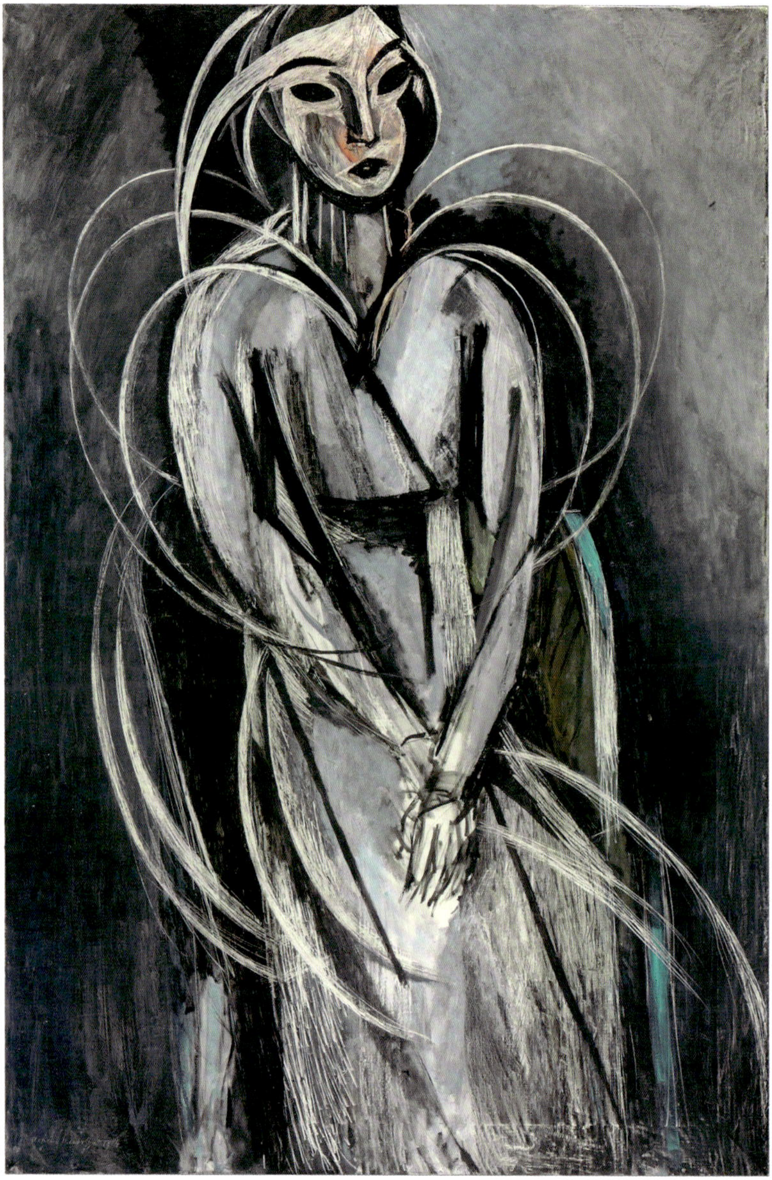

Figure 45. Henri Matisse, *Mademoiselle Yvonne Landsberg*, 1914. Oil on canvas. 58″ × 38⅜″ (147.3 × 97.5 cm). The Louise and Walter Arensberg Collection, 1950. The Philadelphia Museum of Art. © 2014 Succession H. Matisse / Artists Rights Society (ARS), New York.

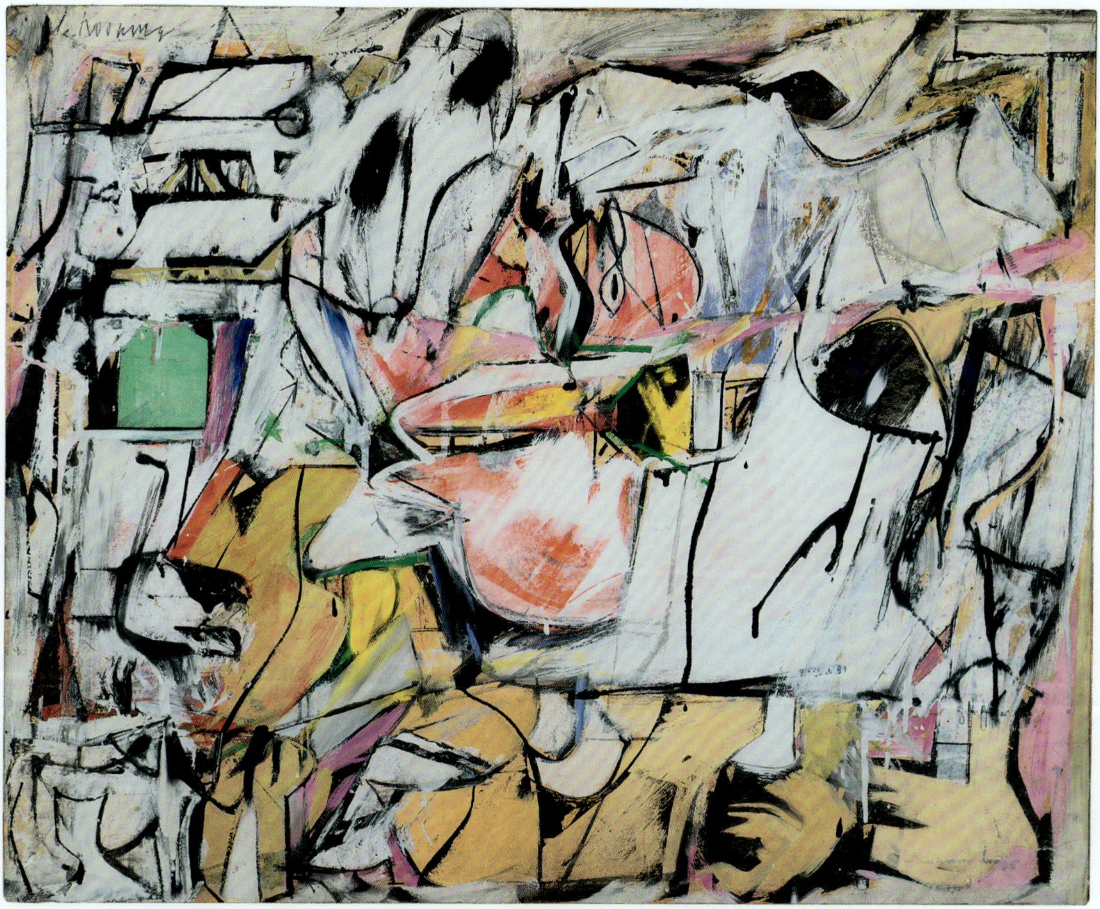

Figure 46. Willem de Kooning, *Asheville*, 1948. Oil and enamel on cardboard. $25\frac{9}{16}$" × $31\frac{7}{8}$" (64.92875 × 80.9625 cm). The Phillips Collection, Washington, DC, acquired 1952. © 2014 The Willem de Kooning Foundation / Artists Rights Society (ARS), New York.

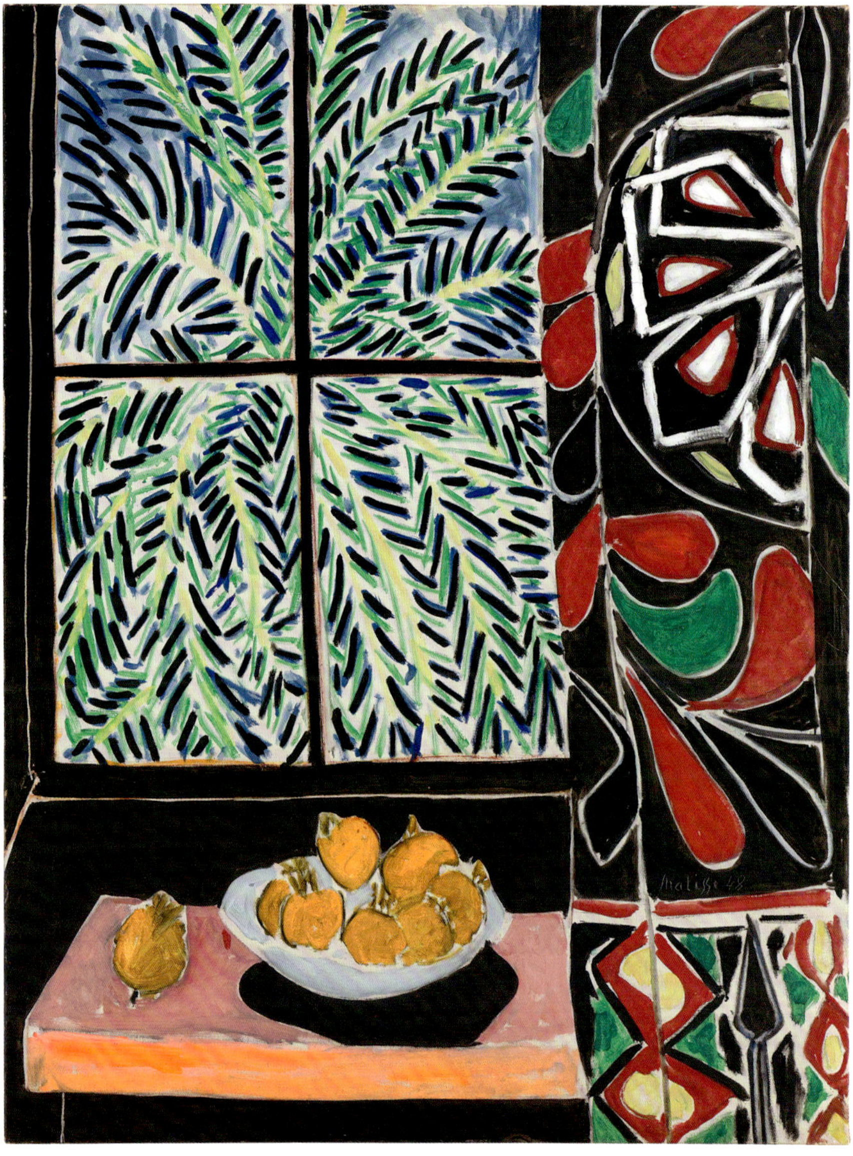

Figure 47. (above) Matisse, *Interior with Egyptian Curtain*, 1948. Oil on canvas. Framed: 38¼″ × 48⅝″ × 2″ (97.15 cm × 123.51 cm × 5.08 cm). Image: 45¾″ × 35⅛″ (116.205 × 89.2175 cm). The Phillips Collection, Washington, DC, acquired 1950. © 2014 Succession H. Matisse / Artists Rights Society (ARS), New York.

Figure 48. (facing) Matisse, *View of Notre-Dame*, Paris, quai Saint-Michel, spring 1914. Oil on canvas. 58″ × 37⅛″ (147.3 × 94.3 cm). Acquired through the Lillie P. Bliss Bequest; the Henry Ittleson, A. Conger Goodyear, and Mr. and Mrs. Robert Sinclair Funds; and the Anna Erickson Levene Bequest given in memory of her husband, Dr. Phoebus Aaron Theodor Levene. Digital image © The Museum of Modern Art / Licensed by SCALA / Art Resource, NY. © 2014 Succession H. Matisse / Artists Rights Society (ARS), New York.

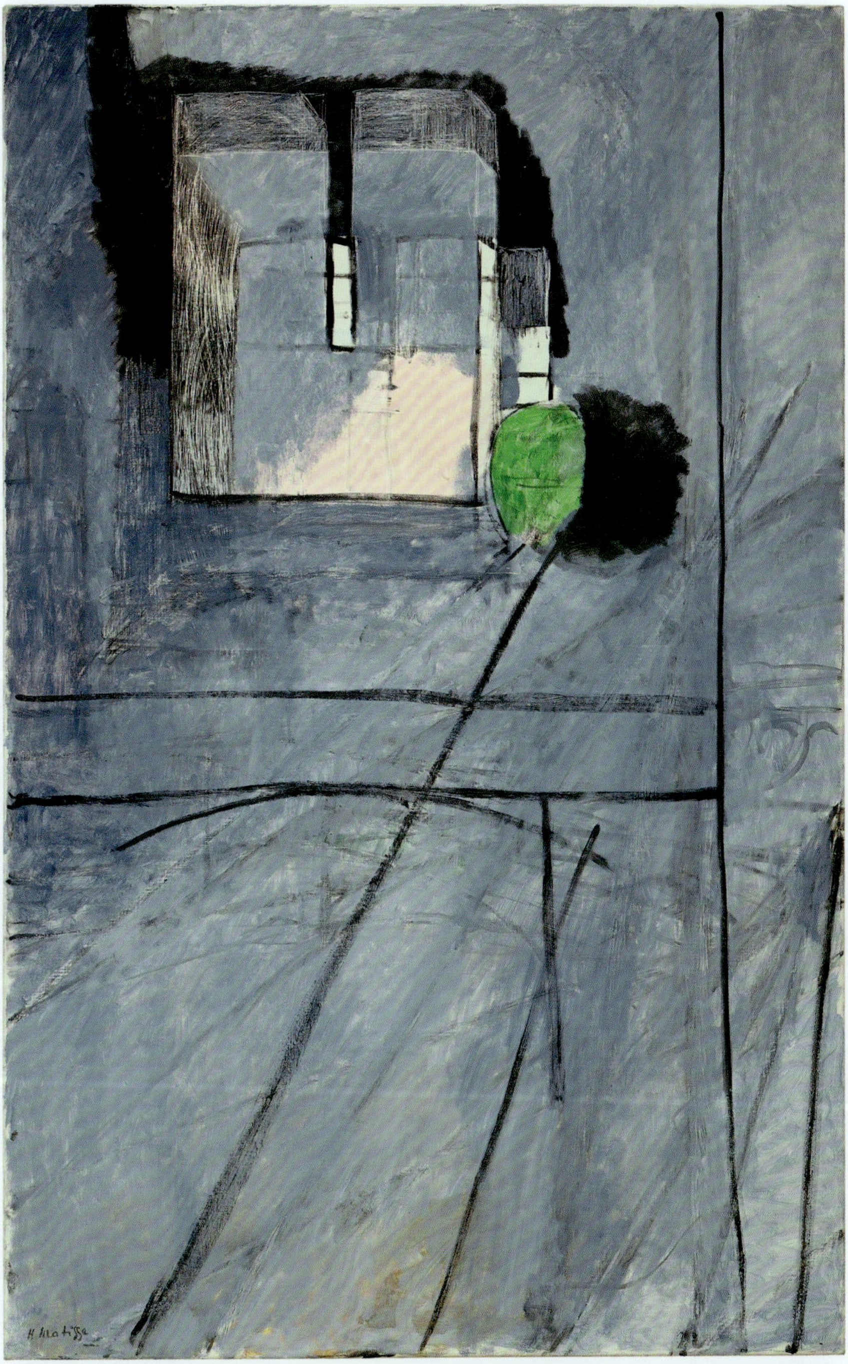
H. Matisse

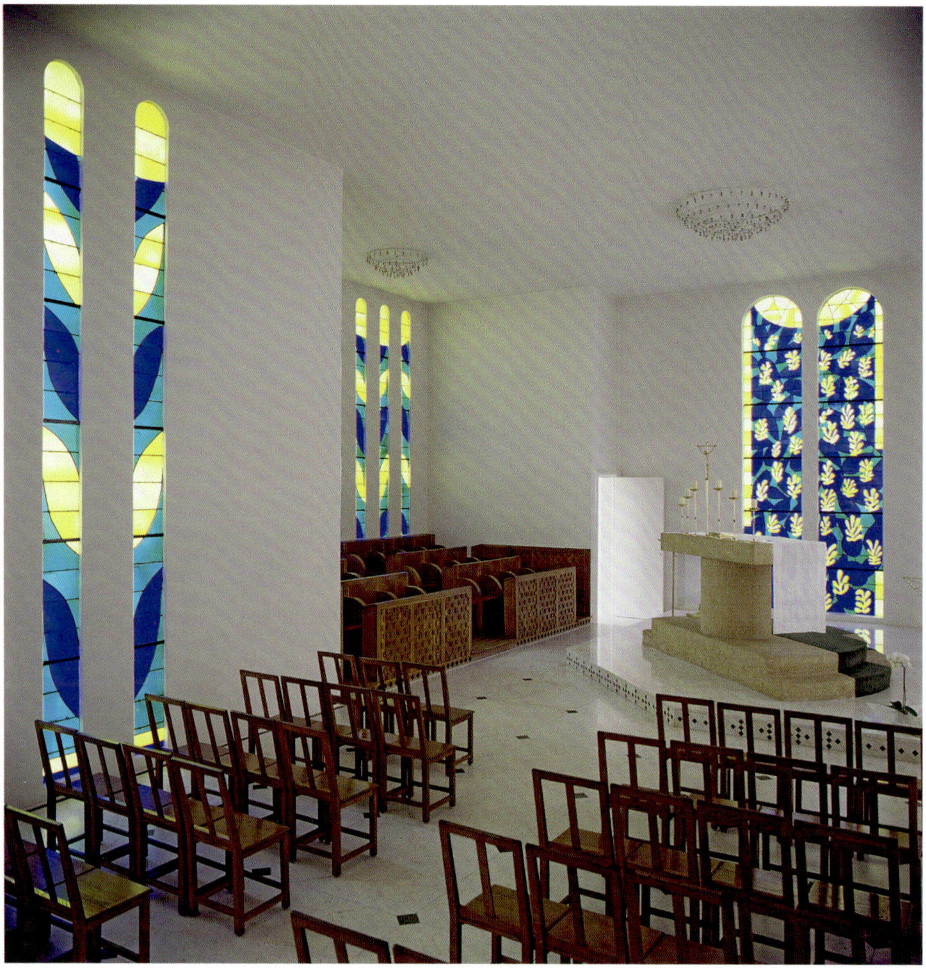

Figure 49. (above) Matisse, Chapelle du Rosaire (Chapel of the Rosary), Vence, France 1948–51, general view of the interior (mixed media). DACS, London / Bridgeman Images. © 2014 Succession H. Matisse / Artists Rights Society (ARS), New York.

Figure 50. (facing) Matisse, *The Painter in His Studio*, late 1916–early 1917. Oil on canvas. 146.5 × 97 cm. AM 2585 P. Photo: Philippe Migeat. © CNAC /MNAM / Dist. RMN-Grand Palais / Art Resource, NY. © 2014 Succession H. Matisse / Artists Rights Society (ARS), New York.

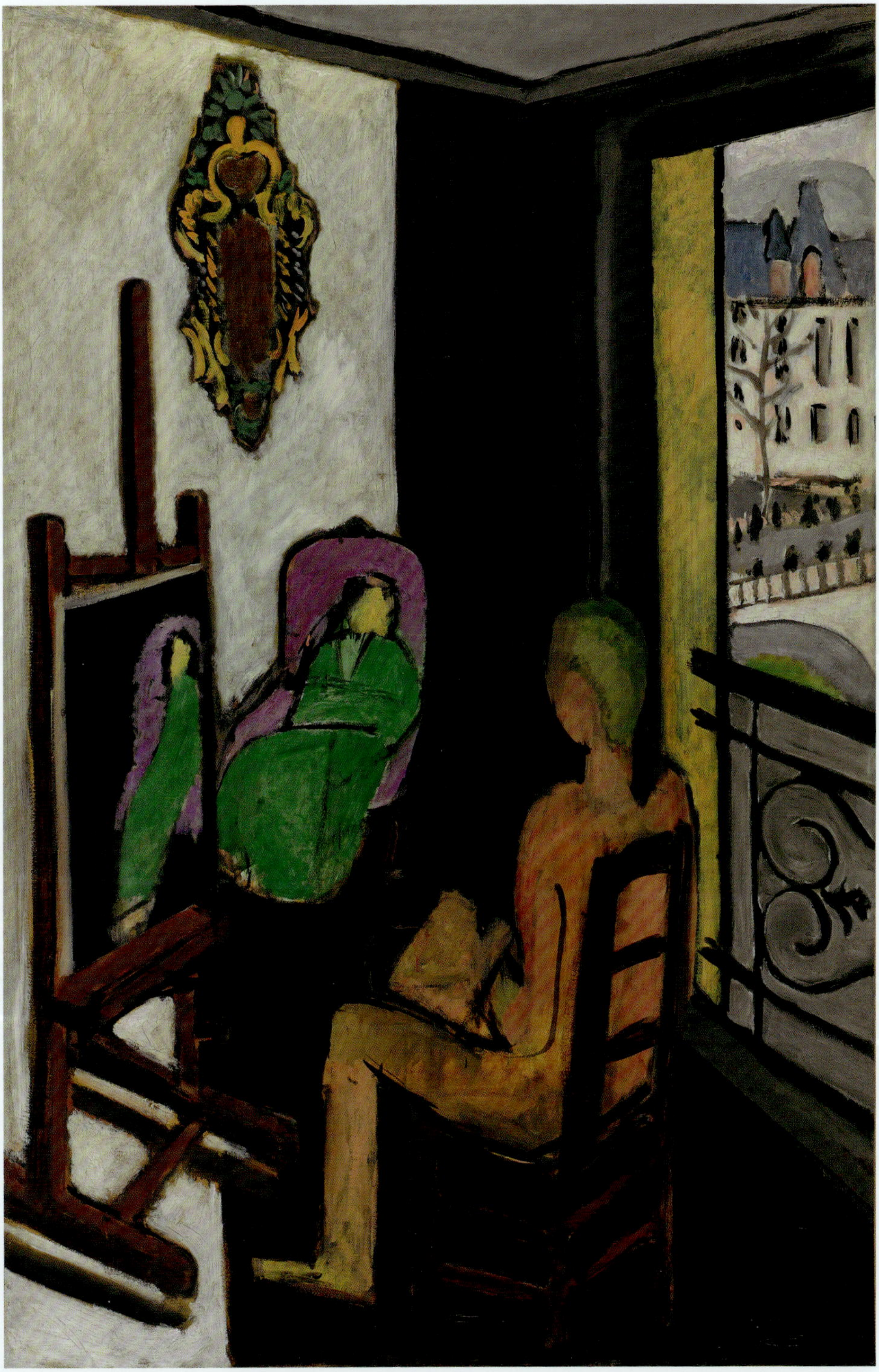

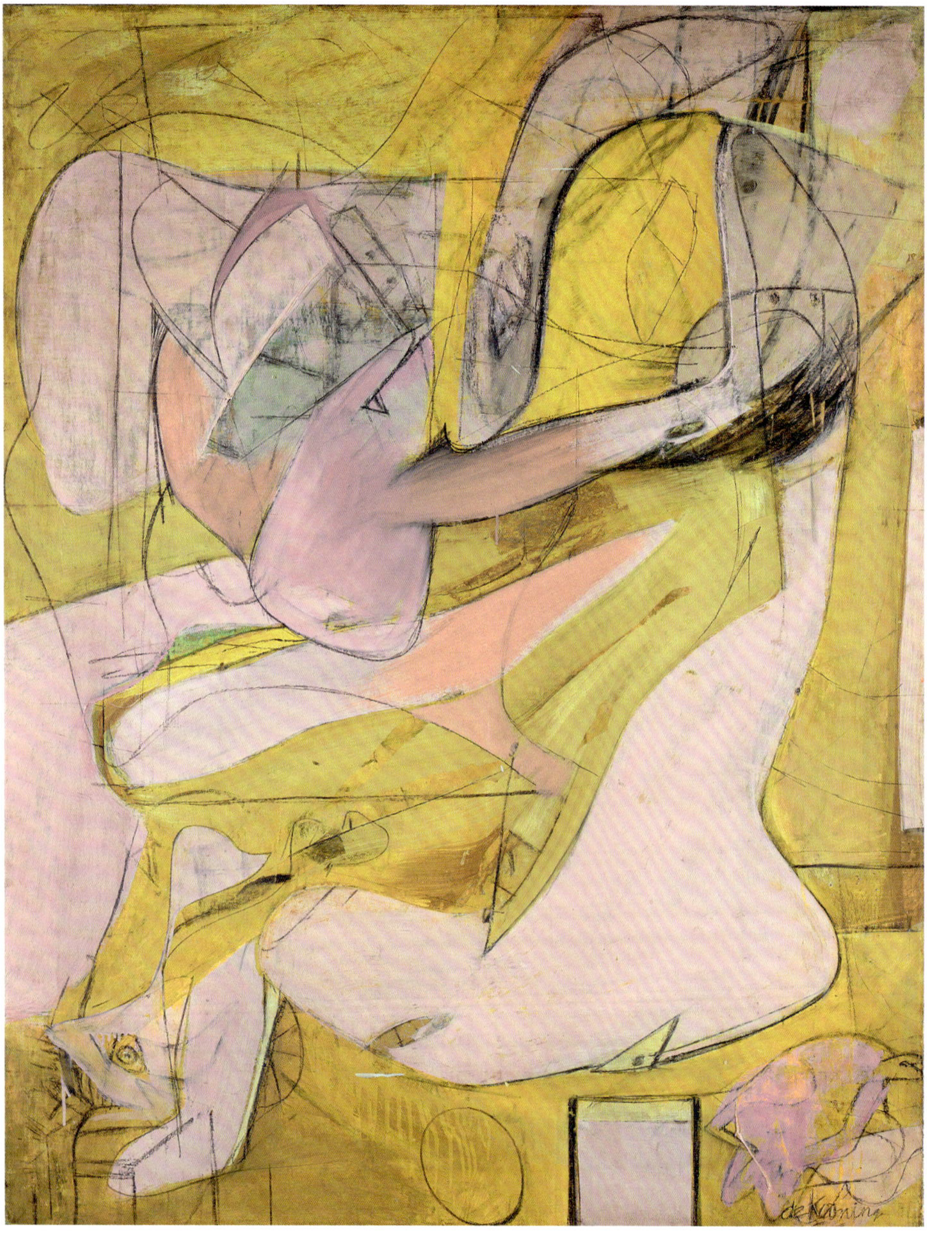

Figure 51. Willem de Kooning, *Pink Angels*, circa 1945. Oil and charcoal on canvas. 132.1 × 101.6 cm. Frederick R. Weisman Art Foundation, Los Angeles, CA, USA / Bridgeman Images. © 2014 The Willem de Kooning Foundation / Artists Rights Society (ARS), New York.

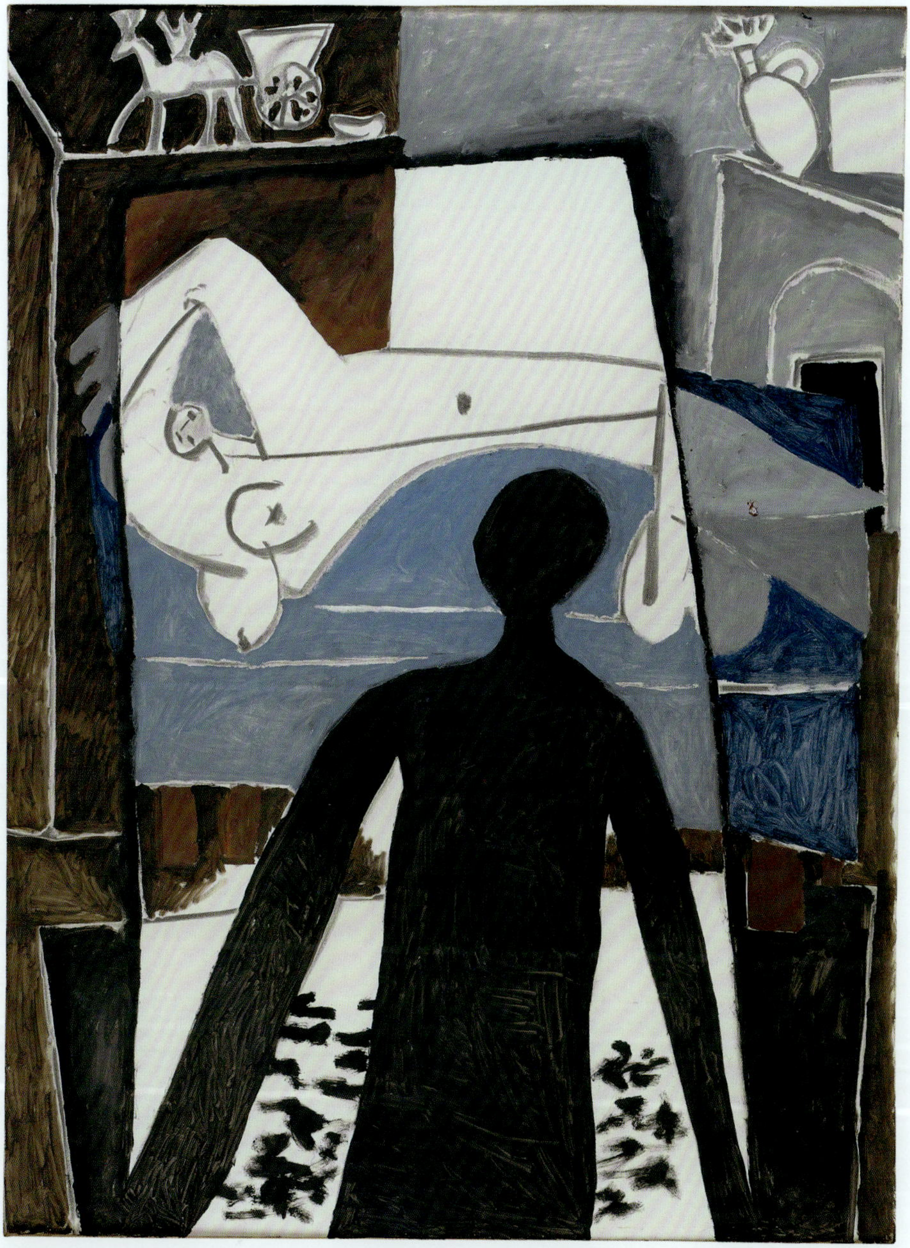

Figure 52. Picasso, *The Shadow* (*L'Ombre*), December 29, 1953, Vallauris. Oil and charcoal on canvas. 49½" × 38". MP 208. Photo: J. G. Berizzi. © RMN-Grand Palais / Art Resource, NY. © 2014 Estate of Pablo Picasso / Artists Rights Society (ARS), New York.

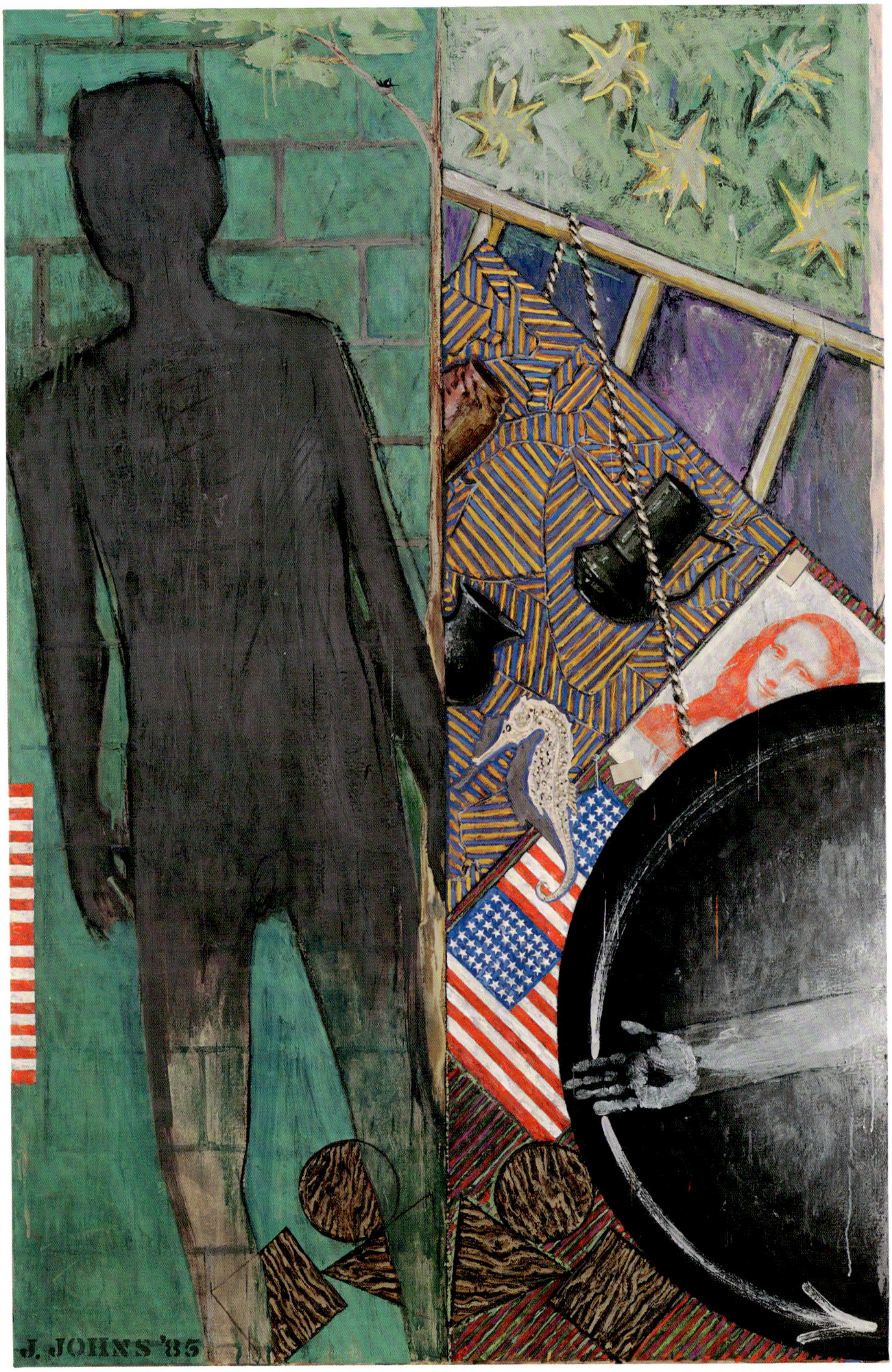
J. JOHNS '85

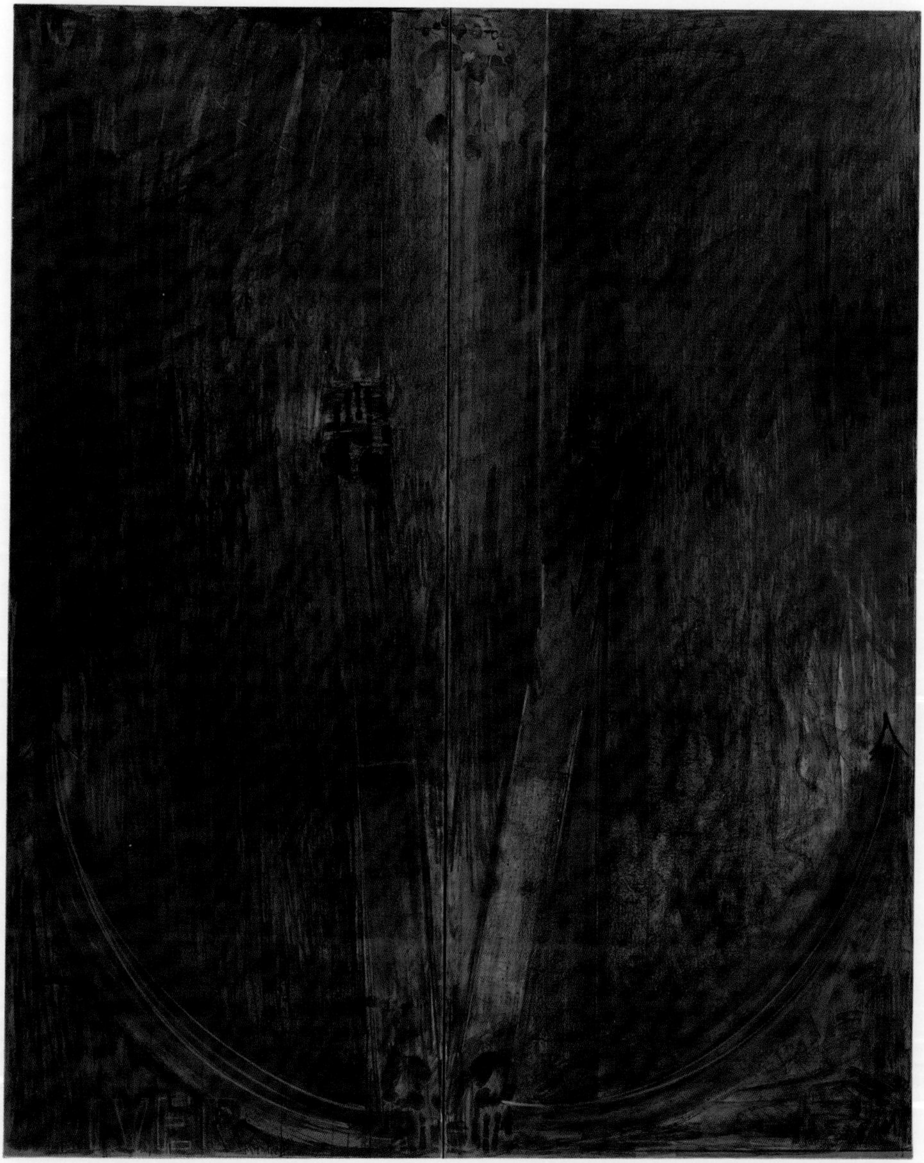

Figure 53. (facing) Jasper Johns, *Summer*, 1985. Encaustic on canvas. 6′3″ × 50″. Gift of Philip Johnson. Digital image © The Museum of Modern Art / Licensed by SCALA / Art Resource, NY. Art © Jasper Johns / Licensed by VAGA, New York, NY.

Figure 54. (above) Johns, *Diver*, 1962–63. Charcoal, pastel, and watercolor on paper mounted on canvas, two panels. 7′2½″ × 7′1¾″ (219.7 × 182.2 cm). Partial gift of Kate Ganz and Tony Ganz in memory of their parents, Victor and Sally Ganz, and in memory of Kirk Varnedoe; Mrs. John Hay Whitney Bequest Fund; gift of Edgar Kaufmann Jr. and Philip L. Goodwin (both by exchange). Acquired by the Trustees of The Museum of Modern Art in memory of Kirk Varnedoe. Digital image © The Museum of Modern Art / Licensed by SCALA / Art Resource, NY. Art © Jasper Johns / Licensed by VAGA, New York, NY.

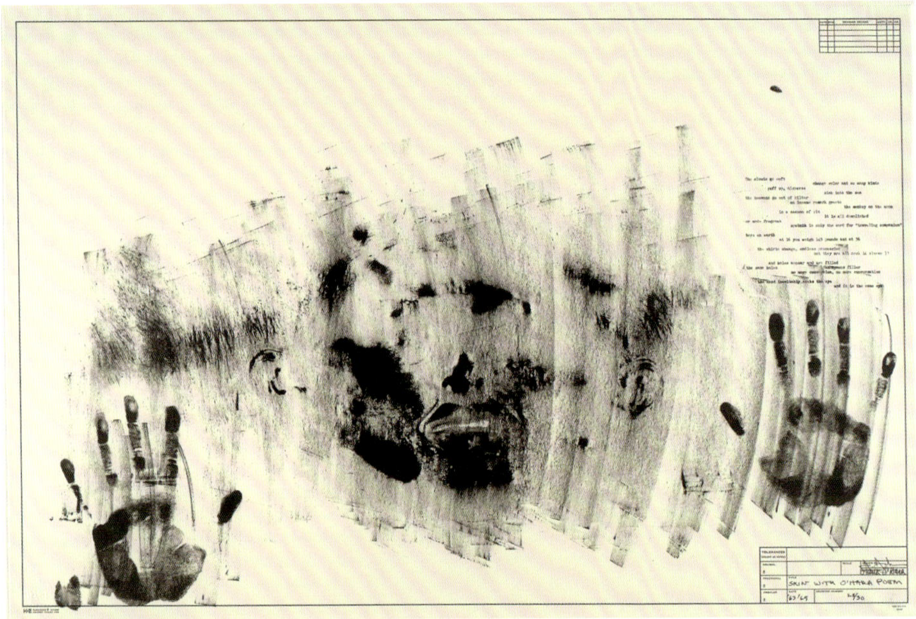

Figure 55. Johns with poetry by Frank O'Hara, *Skin with O'Hara Poem,* 1963–65. Lithograph in black from two stones on commercially printed off-white semitransparent wove paper. 539 × 839 mm (image); 559 × 863 mm (sheet). Collection acquired through a challenge grant of Mr. and Mrs. Thomas Dittmer; restricted gift of supporters of the Department of Prints and Drawings; Centennial Endowment; Margaret Fisher Endowment Fund, 1982.949, The Art Institute of Chicago. Art © Jasper Johns and ULAE / Licensed by VAGA, New York, NY. Published by Universal Limited Art Editions.

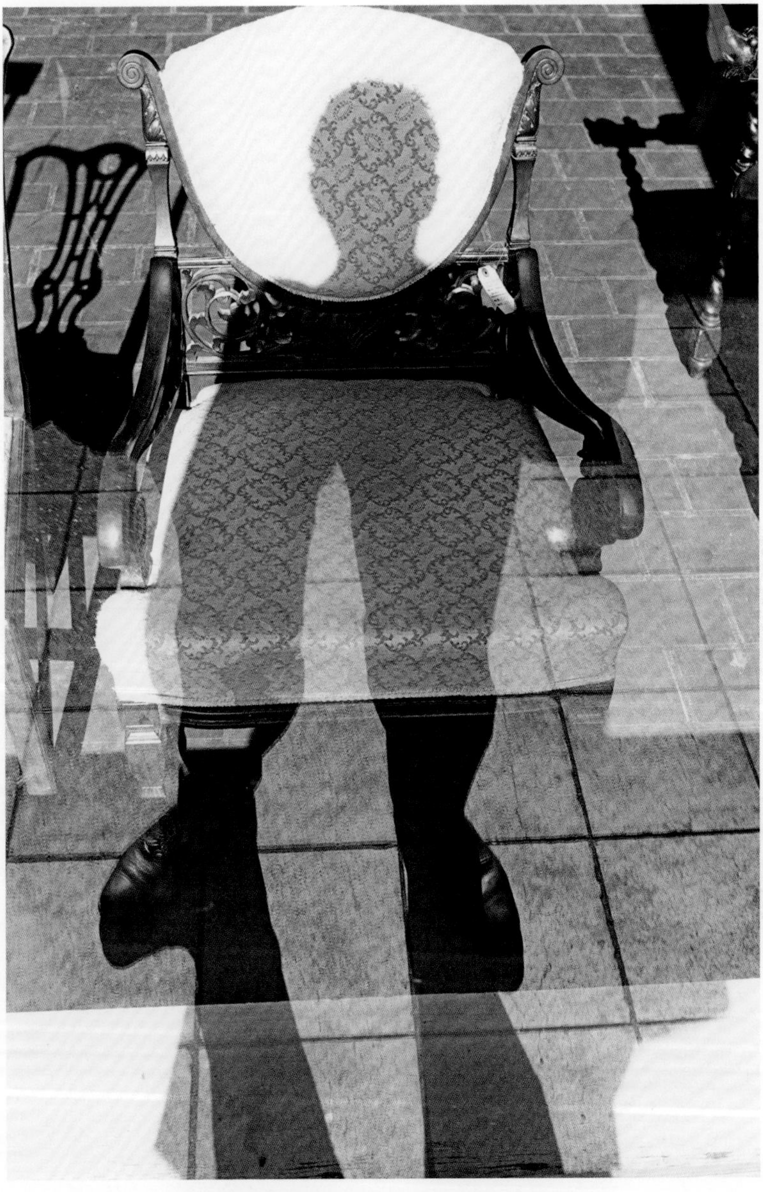

Figure 56. Lee Friedlander, *Wilmington, Delaware*, 1965. Gelatin silver print. 9 1/16″ × 5⅞″ (24.3 × 15.4 cm). © Lee Friedlander, courtesy Fraenkel Gallery, San Francisco.

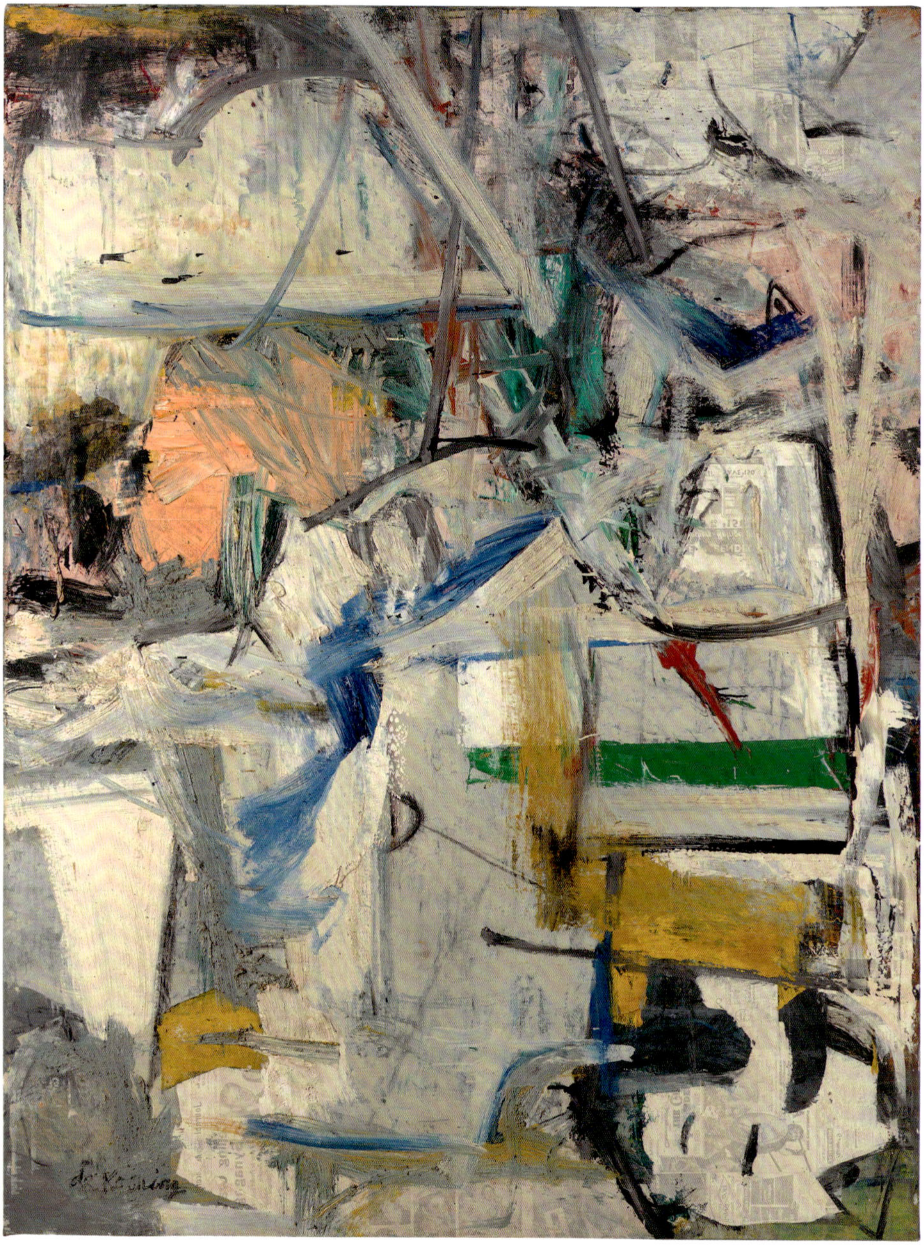

Figure 57. Willem de Kooning, *Easter Monday*, 1955–56. Oil and newspaper transfer on canvas. 96″ × 74″ (243.8 × 188cm). Rogers Fund, 1956, 56.205.2. Photograph by Malcom Varon. Image copyright © The Metropolitan Museum of Art. Image source: Art Resource, NY. © 2014 The Willem de Kooning Foundation / Artists Rights Society (ARS), New York.

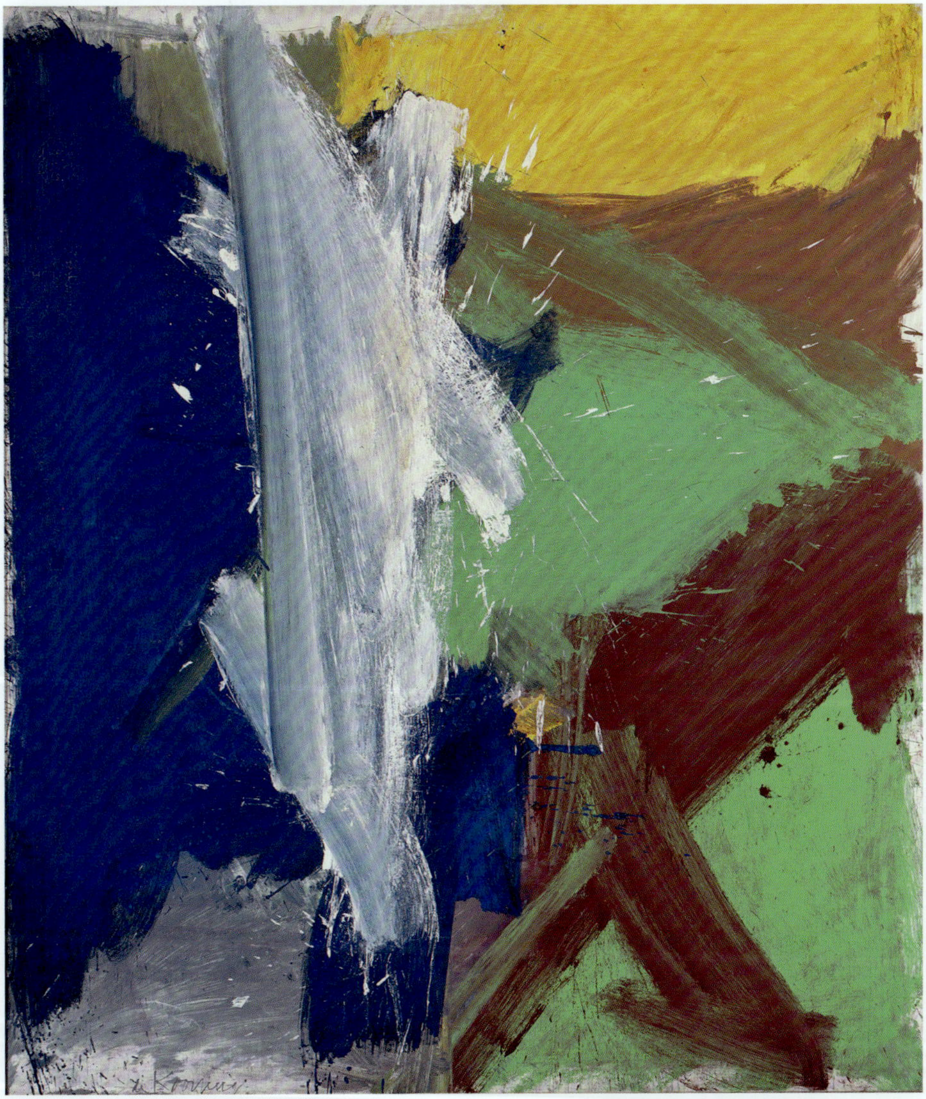

Figure 58. Willem de Kooning, *Merritt Parkway*, 1959. Oil on canvas. 203.2 × 179.1 cm. Detroit Institute of Arts, USA / Gift of W. Hawkins Ferry / Bridgeman Images. © 2014 The Willem de Kooning Foundation / Artists Rights Society (ARS), New York.

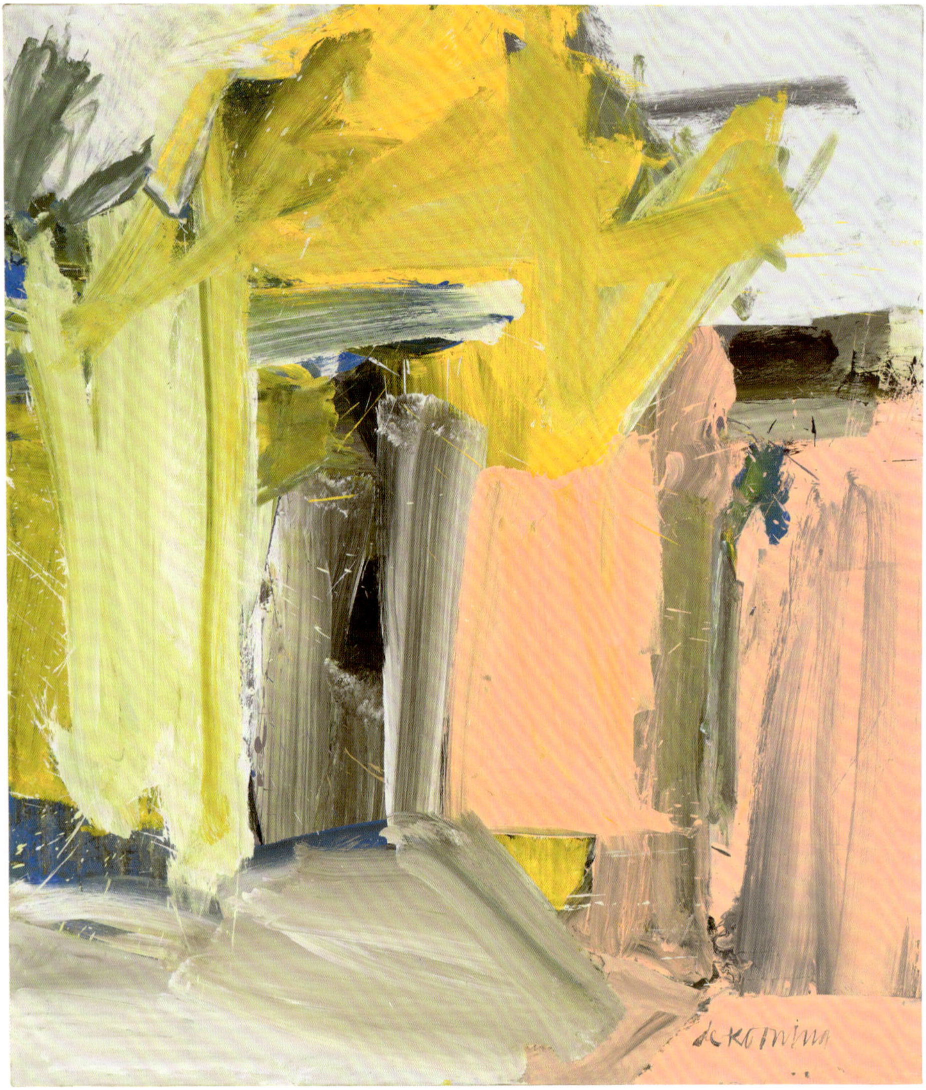

Figure 59. Willem de Kooning, *Door to the River*, 1960. Oil on linen. 80⅛" × 70⅛" (203.5 × 178.1 cm). Whitney Museum of American Art, New York; purchase, with funds from the Friends of the Whitney Museum of American Art, 60.63. Digital image © Whitney Museum, New York. © 2014 The Willem de Kooning Foundation / Artists Rights Society (ARS), New York.

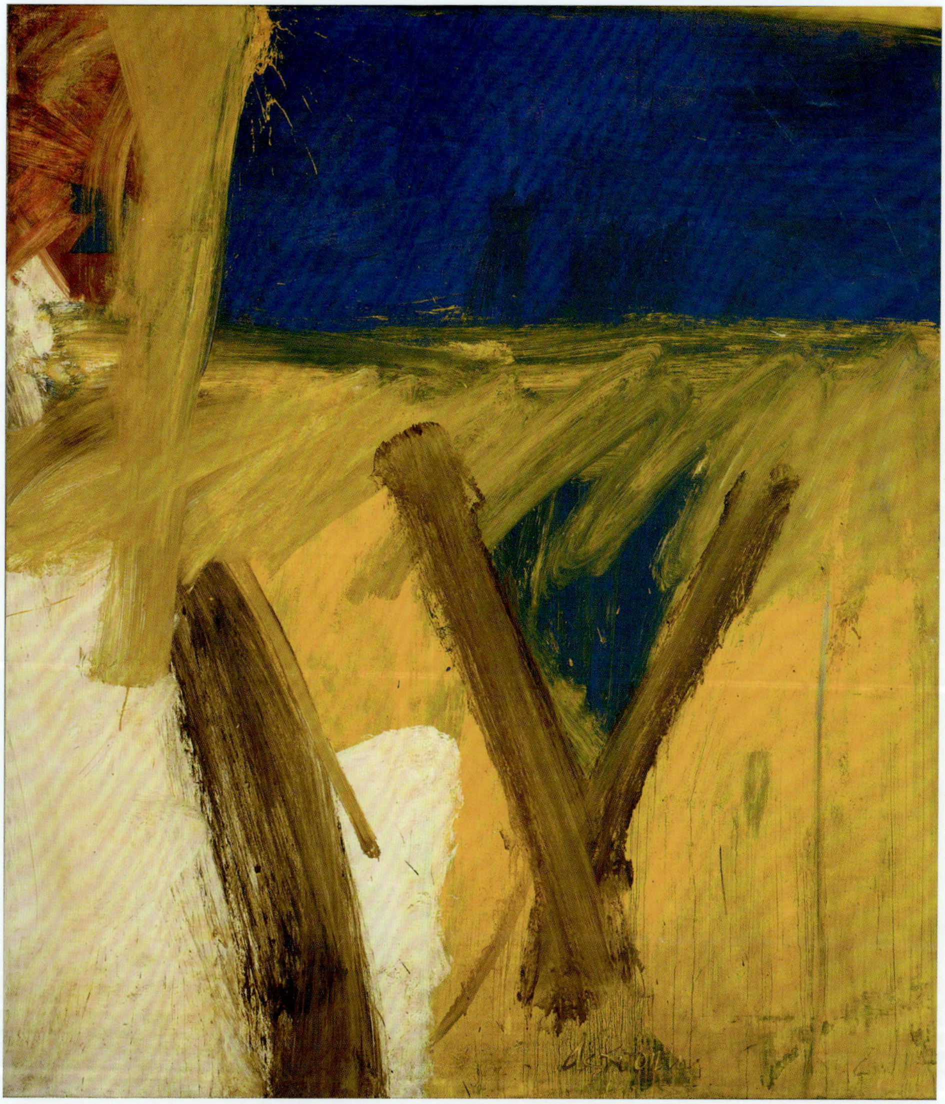

Figure 60. Willem de Kooning, *Suburb in Havana*, 1958. Oil on canvas. 80″ × 70″ (203.2 × 177.8 cm). Courtesy Gagosian Gallery. © 2014 The Willem de Kooning Foundation / Artists Rights Society (ARS), New York.

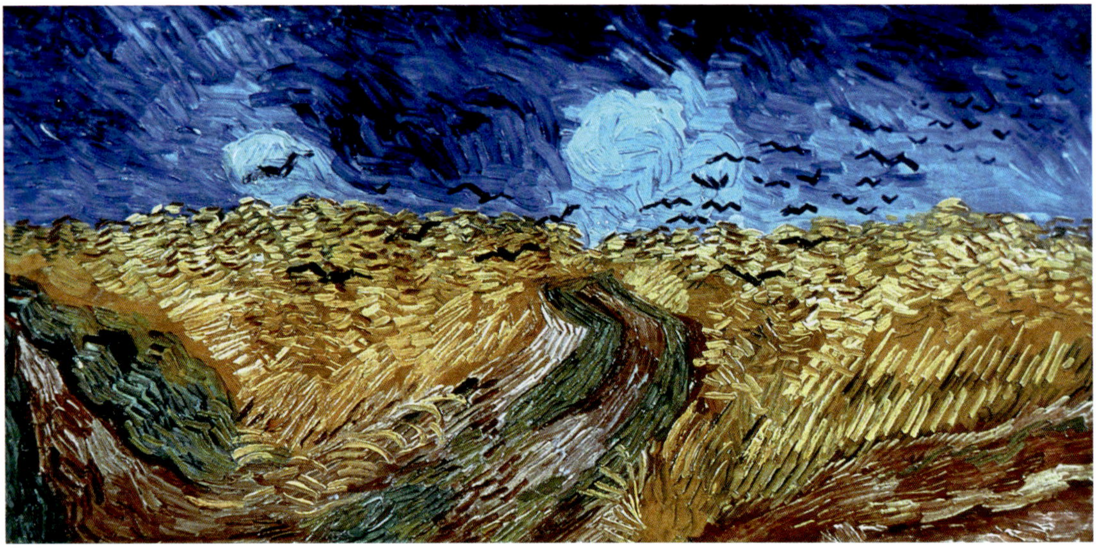

Figure 61. Vincent van Gogh, *Wheatfield with Crows*, July 1890. Oil on canvas. 50.5 × 103 cm. Van Gogh Museum. Art Resource, NY.

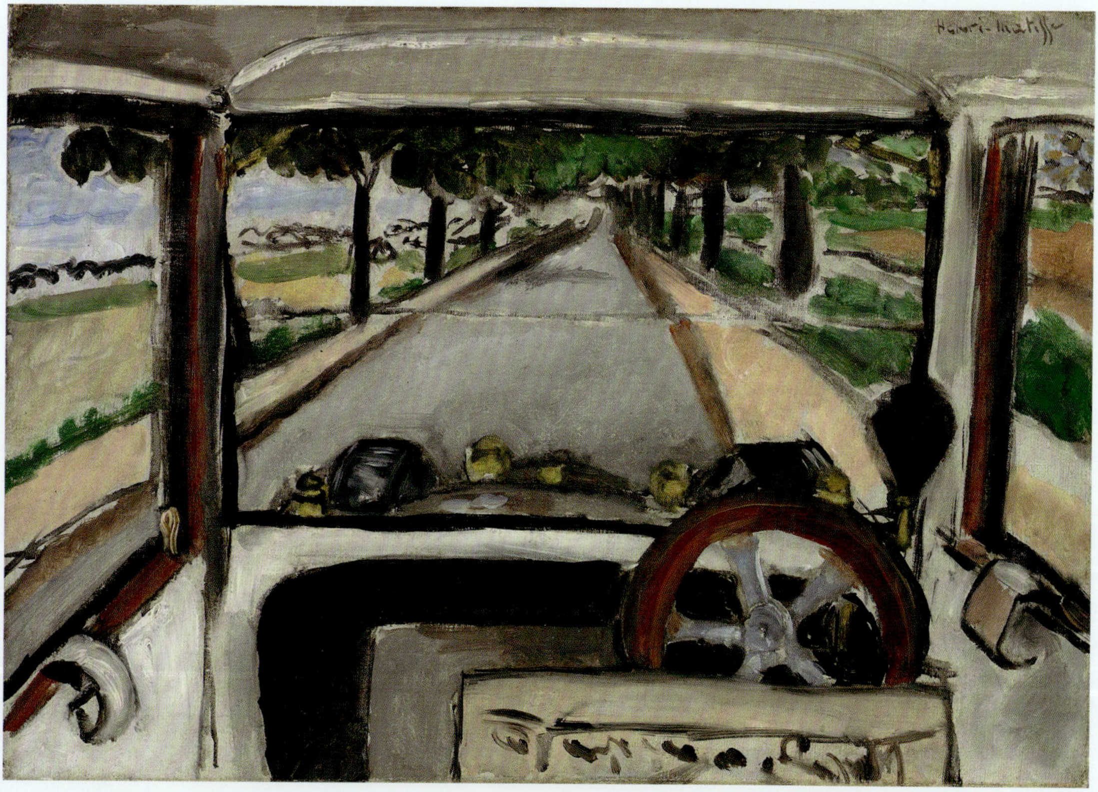

Figure 62. Matisse, *The Windshield, On the Road to Villacoublay*, 1917. Oil on canvas. 38.2 × 55.2 cm. The Cleveland Museum of Art, Bequest of Lucia McCurdy McBride in memory of John Harris McBride II, 1972.225. © 2014 Succession H. Matisse / Artists Rights Society (ARS), New York.

Figure 63. Robert Rauschenberg, *Erased de Kooning Drawing*, 1953. Traces of drawing media on paper with label and gilded frame. 25¼″ × 21¾″ × ½″ (64.14 × 55.25 × 1.27 cm). San Francisco Museum of Modern Art, purchase through a gift of Phyllis Wattis. Art © Robert Rauschenberg Foundation / Licensed by VAGA, New York, NY.

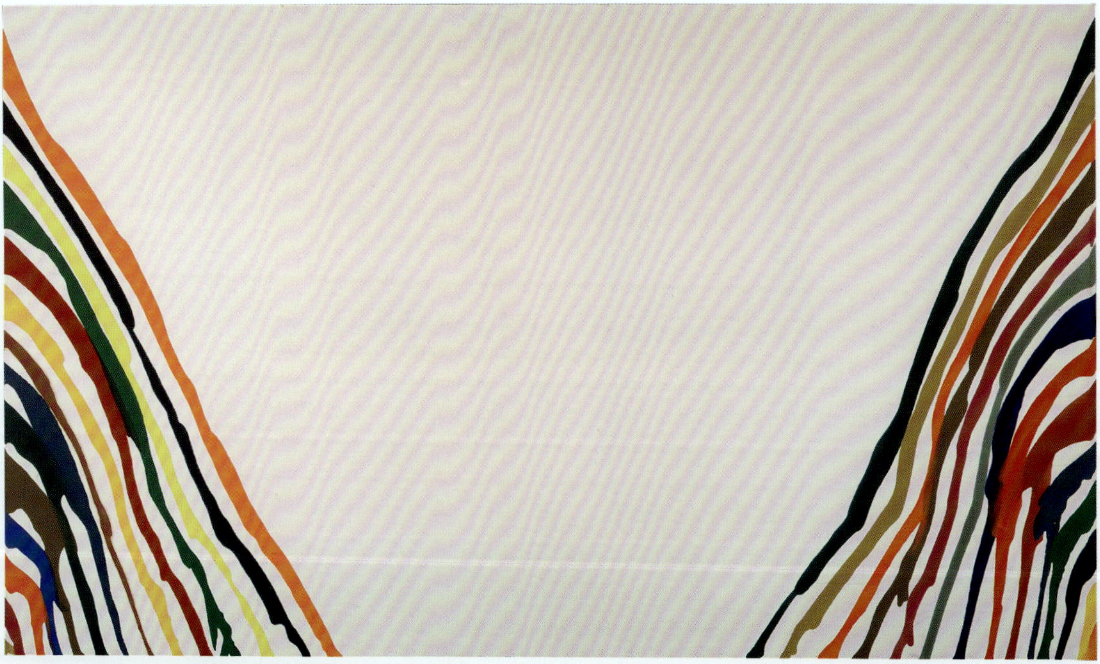

Figure 64. Morris Louis, *Alpha-Pi*, 1960. Magna on canvas. 102½" × 177" (260.4 × 449.6 cm). Arthur Hoppock Hearn Fund, 1967, 67.232. Image copyright © The Metropolitan Museum of Art. Image source: Art Resource, NY. © 2014 Maryland Institute College of Art (MICA), rights administered by Artist Rights Society (ARS), New York, all rights reserved.

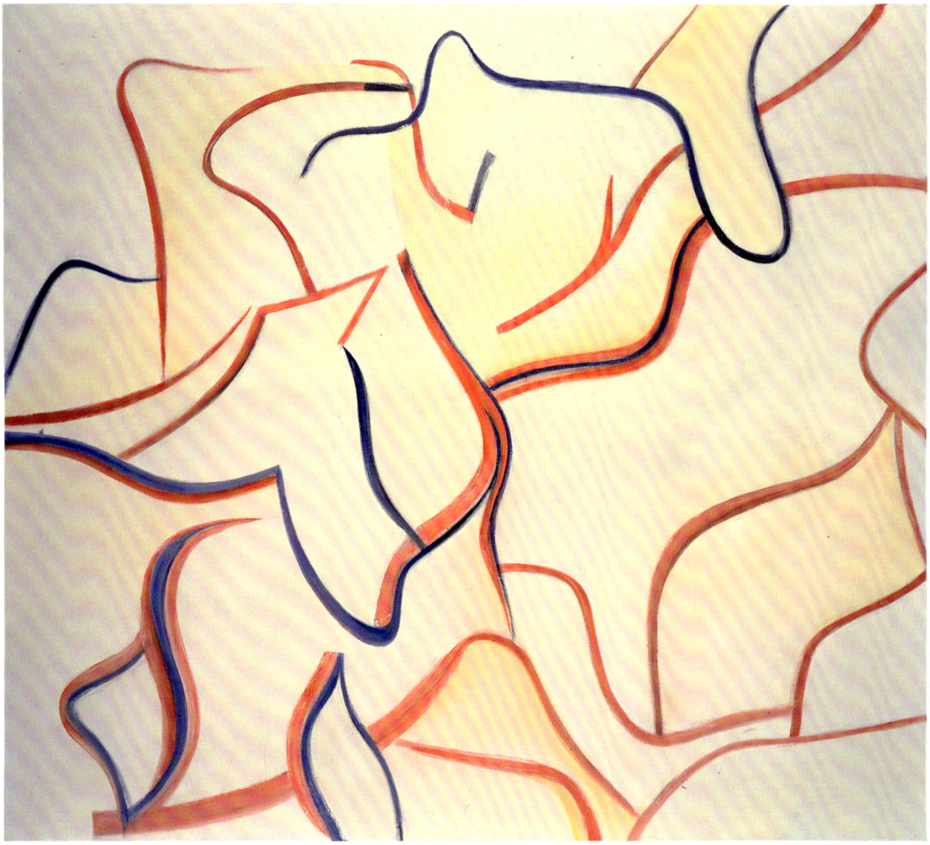

Figure 65. Willem de Kooning, *Untitled I*, 1985. Oil on canvas. 70″ × 80″ (177.8 × 203.2 cm). Courtesy Gagosian Gallery. © 2014 The Willem de Kooning Foundation / Artists Rights Society (ARS), New York.

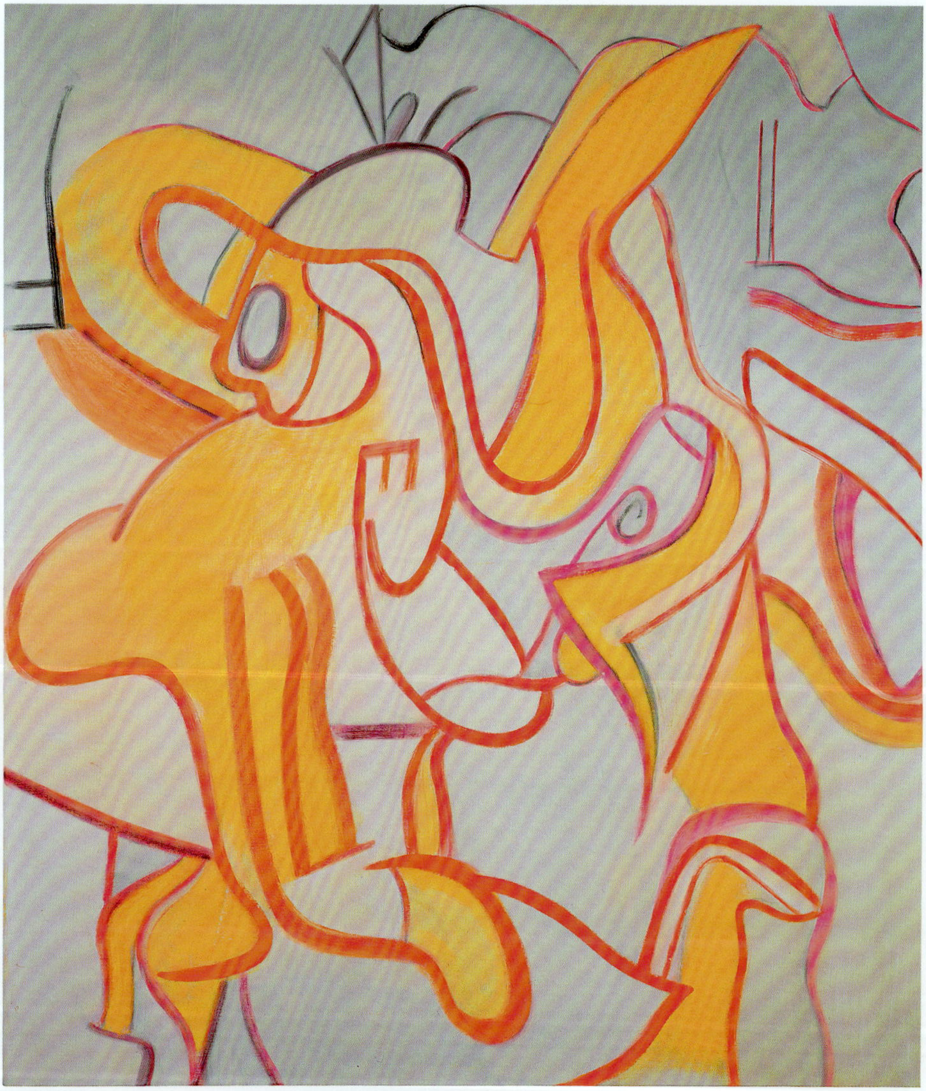

Figure 66. Willem de Kooning, *The Cat's Meow*, 1987. Oil on canvas. 88″ × 77″. Collection Jasper Johns. Courtesy Matthew Marks Gallery. © 2014 The Willem de Kooning Foundation / Artists Rights Society (ARS), New York.

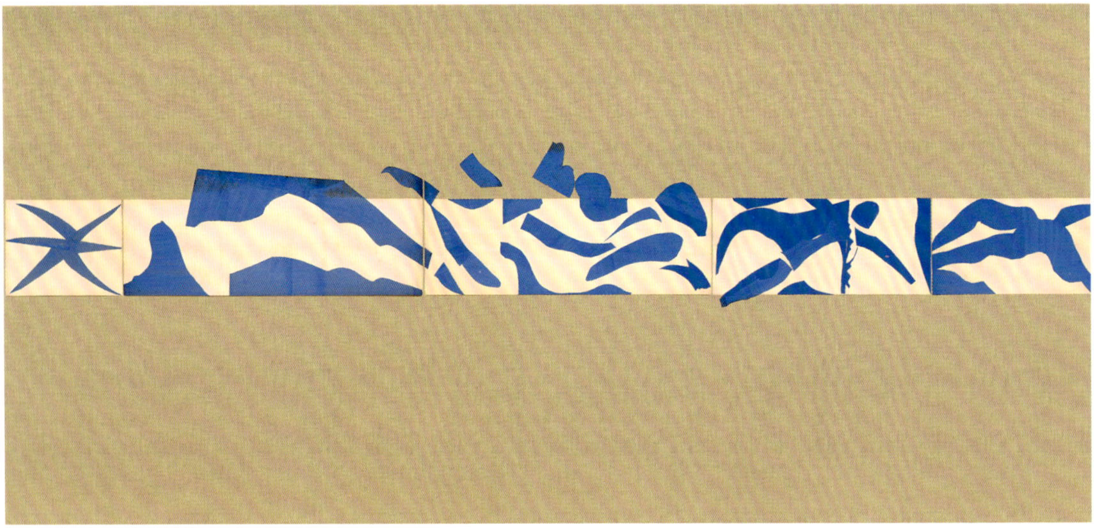

Figure 67. (above) Matisse, *The Swimming Pool Maquette for Ceramic* (realized 1999 and 2005), Nice-Cimiez, Hôtel Régina, late summer 1952. Gouache on paper, cut and pasted, on painted paper. Overall 73″ × 53′11″ (185.4 × 1643.3 cm). Installed as nine panels in two parts on burlap-covered walls 11′4″ (345.4 cm) high. Frieze installed at a height of 5′5″ (165 cm). Mrs. Bernard F. Gimbel Fund. Digital image © The Museum of Modern Art / Licensed by SCALA / Art Resource, NY. © 2014 Succession H. Matisse / Artists Rights Society (ARS), New York.

Figure 68. (facing) Alberto Giacometti, *Walking Man, I*, 1960. Bronze. 180.5 × 27 × 97 cm. Collection Fondation Alberto & Annette Giacometti. © 2014 Alberto Giacometti Estate / Licensed by VAGA and ARS, New York, NY.

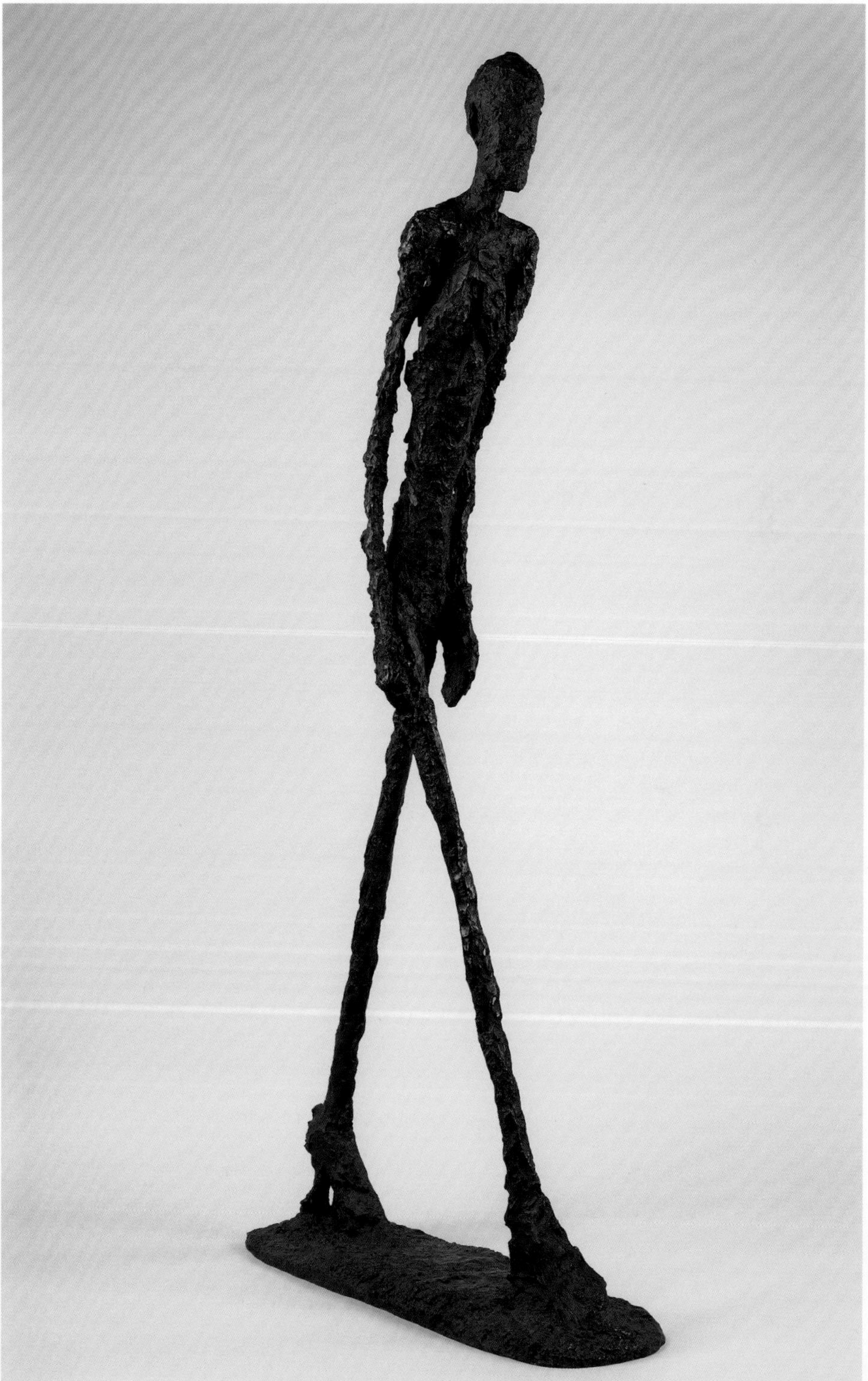

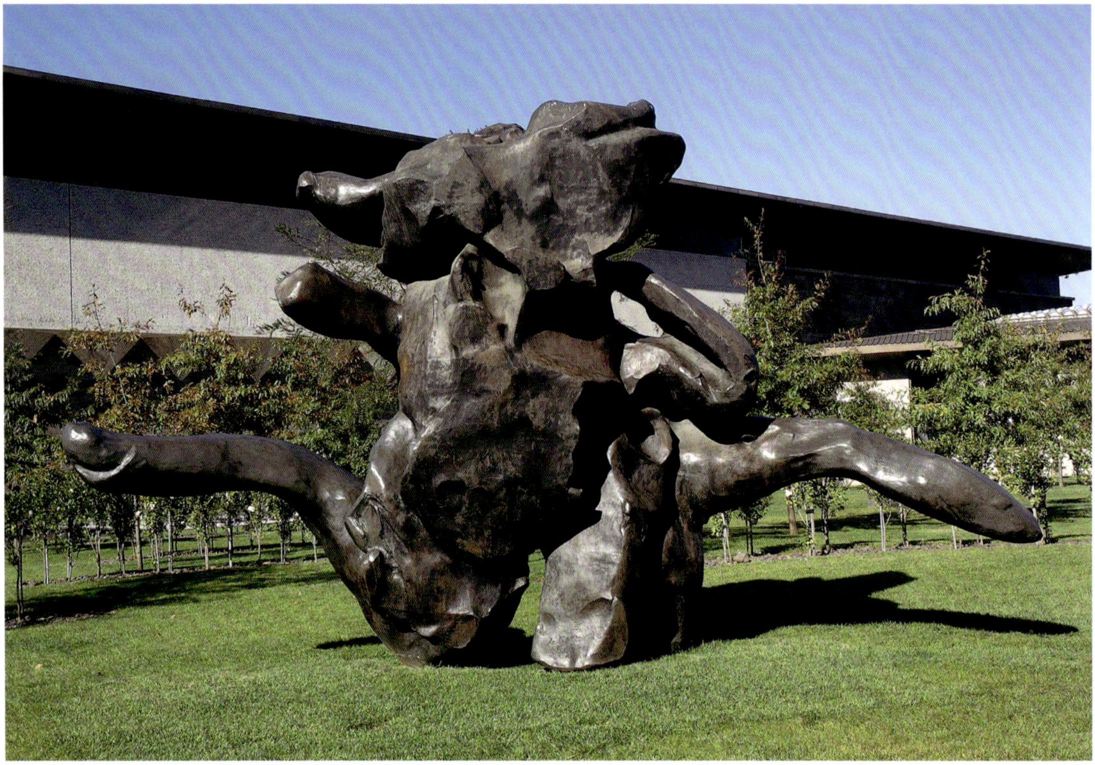

Figure 69. Willem de Kooning, *Standing Figure*, 1969, cast 1984. Bronze. 380.0 × 630.0 × 97.0 cm. National Gallery of Victoria, Melbourne. Presented through The Art Foundation of Victoria to the people of Australia in celebration of the Bicentenary, 1788–1988, by the National Australia Bank Limited, Founder Benefactor, in association with the Victorian Arts Centre Trust, 1987, S10-1987. © 2014 The Willem de Kooning Foundation / Artists Rights Society (ARS), New York.

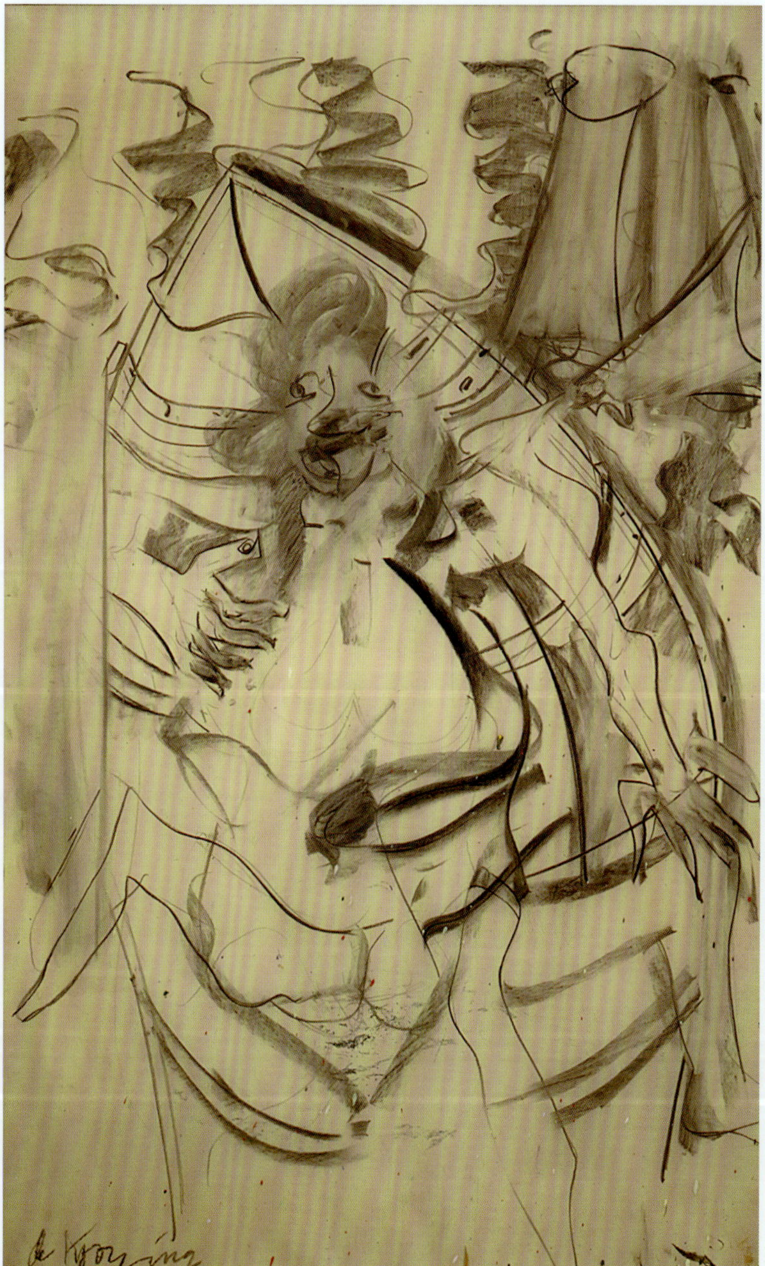

Figure 70. Willem de Kooning, *Woman in a Rowboat*, 1964. Charcoal on vellum. 58″ × 35½″ (147.3 × 90.2 cm). Collection James and Catherine Goodman. Courtesy Goodman Gallery. © 2014 The Willem de Kooning Foundation / Artists Rights Society (ARS), New York.

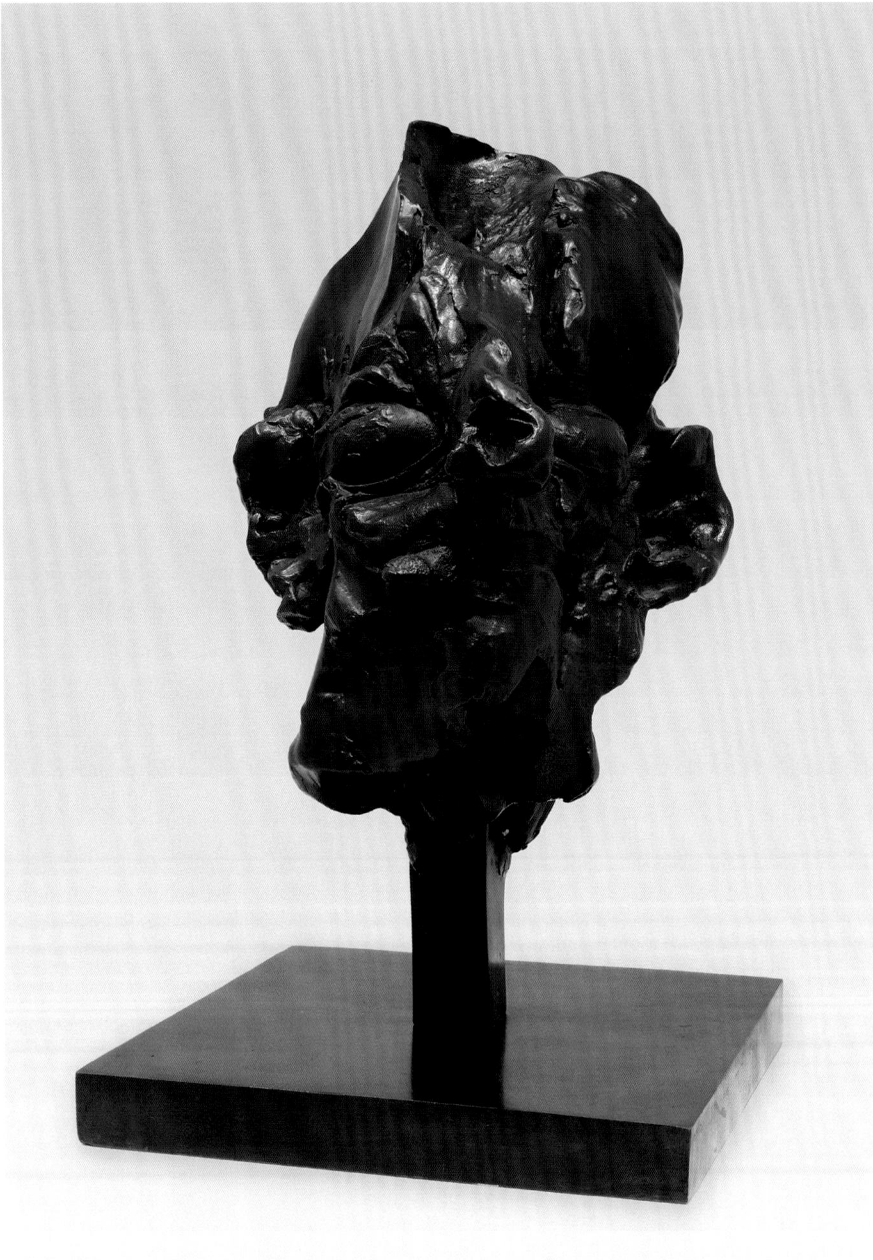

Figure 71. Willem de Kooning, *Head #3*, 1973. Bronze; edition number five of twelve. 49.5 × 29.2 × 29.2 cm (19½″ × 11½″ × 11½″). Restricted gift of Margaret Fisher, 1975.129, The Art Institute of Chicago. © 2014 The Willem de Kooning Foundation / Artists Rights Society (ARS), New York.

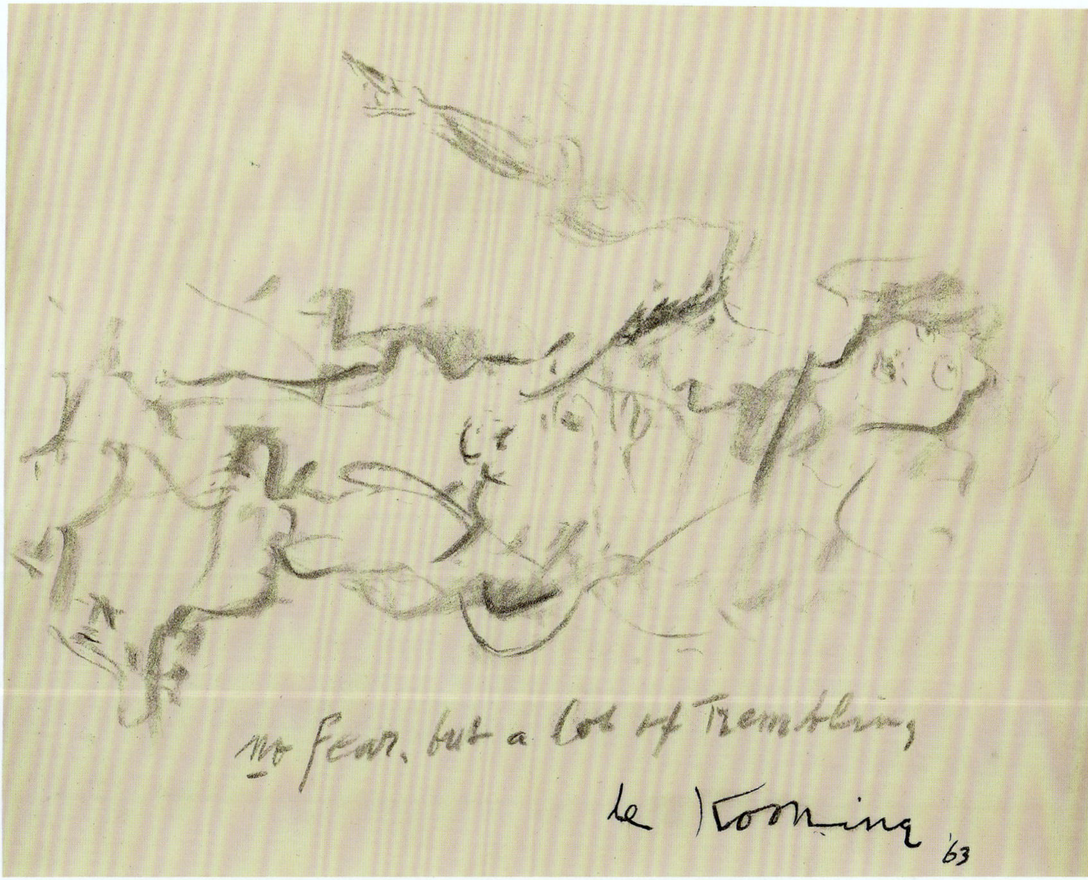

Figure 72. Willem de Kooning, *Untitled* (*No Fear but a Lot of Trembling*), 1963. Charcoal on paper. 8⅜" × 10⅞" (21.3 × 27.6 cm). Private collection. Photo courtesy of Allan Stone Collection, New York. © 2014 The Willem de Kooning Foundation / Artists Rights Society (ARS), New York.

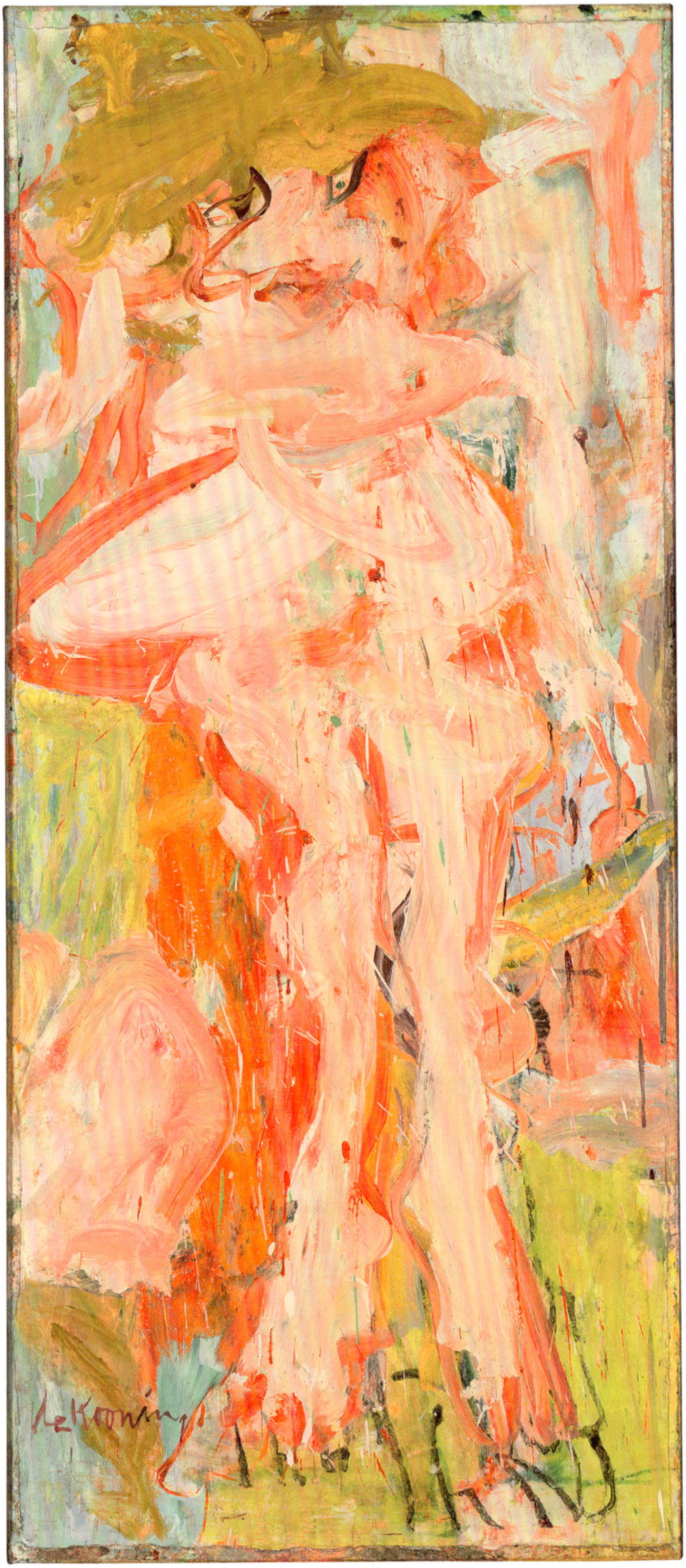

Figure 73. Willem de Kooning, *Woman Accabonac*, 1966. Oil on paper mounted on canvas. 79″ × 35⅛″ (200.7 × 89.2 cm). Whitney Museum of American Art, New York; purchase, with funds from the artist and Mrs. Bernard F. Gimbel, 67.75. Digital image © Whitney Museum, New York. © 2014 The Willem de Kooning Foundation / Artists Rights Society (ARS), New York.

Index

Italicized page locators refer to plates.